Diabetes Cookbook

FOR

DUMMIES®

3RD EDITION

by Alan L. Rubin, MD
with Cait James, MS

WILEY

Wiley Publishing, Inc.

Diabetes Cookbook For Dummies,® 3rd Edition

Published by
Wiley Publishing, Inc.
111 River St.
Hoboken, NJ 07030-5774
www.wiley.com

Copyright © 2010 by Wiley Publishing, Inc., Indianapolis, Indiana

Published by Wiley Publishing, Inc., Indianapolis, Indiana

Published simultaneously in Canada

For general information on our other products and services, please contact our Customer Care Department within the U.S. at 877-762-2974, outside the U.S. at 317-572-3993, or fax 317-572-4002.

For technical support, please visit www.wiley.com/techsupport.

Wiley also publishes its books in a variety of electronic formats. Some content that appears in print may not be available in electronic books.

Library of Congress Control Number: 2009940870

ISBN: 978-0-470-53644-5

Manufactured in the United States of America

10 9 8 7 6 5 4 3 2 1

WILEY

About the Authors

Alan L. Rubin, MD, is one of the nation's foremost experts on diabetes. He is a professional member of the American Diabetes Association and the Endocrine Society and has been in private practice specializing in diabetes and thyroid disease for over 30 years. Dr. Rubin was assistant clinical professor of medicine at University of California Medical Center in San Francisco for 20 years. He has spoken about diabetes to professional medical audiences and nonmedical audiences around the world. He has been a consultant to many pharmaceutical companies and companies that make diabetes products.

Dr. Rubin was one of the first specialists in his field to recognize the significance of patient self-testing of blood glucose, the major advance in diabetes care since the advent of insulin. As a result, he has been on numerous radio and television programs, talking about the cause, prevention, and treatment of diabetes and its complications. His first book, *Diabetes For Dummies,* now in a third edition, is a basic reference for any nonprofessional who wants to understand diabetes. It has sold more than 1 million copies and has been translated into 15 languages including French, Chinese, Spanish, and Russian. He is also the author of *Thyroid For Dummies, High Blood Pressure For Dummies, Type 1 Diabetes For Dummies,* and *Prediabetes For Dummies.*

Cait L. James, MS, is a Senior Health Educator at Kaiser Permanente in San Francisco. After receiving her undergraduate degree in Journalism and Health from the University of Oregon, she spent several years counseling clients in individualized nutrition and personal fitness plans. Her Master of Science degree in Health Education focused on the prevention and treatment of obesity. This led her to Kaiser Permanente's Pediatric Clinic, working with children suffering from or at risk of medical complications due to weight. While she now oversees a wide variety of health promotion programs for patients and staff, the promotion of healthy nutrition choices continues to be her biggest passion. She loves great food and wine, so thankfully she balances it with avid running and yoga!

Dedication

This book is dedicated to the great chefs and restaurant owners, especially the ones in this book, who spend all their time and creative energy producing delicious and nutritious food in a beautiful environment and making sure that it is served in a way that complements the taste.

Authors' Acknowledgments

Acquisitions editor Michael Lewis, who shepherded this third edition through all the committees that had to approve it, deserves special commendation. Our project editor, Jennifer Connolly, made certain that the book is understandable and readable in the great *For Dummies* tradition.

Heather Dismore is responsible for most of the discussions of food and the organization of the recipes in the book, and she also contributed a number of excellent recipes. Her tremendous skill in doing so is apparent in this book and in another book that she helped author, *Cooking Around the World All-in-One For Dummies*.

Reviewers Dawn Ayers, MD, Emily Nolan, and Patty Santelli did a fantastic job of ensuring that the information in the book is accurate.

Publisher's Acknowledgments

We're proud of this book; please send us your comments at http://dummies.custhelp.com. For other comments, please contact our Customer Care Department within the U.S. at 877-762-2974, outside the U.S. at 317-572-3993, or fax 317-572-4002.

Some of the people who helped bring this book to market include the following:

Acquisitions, Editorial, and Media Development

Project Editor: Jennifer Connolly

(Previous Edition: Georgette Beatty)

Acquisitions Editor: Michael Lewis

Copy Editor: Jennifer Connolly

Assistant Editor: Erin Calligan Mooney

Editorial Program Coordinator: Joe Niesen

Technical Editor: Dawn Ayers, M.D.

Recipe Tester: Emily Nolan

Nutritional Analyst: Patty Santelli

Editorial Manager: Jennifer Ehrlich

Editorial Supervisor: Carmen Krikorian

Editorial Assistants: Jennette Elnaggar, David Lutton

Art Coordinator: Alicia B. South

Photos: © T.J. Hine Photography

Food Stylist: Lisa Bishop

Cartoons: Rich Tennant (www.the5thwave.com)

Composition Services

Project Coordinator: Katie Crocker

Layout and Graphics: Claudia Bell, Ashley Chamberlain, Ronald G. Terry, Julia Trippetti, Christine Williams

Proofreader: Penny L. Stuart

Indexer: BIM Indexing & Proofreading Services

Publishing and Editorial for Consumer Dummies

Diane Graves Steele, Vice President and Publisher, Consumer Dummies

Kristin Ferguson-Wagstaffe, Product Development Director, Consumer Dummies

Ensley Eikenburg, Associate Publisher, Travel

Kelly Regan, Editorial Director, Travel

Publishing for Technology Dummies

Andy Cummings, Vice President and Publisher, Dummies Technology/General User

Composition Services

Debbie Stailey, Director of Composition Services

Contents at a Glance

Table of Contents

Introduction

*P*eople with diabetes *can* eat great food! We don't have to prove that statement anymore. The recipes in Dr. Rubin's previous book, *Diabetes For Dummies,* 3rd Edition (Wiley), and the second edition of this book show that people can follow a diabetic diet at home or anywhere they travel and still enjoy a five-star meal. They just have to know how to cook it or where to go to get it.

More and more eating is being done away from home or, if at home, from food in the form of take-out from a local supermarket or restaurant, and people with diabetes want to know what they can and can't eat.

If you bought *Diabetes For Dummies,* 3rd Edition, you know that you can find such food in Chicago, New York City, Santa Monica, and San Francisco. But what about the rest of the world? This book is both a cookbook that shows you how to prepare great foods in your own home and a guide to eating out in restaurants and fast-food places.

Is diet important for a person with diabetes? Do salmon swim upstream? The Diabetes Control and Complications Trials showed that a good diabetic diet could lower the hemoglobin A1c, a test of overall blood glucose control, by over 1 percent. That much improvement will result in a reduction of complications of diabetes such as eye disease, nerve disease, and kidney disease by 25 percent or more. The progression of complications that have already started to occur can be significantly slowed.

Of course, there's much more to managing diabetes than diet alone. In this book, you can discover the place of diet in a complete program of diabetes care.

This edition will feature a lot more about vegetarian eating. People who eat that way tend to be lighter and healthier. Many of the animal protein recipes in previous editions will be replaced by vegetarian food. We have tried them all, and they are delicious. We hope you will agree.

Cherry pie is good. But if you eat a whole lot of it, it's going to make you sick.

About This Book

You wouldn't read a cookbook from cover to cover, and this book is no exception to that rule. There's no reason to read about setting up your kitchen if you simply want a place to eat in New York where you can find healthy nutrition for your diabetes. You may want to read the first few chapters to get an overview of the place of diet in your overall diabetes management, but if you just need a great entree for tonight's supper or a great restaurant wherever you are, go right to that information. The book is written to be understood no matter where you find yourself in it.

Conventions Used in This Book

The recipes in this book are produced in a standard form that tells you what you're cooking, how much you're cooking, and how to cook it. The preparation time, cooking time (which is in addition to the prep time), and *yield,* or number of servings, are all presented at the beginning of the recipe, followed by a list of ingredients. We suggest that you always read through a recipe completely before you start preparing it so that you can make sure you have all the ingredients and equipment you need.

Chefs sometimes use exotic ingredients that may not be easily available to you. With the permission of the chefs, we have tried to substitute more common ingredients. On the other hand, walking into a store that sells special ingredients for a Chinese meal or an Indian meal, for example, can be a fascinating experience. We always define ingredients that are unfamiliar to English-speaking eaters in the introduction to the recipe.

You can find nutrition information at the end of every recipe so that you can incorporate the recipe into your nutrition plan. The nutrition information is always given in the following order:

- ✔ Kcalories (see Chapter 1)
- ✔ Kcalories from fat
- ✔ Grams of fat
- ✔ Grams of saturated fat
- ✔ Milligrams of cholesterol
- ✔ Milligrams of sodium

- Grams of carbohydrate
- Grams of fiber
- Grams of protein

If salt is listed in a recipe as an optional ingredient or listed "to taste," it isn't figured into the nutritional information; but if a specific amount of salt is listed in the recipe, that amount is calculated into the nutritional information. Serving sizes are always calculated as the total recipe divided by the number of servings listed at the beginning of the recipe.

Here are a few other guidelines to keep in mind about the recipes:

- All butter is unsalted. Margarine is not a suitable substitute for butter, because of the difference in flavor and nutritional value. Butter is a natural product, while margarine is man-made and contains trans fatty acids.
- All eggs are large.
- All flour is all-purpose unless otherwise specified.
- All milk is lowfat unless otherwise specified.
- All onions are yellow unless otherwise specified.
- All pepper is freshly ground black pepper unless otherwise specified.
- All salt is table salt unless otherwise specified.
- All mentions of Splenda refer to the regular sugar substitute unless Splenda for Baking is specified.
- All dry ingredient measurements are level — use a dry ingredient measuring cup, fill it to the top, and scrape it even with a straight object, such as the flat side of a knife.
- All temperatures are Fahrenheit. (See Appendix D for information about converting temperatures to Celsius.)
- A handful of recipes that appeared in the first edition of this book are featured in this edition and called "Classics" in their recipe names.
- If you need or want vegetarian recipes, scan the list of "Recipes in This Chapter" on the first page of each chapter in Part II. A little tomato, rather than a triangle, in front of the name of a recipe marks that recipe as vegetarian. (See the tomato to the left of this paragraph.)

This isn't a complete book about diagnosing and treating diabetes and its complications. Check out *Diabetes For Dummies,* 3rd Edition, if you need diagnosis and treatment information.

What You're Not to Read

All *For Dummies* books have shaded areas called *sidebars*. They contain interesting but nonessential information. If you aren't interested in the nitty-gritty, you can skip these sidebars. We promise not to include that information on the test.

Foolish Assumptions

The book assumes that you've done some cooking, you're familiar with the right knife to use to slice an onion without cutting your finger, and you can tell one pot from another. Beyond that, you can find many cooking terms in Appendix C at the end of the book.

How This Book Is Organized

The book is divided into five parts to help you incorporate the benefits of a good diet into your diabetes management program, while showing you that the food can be great.

Part I: Thriving with Diabetes

This part takes you on the road to long life and great health as you incorporate the needs of being a person with diabetes into the rest of your life. It begins by showing you all aspects of a healthy lifestyle and continues by focusing on food and its importance to you. When you cook for a person with diabetes (either yourself or a loved one), you must keep some special considerations in mind, but this part shows you that a diet for diabetes is an excellent diet for anyone. We guide you around the kitchen and take you to the supermarket to find out about meal-enhancing ingredients, as well as the ones to bypass as you navigate the aisles.

Part II: Healthy Recipes That Taste Great

This part presents recipes from A to Z (apples to zucchini) and everything in between. The chapters take you through your eating day, starting with your breakfast, providing snacks for midmorning and midafternoon, and offering larger meals at lunch and dinner. They end, naturally, with wonderful desserts, which show that you're not doomed to give up what you may consider the best part of the meal. You just need to be careful about calories. In this part, we feature the recipes from the great restaurants that have participated in the creation of this book.

Part III: Eating Away from Home

In this book, we can't cover every city and every restaurant you may visit. What do you do if you find yourself without a suggestion from this book? Part III tells you how to eat well and stay healthy wherever you are. You can always visit a fast-food franchise, but a lot of that food isn't good for you. If you pick and choose well, however, you'll be able to select a meal even when your only choice is the one fast-food restaurant off the next exit on the freeway.

Part IV: The Part of Tens

We love to help you solve your problems in groups of ten. If you have 13 problems, you'll just have to wait for the next book to solve the last 3. In this part, we provide ten steps to improve your eating habits and ten food substitutions that you can easily make within a recipe. You can explore ten strategies to normalize your blood glucose and ten ways to promote healthy eating in children.

Part V: Appendixes

Appendix A has info about the restaurants that provided many of the delicious recipes in this book. You find out about their particular style of cooking and the chefs who make this possible. Appendix B contains a glossary of key cooking terms. In Appendix C, you can find guidelines if you want to substitute other sweeteners for sugar, as well as cooking equivalents, such as how many tablespoons make up a cup. Appendix D offers other resources in books and on the Web for recipes and nutritional information for people with diabetes.

Icons Used in This Book

The icons in this book are like bookmarks, pointing out information that we think is especially important. You may want to pick out one particular icon that appeals to you. For example, if you like stories about people, the Anecdote icon is for you. The Anecdote icon points you to a lot of interesting stories about others with diabetes and how they cope with their diets. If your interests lie in the direction of very mild fear, look for the Warning icon. Here are the icons used in this book:

We use this icon whenever Dr. Rubin tells a story about his patients.

Whenever we want to emphasize the importance of the current information to your nutritional plan, we use this icon.

When you see the Remember icon, pay special attention because the information is essential.

This icon flags situations when you should see your doctor (for example, if your blood glucose level is too high or you need a particular test done).

This helpful icon marks important information that can save you time and energy.

Watch for this icon; it warns about potential problems (for example, the possible results if you don't treat a condition).

Where to Go from Here

Where you go from here depends on your immediate needs. If you want an introduction to the place of nutrition in diabetes management, start with Chapter 1. If you are hungry and want some lunch, go to Chapter 8 or 9. If you are about to travel or eat out, head for Part III. At any time, the Part of Tens can provide useful tips for healthy eating. Finally, the appendixes help you cook for yourself or choose a restaurant. Feel free to jump around, but take the time to go through Part II so that you realize that diabetes and great food are not mutually exclusive.

Part I
Thriving with Diabetes

The 5th Wave   By Rich Tennant

"No, diabetes is not fatal, it's not contagious, and it doesn't mean you'll always get half my desserts."

In this part . . .

The chapters in this part begin by showing you all aspects of a healthy lifestyle and continue by focusing on food and its importance to you. When you cook for a person with diabetes (either yourself or a loved one), you must keep some special considerations in mind, but this part shows you that a diet for diabetes is an excellent diet for anyone. I guide you around the kitchen and take you to the supermarket to find out about meal-enhancing ingredients, as well as the ones to bypass as you navigate the aisles.

Chapter 1

What It Means to Thrive with Diabetes

In This Chapter

▶ Getting a grip on diabetes

▶ Controlling calories

▶ Working exercise into your schedule

▶ Keeping your blood pressure down

▶ Making lifestyle changes that count

Since the second edition of *Diabetes Cookbook For Dummies* came out, there have been a number of studies that indicate that a vegetarian diet may be beneficial in the prevention and treatment of diabetes. In this new edition, we provide some of the rationale for that type of diet. You will also find 28 new recipes from some of the finest vegetarian restaurants in the country. They and the older vegetarian recipes will be marked with a tomato.

In this chapter, you get the latest information about what diabetes means, how diabetes is diagnosed, and the things you need to do to thrive with diabetes. Don't waste another minute. Get started right away.

Recognizing Diabetes

With so much diabetes around these days, you may think that recognizing it should be easy. The truth is that it's not easy, because diabetes is defined by blood tests. You can't just look at someone and know the level of glucose — blood sugar — in his or her blood.

Diabetes by the numbers

The level of glucose that means you have diabetes is as follows:

- A *casual* blood glucose of 200 milligrams per deciliter (mg/dl) or more at any time of day or night, along with symptoms such as fatigue, frequent urination and thirst, slow healing of skin, urinary infections, and vaginal itching in women. A normal casual blood glucose should be between 70 and 139 mg/dl.

- A *fasting* blood glucose of 126 mg/dl or more after no food for at least eight hours. A normal fasting blood glucose should be less than 100 mg/dl.

- A blood glucose of 200 mg/dl or greater two hours after consuming 75 grams of glucose.

A diagnosis of diabetes requires at least two abnormal levels on two different occasions. Don't accept a lifelong diagnosis of diabetes on the basis of a single test.

A fasting blood glucose between 100 and 125 mg/dl or casual blood glucose between 140 and 199 mg/dl is *prediabetes.* See Dr. Rubin's book *Prediabetes For Dummies* (Wiley). Most people with prediabetes will develop diabetes within ten years. Although people with prediabetes don't usually develop small blood vessel complications of diabetes like blindness, kidney failure, and nerve damage, they're more prone to large vessel disease like heart attacks and strokes, so you want to get that level of glucose down. Sixty million people in the United States have prediabetes.

Types of diabetes

The following list describes the three main types of diabetes:

- **Type 1 diabetes:** This used to be called *juvenile diabetes* or *insulin-dependent diabetes.* It mostly begins in childhood and results from the body's self-destruction of its own pancreas. The pancreas is an organ of the body that sits behind the stomach and makes insulin, the chemical or "hormone" that gets glucose into cells where it can be used. You can't live without insulin, so people with type 1 diabetes must take insulin shots. Of the 24 million Americans with diabetes, about 10 percent have type 1.

- **Type 2 diabetes:** Once called *adult-onset diabetes,* type 2 used to begin around the age of 40, but it is occurring more often in children, many of whom are getting heavier and heavier and exercising less and less. The problem in type 2 diabetes is not a total lack of insulin, as occurs in type 1, but a resistance to the insulin, so that the glucose still doesn't get into cells but remains in the blood.

✔ **Gestational diabetes:** This type of diabetes is like type 2 diabetes but occurs in women during pregnancy, when a lot of chemicals in the mother's blood oppose the action of insulin. About 4 percent of all pregnancies are complicated by gestational diabetes. If the mother isn't treated to lower the blood glucose, the glucose gets into the baby's bloodstream. The baby produces plenty of insulin and begins to store the excess glucose as fat in all the wrong places. If this happens, the baby may be larger than usual and therefore may be hard to deliver. When the baby is born, he is cut off from the large sugar supply but is still making lots of insulin, so his blood glucose can drop severely after birth. The mother is at risk of gestational diabetes in later pregnancies and of type 2 diabetes as she gets older.

✔ **Other types:** A small group of people with diabetes suffer from one of these much less common varieties of diabetes:

- Latent autoimmune diabetes on adults (LADA), which has characteristics of both type 1 and type 2 diabetes

- Genetic defects of the beta cell, which makes insulin

- Medications that affect insulin action like cortisol or prednisone

- Diseases or conditions that damage the pancreas like pancreatitis or cystic fibrosis

- Genetic defects in insulin action

Consequences of diabetes

If your blood glucose isn't controlled — that is, kept between 70 and 139 mg/dl after eating or under 100 mg/dl fasting — damage can occur to your body. The damage can be divided into three categories: irritations, short-term complications, and long-term complications.

Irritations

Irritations are mild and reversible but still unpleasant results of high blood glucose levels. The levels aren't so high that the person is in immediate life-threatening danger. The most important of these irritations are the following:

✔ Blurred vision

✔ Fatigue

✔ Frequent urination and thirst

✔ Genital itching, especially in females

✔ Gum and urinary tract infections

✔ Obesity

✔ Slow healing of the skin

Short-term complications

These complications can be very serious and lead to death if not treated. They're associated with very high levels of blood glucose — in the 400s and above. The three main short-term complications are the following:

- ✔ **Ketoacidosis:** This complication is found mostly in type 1 diabetes. It is a severe acid condition of the blood that results from lack of insulin, the hormone that is missing. The patient becomes very sick and will die if not treated with large volumes of fluids and large amounts of insulin. After the situation is reversed, however, the patient is fine.

- ✔ **Hyperosmolar syndrome:** This condition is often seen in neglected older people. Their blood glucose rises due to severe dehydration and the fact that the kidneys of the older population can't get rid of glucose the way younger kidneys can. The blood becomes like thick syrup. The person can die if large amounts of fluids aren't restored. They don't need that much insulin to recover. After the condition is reversed, these people can return to a normal state.

- ✔ **Hypoglycemia or low blood glucose:** This complication happens when the patient is on a drug like insulin or a pill that drives the glucose down but isn't getting enough food or is getting too much exercise. After it falls below 70 mg/dl, the patient begins to feel bad. Typical symptoms include sweating, rapid heartbeat, hunger, nervousness, confusion, and coma if the low glucose is prolonged. Glucose by mouth, or by venous injection if the person is unconscious, is the usual treatment. This complication usually causes no permanent damage.

Long-term complications

These problems occur after ten or more years of poorly controlled diabetes or, in the case of the macrovascular complications, after years of prediabetes or diabetes. They have a substantial impact on quality of life. After these complications become established, reversing them is hard, but treatment is available for them early in their course, so watch for them five years after your initial diagnosis of diabetes. See Dr. Rubin's book *Diabetes For Dummies,* 3rd Edition (Wiley), for information on screening for these complications.

The long-term complications are divided into two groups: *microvascular,* which are due at least in part to small blood vessel damage, and *macrovascular,* associated with damage to large blood vessels.

Microvascular complications include the following:

- ✔ **Diabetic retinopathy:** Eye damage that leads to blindness if untreated.
- ✔ **Diabetic nephropathy:** Kidney damage that can lead to kidney failure.

✔ **Diabetic neuropathy:** Nerve damage that results in many clinical symptoms, the most common of which are tingling and numbness in the feet. Lack of sensation in the feet can result in severe injury without awareness unless you carefully look at your feet regularly. Such injury can result in infection and even amputation.

Macrovascular complications also occur in prediabetes and consist of the following:

✔ **Arteriosclerotic heart disease:** Blockage of the blood vessels of the heart. This is the most common cause of death in diabetes due to a heart attack.

✔ **Arteriosclerotic cerebrovascular disease:** Blockage of blood vessels to the brain, resulting in a stroke.

✔ **Arteriosclerotic peripheral vascular disease involving the blood vessels of the legs:** These vessels can become clogged and result in amputation of the feet or legs.

If you control your blood glucose, none of these complications need ever occur. Controlling your blood pressure and your cholesterol also helps prevent these complications.

Treating diabetes

Treatment of diabetes involves three essential elements:

✔ **Diet:** If you follow the recommendations in this book, you can lower your average blood glucose by as much as 30 to 50 mg/dl. Doing so can reduce the complication rate by as much as 33 percent.

✔ **Exercise:** We touch on exercise in Chapter 3 and cover it more extensively in *Diabetes For Dummies,* 3rd Edition (Wiley).

✔ **Medication:** Diabetes medications abound — there are far too many to discuss here, but you can find out about them in *Diabetes For Dummies,* 3rd Edition.

Controlling Calories

Just as the three most important factors in the value of a house are location, location, location, the three most important factors in diet for people with diabetes are moderation, moderation, moderation. If you're overweight or obese, which is true of most people with type 2 diabetes and a lot of people with type 1 diabetes who are on intensive insulin treatment (four shots of insulin daily), weight loss will make a huge difference in your blood glucose levels. If you maintain the weight loss, you'll avoid the complications of diabetes discussed earlier in this chapter.

To successfully lose weight, you need to control your total calories. You must burn up the same amount of calories you take in by mouth, or you will gain weight. To lose weight, you need to burn up more calories than you eat. Sounds simple, eh! And it doesn't matter where the calories come from. Studies that compare diets low in fats, proteins, or carbohydrates result in the same weight loss after a year.

As you reduce your portions, reduce your intake of added sugars, fats, and alcohol. These items contain no nutrients such as vitamins and minerals and are simply sources of empty calories.

If you are predisposed to have diabetes because, for example, your parents both had diabetes, you can prevent it by maintaining a healthy weight. If you already have diabetes, you can minimize its impact by losing weight and keeping it off.

Do you need a highly complicated formula to figure out how to moderate your food intake? No! It's as simple as looking at the portions you currently eat and cutting them in half. At home, where you control the amount of food on your plate, you can start with a small portion, so you may not need to reduce it by half. However, in restaurants, where more and more people are eating their meals, especially the fast-food restaurants, discussed extensively in Chapters 17 and 18, the rule of eating half may not be strong enough. There you may need to eat only a third of the portion. You may need to apply the same portion control when you eat at someone else's home. Figure 1-1 shows you the difference between reasonably sized portions and ones that are too big.

Use these tips to help you visualize portion sizes:

- An ounce of meat is the size of a pack of matches.
- Three ounces of meat is the size of a deck of cards.
- A medium fruit is the size of a tennis ball.
- A medium potato is the size of a computer mouse.
- A medium bagel is the size of a hockey puck.
- An ounce of cheese is the size of a domino.
- A cup of fruit is the size of a baseball.
- A cup of broccoli is the size of a light bulb.

Figure 1-1:
Eating in moderation means choosing the portion sizes on the left, rather than those on the right.

You don't need to take in many extra calories over time to gain weight. Just 100 extra kilocalories (see the "Kilocalories versus calories" sidebar for an explanation of kilocalories) on a daily basis results in a weight gain of 12 pounds in a year. An extra glass of wine is that many kilocalories. On the other hand, if you reduce your daily intake by 100 kilocalories, you can lose those 12 pounds over a year.

Look at a few examples of the portion sizes provided today compared to 20 years ago. Table 1-1 shows the kilocalories in the portions of 20 years ago and today and how much exercise you have to do to burn up the extra kilocalories so you don't gain weight.

Table 1-1	Consequences of Today's Larger Portions		
Food	*Kilocalories 20 years ago*	*Kilocalories today*	*Exercise to burn the difference*
Bagel	140	350	50 minutes raking leaves
Cheeseburger	333	590	90 minutes lifting weights
French fries	210	610	80 minutes walking
Turkey sandwich	320	820	85 minutes biking
Coffee	45	350	70 minutes walking
Chicken Caesar salad	390	790	80 minutes walking
Popcorn	270	630	75 minutes of water aerobics
Chocolate chip cookie	55	275	75 minutes washing the car

Kilocalories versus calories

I use the term *kilocalories* (or *kcalories*) rather than calories because experts in health and medicine measure energy in a diet plan or in food in kilocalories (a kilocalorie is 1,000 times greater than a calorie). Unfortunately, the term *calories* has been established on food labels and in diets, and health officials don't want to confuse the public by attempting to correct this error.

Calorie counts in the text of this book and in the nutritional analyses of the recipes are given in kilocalories.

Including Exercise (And Rest)

Exercise is just as important as diet in controlling your blood glucose. A group of people who were expected to develop diabetes because their parents both had diabetes was asked to walk 30 minutes a day. Eighty percent of those who did walk did not develop the disease. These people didn't necessarily lose weight, but they did exercise.

Too many people complain that they just can't find the time to exercise. But a recent study showed that just 7½ minutes of highly intense exercise a week had a profound effect on the blood glucose. So this excuse isn't acceptable, especially when you realize how much difference exercise can make in your life and your diabetes. Here are some ways that different amounts of exercise can help you:

✔ Thirty minutes of exercise a day will get you in excellent physical shape and reduce your blood glucose substantially.

✔ Sixty minutes of exercise a day will help you to maintain weight loss and get you in even better physical shape.

✔ Ninety minutes of exercise a day will cause you to lose weight.

An exercise partner helps ensure that you get out and do your thing. We find it extremely helpful to have someone waiting for us so that we can exercise together.

Here are some more facts about exercise to keep in mind:

✔ You don't have to get in all your minutes of exercise in one session. Two 30-minute workouts are just as good as and possibly better than one 60-minute workout.

✔ Although walking is excellent exercise, especially for the older population, the benefits of more vigorous exercise and for a longer time are greater still.

✔ Everything counts when it comes to exercise. Your decision to take the stairs instead of the elevator may not seem like much, but if you do so day after day, it makes a profound difference. Another suggestion that may help over time is to park your car farther from your office or bike to the office.

✔ A pedometer (a small gadget worn on your belt that counts your steps) may help you to achieve your exercise goals. The objective is to get up to 10,000 steps a day by increasing your step count every week.

You also want to do something to strengthen your muscles. Larger muscles take in more glucose, providing another way of keeping it under control. You'll be surprised by how much your stamina will increase and how much your blood glucose will fall.

Place a daily limit on activities that are completely sedentary, such as watching television or surfing the Web. Use the time you might have once spent on these activities to exercise. This advice is especially helpful for overweight children who should be limited to two hours a day.

You want to be active, but don't do it at the cost of getting plenty of rest each day. People who sleep eight hours a night tend to be less hungry and leaner than people who sleep less.

Of course, it is possible to overdo it. One French diplomat found the phenomenal energy of President Theodore Roosevelt too much for him. After two sets of tennis at the White House, Roosevelt invited him to go jogging. Then they had a workout with a medicine ball. "What would you like to do now?" the president asked his guest when his enthusiasm for the exercise seem to be flagging. "If it's all the same to you," gasped the exhausted Frenchman, "lie down and die."

Keeping up to speed on treatment developments

By the time you read this book, several months will have passed since we wrote these words. Several important discoveries about diabetes or related medical information may have occurred that you need to know about. How can you keep up with the latest and greatest treatments?

✔ Take a course with a certified diabetes educator (CDE). Here you learn how to manage your diabetes right now and find out about what's coming up.

✔ Go to the Web and do a search for diabetes. If you want to be sure that the sites you

come up with are both accurate and helpful, go to his Web site, www.drrubin.com, where you'll find a page on Useful Diabetes Related Web sites. He has checked all of them out for you, so you know you can rely on them.

✔ Come to your doctor prepared to ask questions. If you don't get a satisfactory answer, see a specialist.

✔ Take another certified course after several years. You'll be amazed at the changes.

Controlling Your Blood Pressure

Keeping your blood pressure in check is particularly important in preventing the macrovascular complications of diabetes. But elevated blood pressure also plays a role in bringing on eye disease, kidney disease, and neuropathy. You should have your blood pressure tested every time you see your doctor. The goal is to keep your blood pressure under 130/80. (See Dr. Rubin's book *High Blood Pressure For Dummies,* 2nd edition, published by Wiley, for a complete explanation of the meaning of these numbers.) You may want to get your own blood pressure monitor so that you can check it at home yourself.

The statistics about diabetes and high blood pressure are daunting. Seventy-one percent of diabetics have high blood pressure, but almost a third are unaware of it. Almost half of them weren't being treated for high blood pressure. Among the treated patients, less than half were treated in a way that reduced their pressure to lower than 130/80.

You can do plenty of things to lower your blood pressure, including losing weight, avoiding salt, eating more fruits and vegetables, and, of course, exercising. But if all else fails, your doctor may prescribe medication. Many blood pressure medicines are available, and one or two will be exactly right for you. See *High Blood Pressure For Dummies,* 2nd Edition, for an extensive discussion of the large number of blood pressure medications.

One class of drugs in particular is very useful for people with diabetes with high blood pressure: angiotensin converting enzyme inhibitors (ACE inhibitors), which are especially protective of your kidneys. If kidney damage is detected early, ACE inhibitors can reverse the damage. Some experts believe that all diabetics should take ACE inhibitors. We believe that if there's no evidence of kidney damage and the diabetes is well controlled, this isn't necessary.

Considering the Rest of Your Lifestyle

Diabetes is just one part of your life. It can affect the rest of your lifestyle, however, and your lifestyle certainly affects your diabetes. In this section, we take up some of these other parts of your lifestyle, all of which you can alter to the benefit of your health and your diabetes. Try making changes one at a time, and when you think you have that one under control, move on to the next.

Drinking alcohol safely

A glass of wine is a pleasant addition to dinner, and studies show that alcohol in moderation can lower the risk of a heart attack. For a diabetic, it is especially important that food accompany the wine because alcohol reduces the blood glucose; a complication called hypoglycemia may occur (see the section "Short-term complications," earlier in this chapter).

Never drink alcohol without food, especially when you're taking glucose-lowering medication.

The following people should not drink alcohol at all:

- ✔ Pregnant women
- ✔ Women who are breastfeeding
- ✔ Children and adolescents
- ✔ People who take medications that interact with alcohol
- ✔ People with medical conditions that are worsened by alcohol, such as liver disease and certain diseases of the pancreas

The amount of wine that is safe on a daily basis is a maximum of two 4-ounce glasses for a man or one 4-ounce glass for a woman. Men metabolize alcohol more rapidly than women, so they can drink more. But you should drink no more than a maximum of five days out of seven.

In terms of alcohol content, 1½ ounces of hard liquor, such as gin, rum, vodka, or whisky, or 12 ounces of light beer are the equivalent of a 4-ounce glass of wine.

Alcohol adds calories without any nutrition. Alcohol has no vitamins or minerals, but you do have to account for the calories in your diet. If you stop drinking alcohol, you may lose a significant amount of weight. For example, a person who has been drinking three drinks a night and stops will lose 26 pounds in a year.

Alcohol can cause cirrhosis of the liver and raises blood pressure. It also worsens diabetic neuropathy. Do you need any more reasons not to drink alcohol?

In addition to drinking alcohol in moderation, here are major ways you can improve the rest of your lifestyle:

- ✔ Avoid tobacco in any form. It is the number-one killer.
- ✔ Avoid illicit drugs.
- ✔ Drive safely.
- ✔ Benefit from relationships.
- ✔ Maintain your sense of humor.

Chapter 2

How What You Eat Affects Your Diabetes

*O*besity is getting bigger. As defined by a body mass index of 30 m^2 or greater, the percent of Americans who were obese went from 23.9 in 2005 to 25.6 in 2007. During the same period, the prevalence of people with a diagnosis of diabetes went from 20.8 million in 2005 to 23.6 million in 2007.

The United States must reverse this trend. Otherwise, millions of people will become blind, develop kidney failure, and require amputations. In addition, millions of people will become heart attack victims, many of whom will not survive their first heart attack.

Diet can lower the hemoglobin A1c, a measure of the average glucose in the blood for the last 90 days, by 1 percent or more. For every 1 percent reduction in hemoglobin A1c, there is a 33 percent reduction in complications of diabetes. See *Diabetes For Dummies,* 3rd Edition (Wiley), for more information on hemoglobin A1c.

This chapter tells you how much to eat, what to eat, and when to eat. Because most people with diabetes are overweight, I provide advice so that eating healthy becomes a way of life for you. And don't forget the important value of exercise, particularly "skipping" soda, "skipping" fatty foods, and "skipping" desserts.

The first thing you need to know when you plan your diet is how much you should be eating. To find out how many *kilocalories* (commonly called *calories*) you need, you have to do a little math. Chapter 3 shows you how to determine your ideal weight and the number of kilocalories you need, depending on your lifestyle and weight goals.

After you know your total calorie intake objective, break it down into the three sources of energy: carbohydrates, protein, and fat.

Considering a Vegetarian Diet

The evidence for the benefits of vegetarian eating for your health is growing. There are several degrees of vegetarian eating:

- ✔ Vegan leaves out all animal meats and products including dairy.

- ✔ Lacto-ovo vegetarian includes eggs, milk, and milk products.

- ✔ Pesco-vegetarian includes fish with eggs, milk, and milk products.

A study in the May 2009 issue of *Diabetes Care* compared the eating patterns in Seventh Day Adventists, a group in whom there were different patterns of vegetarianism. The study found that the group that followed a vegan diet had the lowest average *body mass index* (BMI), 23.6, while lacto-ovo vegetarians had a BMI of 25.7, pesco-vegetarians had a BMI of 26.3, and nonvegetarians had an average BMI of 28.8. The prevalence of diabetes increased from 2.9 percent in vegans to 7.6 percent in nonvegetarians.

A second key study in the March 2007 issue of *The Archives of Internal Medicine* looked at 322,263 men and 223,390 women who provided detailed histories of their diet and other habits including smoking, exercise, alcohol consumption, education, weight, and family history of cancer. Over the course of ten years, 47,976 men and 23,276 women died. Their meat consumption varied from 1 ounce to 4 ounces a day and processed meat (like hot dogs, salami, etc.) ranged from once a week to one and one half ounces a day. The number of excess deaths attributed to high meat consumption was large. The authors drew the following conclusions:

- ✔ If these groups are representative of all Americans, over the course of a decade, the deaths of 1 million men and half a million women could be prevented by eating less red and processed meats.

- ✔ People should eat a hamburger only once or twice a week maximum.

- ✔ People should eat steak only once a week maximum.

- ✔ People should eat processed meats less than once in six weeks.

The study didn't begin to calculate the benefits to the environment of producing much less meat, which are enormous.

As a result of studies like these and many others, we are emphasizing vegetarian eating much more in this edition and may, perhaps, publish a whole edition of vegetarian recipes. Whether you will benefit is entirely up to you.

Calculating Carbohydrates — Precursors of Glucose

When you eat a meal, the immediate source of glucose in your blood comes from the carbohydrates in that meal. One group of carbohydrates is the starches, such as cereals, grains, pastas, breads, crackers, starchy vegetables, beans, peas, and lentils. Fruits make up a second major source of carbohydrate. Milk and milk products contain not only carbohydrate but also protein and a variable amount of fat, depending on whether the milk is whole, lowfat, or fat-free. Other sources of carbohydrate include cakes, cookies, candies, sweetened beverages, and ice cream. These foods also contain a variable amount of fat.

To determine what else is found in food, check a source such as *The Official Pocket Guide to Diabetic Exchanges,* published by the American Diabetes Association and the American Dietetic Association, or *The Diabetes Carbohydrate and Fat Gram Guide,* published by the American Diabetes Association.

Determining the amount of carbohydrate

How much carbohydrate should you have in your diet? The current recommendation is between 40 to 65 percent of daily calories. In our experience, those who keep their carbohydrate intake on the lower side of that range have less trouble controlling their blood glucose levels and maintaining lower levels of blood fats. Your registered dietitian may recommend more. We wouldn't argue as long as you can maintain satisfactory blood glucose levels while not increasing the level of *triglyceride,* a blood fat.

Considering the glycemic index

The various carbohydrate sources differ in the degree to which they raise the blood glucose. This difference is called the *glycemic index* (GI), and it refers to the glucose-raising power of a food compared with white bread.

In general, choose foods with a lower glycemic index in order to keep the rise in blood glucose to a minimum. Predicting the glycemic index of a mixed meal (one that contains an appetizer, a main dish, and a dessert) is nearly impossible, but you can make some simple substitutions to lower the glycemic index of your diet, as shown in Table 2-1.

Table 2-1	Simple Diet Substitutions to Lower GI
High GI foods	*Low GI foods*
Whole meal or white bread	Whole-grain bread
Processed breakfast cereal	Unrefined cereals like oats or processed low-GI cereals
Plain cookies and crackers	Cookies made with dried fruits or whole grains like oats
Cakes and muffins	Cakes and muffins made with fruits, oats, and whole grains
Tropical fruits like bananas	Temperate-climate fruits like apples and plums
Potatoes	Pasta or legumes
Rice	Basmati or other low-GI rice

Many of these lower glycemic index foods contain a lot of fiber. Fiber is a carbohydrate that can't be broken down by digestive enzymes, so it doesn't raise blood glucose and adds no calories. Fiber has been shown to reduce the risk of coronary heart disease and diabetes while it improves bowel function, preventing constipation. For the person who has diabetes already, fiber reduces blood glucose levels. The riper the fruit, the higher the GI.

If a food has a lot of fiber in it (more than 5 grams per serving), you can subtract the grams of fiber from the grams of carbohydrates in that food in determining the calories from carbohydrate.

The best sources of fiber are fruits, whole grains, and vegetables, especially the legumes. Animal food sources don't provide fiber. It is recommended that you consume 25 grams of fiber daily. Table 2-2 shows some sources of larger amounts of fiber.

Table 2-2	Sources of Fiber	
Food, Amount	*Fiber (gm)*	*Kcalories*
Navy beans, cooked, ½ cup	9.5	128
Bran cereal, ½ cup	8.8	78
Kidney beans, ½ cup	8.2	109

Food, Amount	Fiber (gm)	Kcalories
Split peas, cooked, ½ cup	8.1	116
Lentils, cooked ½ cup	7.8	115
Black beans, cooked, ½ cup	7.5	114
Whole-wheat English muffin	4.4	134
Pear, raw, small	4.3	81
Apple, with skin, 1 medium	3.3	72

Fiber can be present in two forms:

✔ **Insoluble:** It doesn't dissolve in water but stays in the intestine as *roughage,* which helps to prevent constipation; for example, fiber found in whole-grain breads and cereals, and the skin of fruits and vegetables.

✔ **Soluble:** It dissolves in water and enters the blood, where it helps lower glucose and cholesterol; for example, fiber found in barley, brown rice, and beans, as well as vegetables and fruits.

You can take a spoonful of sugar in your coffee and have a little sugar in your food, but be aware of the number of calories you are adding with no micronutrients (vitamins and minerals present in tiny amounts but essential). See "Monitoring Your Micronutrients," later in this chapter, for more info.

Choosing sugar substitutes

Although people with diabetes are allowed to have some sugar in their diet, sugar is more appropriate for a diabetic who is at normal weight than an obese diabetic. Preventing obesity may be a matter of avoiding as little as 50 extra calories a day. If this can be accomplished by using artificial sweeteners, which provide sweetening power but no calories, so much the better.

Some of the recipes in this book call for ¼ cup or more of sugar. These are perfect opportunities to use a sugar substitute and significantly lower the calories from sugar.

Kilocalorie-containing sweeteners

Several sugars besides sucrose (table sugar) are present in food. These sugars have different properties than glucose, are taken up differently from the intestine, and raise the blood level at a slower rate or not at all if they're not ultimately converted into glucose. They sometimes cause diarrhea.

Although these kilocalorie-containing sweeteners are sweeter than sugar and you use them in smaller amounts, they *do* have calories that you must count in your daily intake.

The following sweeteners contain kilocalories but act differently in the body than sucrose:

- ✔ **Fructose, found in fruits and berries:** Fructose is sweeter than table sugar and is absorbed more slowly than glucose, so it raises the glucose level more slowly. When it enters the bloodstream, it is taken up by the liver, where it is converted to glucose.

- ✔ **Xylitol, found in strawberries and raspberries:** Xylitol is also sweeter than table sugar and has fewer kilocalories per gram. It is absorbed more slowly than sugar. When used in gum, for example, it reduces the occurrence of dental caries (tooth decay).

- ✔ **Sorbitol and mannitol, sugar alcohols occurring in plants:** Sorbitol and mannitol are half as sweet as table sugar and have little effect on blood glucose. They change to fructose in the body.

Sweeteners without calories

This group of non-nutritive or artificial sweeteners (with the exception of Stevia, which comes from a plant) is much sweeter than table sugar and contains no calories at all. Much less of these sweeteners will provide the same level of sweetness as a larger amount of sugar. However, the taste of some of them may seem a little "off" compared to sugar or honey. They include the following:

- ✔ **Saccharin:** This has 300 to 400 times the sweetening power of sugar, and it is heat stable so it can be used in baking and cooking. Brand names for saccharin are Sucaryl, SugarTwin, and Sweet'N Low.

- ✔ **Aspartame:** This is more expensive than saccharin, but people often prefer its taste. It is 150 to 200 times as sweet as sugar. Equal and Sweetmate are two of the brands. It loses its sweetening power when heated, so it can't be used if food has to be cooked for longer than 20 minutes.

- ✔ **Acesulfame-K:** This is 200 times sweeter than sugar and is heat stable, so it is used in baking and cooking.

- ✔ **Stevia:** This is 250 to 300 times sweeter than sugar. It was approved by the FDA in 2008 and marketed as Rebiana in Coca-Cola.

- ✔ **Sucralose:** This sweetener, which is made from sugar, is 600 times sweeter than its parent, sucrose. The brand name is Splenda. It remains stable when heated and has become a favorite sweetener in the food industry. Because foods don't bake the same when made with Splenda, a combination of Splenda and sugar called "Pure Magic" is sold to reduce calories while providing the baking characteristics of sugar.

Appendix C shows the amount of these various sweeteners that will give the sweetening power of a measured amount of sucrose (table sugar). Feel free to substitute calorie-free sweeteners whenever sugar is called for. The calories you save could make a big difference in your diabetes.

Contrary to opinions that you may hear or read, there is no scientific evidence that these sweeteners are associated with a higher incidence of cancer.

Getting Enough Protein (Not Just from Meat)

Most Americans are already eating more than the recommended daily intake of protein. Protein comes from meat, fish, poultry, milk, and cheese. It can also be found in beans, peas, and lentils, which we mention in the carbohydrate discussion in the preceding section. Meat sources of protein can be low or very high in fat, depending on the source. Because people with diabetes should be trying to keep the fat content of their diets fairly low, lowfat sources of protein, such as skinless white meat chicken or turkey, flounder or halibut, and fat-free cheese are preferred. Beans, peas, and lentils, which can be very good sources of protein, don't contain fat but do contain carbohydrate.

How much protein should you eat? We recommend that 40 percent of your calories should be carbohydrate, and in the next section, we suggest that you limit your fat intake to 30 percent of your calories. The remaining 30 percent is protein.

Protein doesn't cause an immediate rise in blood glucose, but it can raise glucose levels several hours later, after your liver processes the protein and converts some of it into glucose. Therefore, protein isn't a good choice if you want to treat low blood glucose, but a snack containing protein at bedtime may help prevent low blood glucose during the night.

Focusing on Fat

Fat comes in many different forms. The one everyone talks about is cholesterol, the type found in the yolk of an egg. However, most of the fat that people eat comes in a chemical form known as triglyceride. This term refers to the chemistry of the fat, and we don't have to get into the details of it for you to understand how to handle fat in your diet. In the following sections, we start with a discussion of cholesterol and then turn to other forms of fat.

Zeroing in on cholesterol

These days, just about everyone knows his or her cholesterol level. You usually find out your total cholesterol level, a combination of so-called good cholesterol and bad cholesterol. If your total is high, much of that cholesterol may be the good kind — *HDL (high-density lipoprotein)* cholesterol. If you're interested in knowing the balance between good and bad cholesterol in your body, talk with your medical practitioner, who may recommend a lipid panel that delivers more details.

The Framingham Study, an ongoing study of the health of the citizens of Framingham, Massachusetts, has shown that the total cholesterol amount divided by the good cholesterol figure gives a number that is a reasonable measure of the risk of a heart attack. People who had results that were less than 4.5 were at lower risk of heart attacks, while those with results of more that 4.5 were at higher risk. The risk increases as the number rises.

More recently, another component of the total cholesterol in your blood, the so-called bad cholesterol or *LDL-C (low-density lipoprotein cholesterol)* has been found to have a very important role in causing heart attacks. For people at high risk of a heart attack, the recommended level for LDL used to be less than 100 mg/dl but has recently been lowered to less than 70 mg/dl.

Most foods don't contain much cholesterol — with the exception of eggs. The daily recommendation for cholesterol is less than 300 milligrams, and one egg almost reaches that level. Some doctors say that eating an egg two or three times a week won't hurt you, but this isn't true if you have diabetes. Avoid eggs and foods such as organ meats that are high in cholesterol, or use egg substitutes instead.

Taking a look at other types of fat

Although cholesterol gets all the press, most of the fat you eat is in the form of triglyceride, the fat you see on fatty meats, contained in whole-fat dairy products, and in many processed foods. There are several forms of triglyceride:

- **Saturated fat** is the kind of fat that comes from animal sources like that big piece of rib-eye steak you ate the other night. Butter, bacon, cream, and cream cheese are other examples. Saturated fat increases your bad cholesterol levels and should be avoided.

- **Trans fats** were invented by food manufacturers to replace butter, which is more expensive. Unfortunately trans fats, which are currently listed as partially hydrogenated oil on food labels, may be worse than saturated fat in causing coronary heart disease. They're found in margarine, cake mixes, dried soup mixes, many fast foods, and many frozen foods, doughnuts, cookies, potato chips, breakfast cereals, candies, and whipped toppings. Keep them out of your diet by reading food labels, which must list them.

✔ **Unsaturated fats** come from vegetable sources such as olive oil and canola oil. There are two forms of unsaturated fats:

   • **Monounsaturated fats,** which don't raise cholesterol in the blood. Olive oil, canola oil, and avocado are some examples. The oil in nuts is also monounsaturated.

   • **Polyunsaturated fats,** which don't raise cholesterol but can lower good or HDL cholesterol. Corn oil, mayonnaise, and some margarines have this form of fat.

Curbing your fat intake

Fat has concentrated calories, so don't eat too much fat in your diet. However, monounsaturated fats seem to protect against heart disease. The increased intake of olive oil by people living around the Mediterranean Sea may be the reason for their lower incidence of heart disease.

Although vegetable sources of fat are generally better than animal sources, the exceptions are palm oil and coconut oil, which are highly saturated fats.

Demystifying fatspeak

If you're concerned about the amount of fat in your diet (and of course you are), you should understand the government definitions of words describing the amounts of fat in various foods.

Here are the definitions:

✔ **Fat-free:** Less than 0.5 grams of fat per serving

✔ **Lowfat:** Less than 3 grams of fat per serving

✔ **Reduced fat:** 25 percent less fat when compared with a similar food

✔ **Lean meat:** Less than 10 grams of fat, less than 4 grams of saturated fat, and less than 95 milligrams of cholesterol per serving

✔ **Low saturated fat:** 1 gram or less of saturated fat and no more than 15 percent of calories from saturated fat

✔ **Cholesterol-free:** Less than 2 milligrams of cholesterol per serving or 2 grams or less of saturated fat per serving

✔ **Low cholesterol:** Less than 20 milligrams of cholesterol or less than 2 grams of saturated fat per serving

✔ **Reduced cholesterol:** At least 25 percent less cholesterol compared to a similar food and 2 grams or less of saturated fat

Here's my bottom line recommendation: No more than 30 percent of your kilo-calories should come from fat, and of that, no more than a third should come from saturated fats. For a person eating 1,500 kilocalories a day, this recommendation would mean 450 kilocalories from fat, and 150 of those kilocalories from saturated fat.

Use vegetable oils, preferably canola oil and olive oil, as your primary sources of fat, because these lower cholesterol.

Choose fish or poultry as your source of protein in order to avoid consuming too much fat along with your protein. If you remove the skin from chicken, you'll get little fat. Fish actually has certain fatty acids that lower cholesterol.

There's a little danger in eating too much salmon, however. One man ate so many salmon croquettes, salmon steaks, and salmon salads that he had to fight the urge to go north and spawn.

Figuring Out Your Diet

After you know how much to eat of each energy source (carbohydrate, fat, and protein), how do you translate this into actual foods? You can use two basic approaches and a new, even simpler technique.

Using the food guide pyramid

The federal government, with the assistance of many experts, has come up with a simple way for you to eat a good, balanced diet: the food guide pyramid. This pyramid was recently completely revised so that you can be more specific about food choices and portions depending on your specific needs. For complete information about the new pyramid and how you can use it to your best advantage, be sure to check out www.mypyramid.gov. After you enter some basic information about yourself, using the site's interactive tool, you can get specific portion sizes for each food group. This Web site is full of great nutritional information and tips on how to adapt the pyramid's recommendations to your lifestyle.

The food guide pyramid is probably a good tool for a person with type 2 diabetes who doesn't tend to gain weight, but the person with type 1 diabetes or the person who is obese with type 2 diabetes needs to know the specific number of calories and particularly the carbohydrate calories that he or she is eating. That's the reason I provide information about carbohydrate counting as well as a new calculation method in the next sections.

Working with diabetic exchanges

Diabetic exchanges were first developed by the American Diabetes Association and the U.S. Public Health Service in the 1950s. They were revised in 1976, 1986, and 1995, but dietitians, in general, ignore it in advising patients with diabetes. We believe it is time to drop it from the teaching of good food practices in diabetes. If you have a previous version of this book, please cross it out! Carbohydrate counting, in the next section, is a much simpler and more useful approach.

Counting carbohydrates

People with type 1 diabetes and those with type 2 diabetes who take insulin may find the technique of counting carbohydrates to be the easiest for them. You still need to know how much carbohydrate you should eat in a given day. You divide the total into the meals and snacks that you eat and then, with the help of your doctor or certified diabetes educator, you determine your short-acting insulin needs based upon that amount of carbohydrates and the blood glucose that you measure before that meal.

For example, suppose that a person with diabetes is about to have a breakfast containing 60 grams of carbohydrate. He has found that each unit of lispro insulin controls about 20 grams of carbohydrate intake in his body. Figuring the proper amount of short-acting insulin can be accomplished by a process of trial and error: knowing the amount of carbohydrate intake and determining how many units are needed to keep the blood glucose level about the same after eating the carbohydrate as it was before. (The number of carbohydrate grams that each unit of insulin can control differs for each individual, and another person might control only 15 grams per unit.)

In this example, the person's measured blood glucose is 150 mg/dl (milligrams per deciliter). This result is about 50 mg/dl higher than he wants it to be. He knows that he can lower his blood glucose by 50 mg/dl for every unit of insulin he takes. Therefore, he needs 3 units of lispro for the carbohydrate intake and 1 unit for the elevated blood glucose for a total of 4 units. For more information on lispro, other types of insulin, and figuring out insulin sensitivity, see Dr. Rubin's book *Diabetes For Dummies,* 3rd Edition (Wiley).

He has a morning that is more active than he expected. When lunchtime comes, his blood glucose is down to 60 mg/dl. He's about to eat a lunch containing 75 grams of carbohydrate. He takes 4 units of lispro for the food but reduces it by 1 unit to a total of 3 units because his blood glucose is low.

At dinner, he is eating 45 grams of carbohydrate. His blood glucose is 115 mg/dl. He takes 2 units of lispro for the food intake and needs no change for the blood glucose, so he takes only 2 units.

To be a successful carbohydrate counter, you must

- ✔ Have an accurate knowledge of the grams of carbohydrate in the food you are about to eat and how many units of insulin you need for a given number of grams of carbohydrate.
- ✔ Measure your blood glucose and know how your body responds to each unit of insulin.

You can make this calculation a little easier by using *constant carbohydrates,* which means that you try to choose carbohydrates so that you are eating about the same amount at every meal and snack. This approach makes determining proper amounts of insulin less tricky; just add or subtract units based upon your blood glucose level before that meal. A few sessions with your physician or a certified diabetes educator can help you feel more comfortable about counting carbohydrates.

Using a simple calculation

For patients with type 1 diabetes and those with type 2 diabetes who take a shot of rapid-acting insulin before meals and a shot of long-acting insulin once a day, this may be the easiest way to go. And it is just as effective as carbohydrate counting in lowering the hemoglobin A1c.

The method is based on a study published in *Diabetes Care* in July 2008. The authors compared their method with a group that did traditional carbohydrate counting and found no difference. Both techniques lowered the hemoglobin A1c into the normal range.

The targets were a fasting blood glucose of less than 95 mg/dl, blood glucose before lunch and dinner of less than 100 mg/dl, and bedtime glucose of less than 130 mg/dl.

The initial dose of the long-acting insulin (in this case, insulin glargine) was determined by adding all the insulin taken in a day before the study began. The dose was then started at 50 percent of the previous total daily insulin. The dose was adjusted by taking the mean of the previous three day's fasting glucose levels. The adjustment was then made as follows:

If the mean of the last three-day fasting glucose was

- ✔ **Greater than 180 mg/dl:** Increase 8 units
- ✔ **140 to 180 mg/dl:** Increase 6 units

✔ **120 to 139 mg/dl:** Increase 4 units

✔ **95 to 119 mg/dl:** Increase 2 units

✔ **70 to 94 mg/dl:** No change

✔ **Less than 70 mg/dl:** Decrease by the same units as the previous increase or up to 10 percent of the previous dose

The dose of the rapid-acting insulin before meals (in this case insulin glulisine) at first totaled the other 50 percent of the pre-study daily insulin. It was divided into 50 percent for the meal with the most carbohydrate, 33 percent for the middle meal, and 17 percent for the meal with the least carbohydrate. Table 2-3 shows the adjustments made to the rapid-acting insulin based on the pattern of the pre-lunch, pre-dinner, and bedtime glucose patterns of the previous week.

Table 2-3	Adjustment of Rapid-Acting Insulin	
Mealtime and bedtime dose	**Pattern of mealtime blood glucose below target**	**Pattern of mealtime blood glucose above target**
Less than or equal to 10 units	Decrease by 1 unit	Increase by 1 unit
11 to 19 units	Decrease by 2 units	Increase by 2 units
20 units or greater	Decrease by 3 units	Increase by 3 units

Try this system for yourself. It's easy and it works.

Monitoring Your Micronutrients

Food contains a lot more than just carbohydrate, protein, and fat. Most of the other components are *micronutrients* (present in tiny or micro quantities), which are essential for maintaining the health of human beings. Examples of micronutrients include vitamins (such as vitamin C and vitamin K) and minerals (such as calcium, magnesium, and iron). Most micronutrients are needed in such small amounts that it's extremely unlikely that you would ever suffer a deficiency of them. A person who eats a balanced diet by using the pyramid technique or the exchange technique doesn't have to worry about getting sufficient quantities of micronutrients — with a few exceptions, which follow:

✔ Adults need to be sure to take in at least 1,000 milligrams of calcium each day. If you're a young person still growing, pregnant, or elderly, you need 1,500 milligrams daily. The best food sources of calcium are plain nonfat yogurt, fat-free or lowfat milk, fortified ready-to-eat cereals, and calcium-fortified soy beverages.

✔ Some menstruating women lose more iron than their bodies can spare and need to take iron supplements. The best sources of iron are iron-rich plant foods like spinach and lowfat meats.

✔ You probably take in 20 to 40 times more salt (sodium) than you need and are better off leaving added salt out of your diet.

✔ You should increase your uptake of potassium to help lower blood pressure. The best sources are leafy green vegetables, fruit from vines, and root vegetables. For more information on micronutrients, check out *Diabetes For Dummies,* 2nd Edition.

Recognizing the Importance of Timing of Food and Medication

If you take insulin, the peak of your insulin activity should correspond with the greatest availability of glucose in your blood. To accomplish this, you need to know the time when your insulin is most active, how long it lasts, and when it is no longer active.

✔ *Regular insulin,* which has been around for decades, takes 30 minutes to start to lower the glucose level, peaks at three hours, and is gone by six to eight hours. This insulin is used before meals to keep glucose low until the next meal. The problem with regular insulin has always been that you have to take it 30 minutes before you eat or run the risk of becoming hypoglycemic at first, and hyperglycemic later when the insulin is no longer around but your food is providing glucose.

✔ *Rapid-acting lispro insulin* and *insulin glulisine* are the newest preparations and the shortest acting. They begin to lower the glucose level within five minutes after administration, peak at about one hour, and are no longer active by about three hours. These insulins are a great advance because they free the person with diabetes to take a shot only when he or she eats. Because their activity begins and ends so quickly, they don't cause hypoglycemia as often as the older preparation.

Given a choice, because of its rapid onset and fall-off in activity, I recommend either lispro or glulisine as the short-acting insulins of choice for people with type 1 diabetes and those with type 2 diabetes who take insulin.

If you're going out to eat, you rarely know when the food will be served. Using rapid-acting insulins, you can measure your blood glucose when the food arrives and take an immediate shot. These preparations really free you to take insulin when you need it. They add a level of flexibility to your schedule that didn't exist before.

If you take regular insulin, keep to a more regular schedule of eating. In addition to short-acting insulin, if you have type 1 diabetes, or in some instances type 2 diabetes, you need to take a longer-acting preparation. The reason is to ensure that some insulin is always circulating to keep your body's metabolism running smoothly. Insulin glargine and insulin detemir are preparations that have no peak of activity but are available for 24 hours. You take one shot daily at bedtime, and they cover your needs for insulin except when large amounts of glucose enter your blood after meals. That is what rapid-acting insulins are for.

Each person responds in his or her own way to different preparations of insulin. You need to test your blood glucose to determine your individual response.

An additional factor affecting the onset of insulin is the location of the injection. Because your abdominal muscles are usually at rest, injection of insulin into the abdomen results in more consistent blood glucose levels. If you use the arms or legs, the insulin will be taken up faster or slower, depending on whether you exercise or not. Be sure to rotate sites.

The depth of the injection also affects the onset of activity of the insulin. A deeper injection results in a faster onset of action. If you use the same length needle and insert it to its maximum length each time, you'll ensure more uniform activity.

You can see from the discussion in this section that a great deal of variation is possible in the taking of an insulin shot. It's no wonder that people who must inject insulin tend to have many more ups and downs in their blood glucose. But with proper education, these variations can be reduced.

If you take oral medication, in particular the sulfonylurea drugs like micronase and glucotrol, the timing of food in relation to the taking of your medication must also be considered. For a complete explanation of this balance between food and medication, see *Diabetes For Dummies,* 3rd Edition.

Chapter 3

Planning Meals for Your Weight Goal

*Y*ou can eat wisely, get all the nutrients you need, *and* continue to eat great food, but you do have to limit your portions. In this chapter, we show you how to plan three different daily levels of *kilocalories* (the proper term for what most people call *calories*). You can lose weight rapidly, lose more slowly, or maintain your weight.

We prefer the slower approach to losing weight. With this method, you'll probably feel less hungry, and cutting back a few hundred kilocalories a day doesn't cause a major upheaval in daily life. Also, maintaining a weight loss may be easier if you lose the weight slowly.

Exercise can help speed up weight loss or permit you to eat more and still lose weight. Twenty minutes of walking burns up 100 kilocalories, and 30 minutes of walking burns up 150 kilocalories. Walk for 30 minutes a day, and you lose about ⅓ of a pound per week (7 times 150 equals 1,050 kilocalories divided into 3,500) — without reducing your calories. That activity amounts to an annual weight loss of 17 pounds in a year. Who says you can't lose weight by exercising but not dieting?

Considering the calories you're storing

Patients often worry that they're going to feel hungry if they take in fewer calories than they need. Does a bear feel hungry as it lives off its fat all winter long? No, it sleeps.

One of our favorite tasks is to point out how many calories of energy are stored in the body of an overweight or obese person. Each pound of fat contains 3,500 kilocalories. If you're 25 pounds overweight, you have 87,500 kilocalories (25 times 3,500) of stored energy in your body. We can give you an idea of what you could do with that much energy. You need

100 kilocalories to walk 20 minutes at 4 miles an hour. So a walk of 1⅓ miles (one-third of 4 miles) burns 100 kilocalories. Your stored energy — 87,500 kilocalories — would take you about 1,100 miles (87,500 divided by 100 times 1⅓)!

We certainly don't suggest that you stop eating and fast for any length of time in order to lose weight, but recognize that your stored energy, in the form of fat, will provide all the calories necessary to continue your daily activities without fatigue and often without hunger.

Figuring Out How Many Calories You Need

Before planning a nutritional program, you need to know how much you need to eat on a daily basis to maintain your current weight. Then you can figure how rapidly a deficit of calories will get you to your goal.

Finding your ideal weight range

The ideal weight for your height is a range and not a single weight at each height, but we use numbers that give a weight in the middle of that range. Because people have different amounts of muscle and different size frames, you're considered normal if your weight is plus or minus 10 percent of this number. For example, a person who is calculated to have an ideal weight of 150 pounds is considered normal at a weight of 135 (150 minus 10 percent) to 165 (150 plus 10 percent) pounds.

Because no two people, even twins, are totally alike in all aspects of their lives, we can only approximate your ideal weight and the number of calories you need to maintain that weight. You'll test the correctness of the approximation by adding or subtracting calories. If your daily caloric needs are 2,000 kilocalories and you find yourself putting on weight, try reducing your intake by 100 kilocalories and see whether you maintain your weight on fewer kilocalories.

If you're a male, your approximate ideal weight is 106 pounds for 5 feet of height plus 6 pounds for each inch over 5 feet. If you're a female, your ideal weight is 100 pounds for 5 feet plus 5 pounds for each inch over 5 feet tall. For example, a 5-foot-4-inch male should weigh 130 pounds while the same height female should weigh 120 pounds. Your ideal weight range is then plus or minus 10 percent. The male could weigh 117 to 143 pounds and the female 108 to 132 pounds.

Now you know your ideal weight for your height. What a surprise! Yes, we know. You have big bones, but bear with us. It is amazing how often we have seen big bones melt away as weight is lost.

Determining your caloric needs

After you know about how much you should weigh, figure out how many calories you need to maintain your ideal weight. Start by multiplying your ideal weight by ten. For example, if you're a male, 5 feet, 6 inches tall, your ideal weight is 142 pounds. Your daily kilocalorie allowance is about 1,400. But this number is ideal only if you don't take a breath or have a heartbeat. It is considered your *basal* caloric need. You must increase your calorie intake depending upon the amount of physical activity you do each day. Table 3-1 shows this graduated increase.

Table 3-1	Kilocalories Needed Based on Activity Level	
Level of Activity	*Kilocalories Added*	*5'6" Male*
Sedentary	10% more than basal	1,540 kilocalories
Moderate	20% more than basal	1,680 kilocalories
Very active	40%+ more than basal	1,960+ kilocalories

The "Very active" line displays a plus sign because some people doing hard manual labor need so many extra calories that they should not be held to only 40 percent more than their basal calorie intake. This requirement becomes clear as the person gains or loses weight on his or her food plan.

You gain weight when your daily intake of kilocalories exceeds your daily needs. Each pound of fat has 3,500 kilocalories, so when the excess has reached that number of calories, you are a pound heavier. On the other hand, you lose weight when your daily expenditure of calories exceeds your daily intake. You lose a pound of fat each time you burn up 3,500 kilocalories more than you take in, whether you do it by burning an extra 100 kilocalories per day for 35 days or an extra 500 kilocalories per day for 7 days.

Now you can create a nutritional program and fill in the blanks with carbohydrates, proteins, fats, and real foods.

Losing Weight Rapidly at 1,200 Kilocalories

If you're a moderately active male, 5 feet, 6 inches tall, you need 1,680 or approximately 1,700 kilocalories daily to maintain your weight. (Refer to Table 3-2.) If you eat only 1,200 kilocalories daily, you'll have a daily deficit of approximately 500 kilocalories. By dividing the kilocalories in a pound of fat (3,500) by 500, you can see that you'll lose 1 pound per week (3,500 divided by 500 is 7, so the loss will take 7 days).

In Chapter 3, you find that you want to eat 40 percent of your calories as carbohydrate, 30 percent as protein, and 30 percent as fat. Multiplying 1,200 kilocalories by those percentages, a 1,200 kilocalorie diet would provide 480 kilocalories of carbohydrate, 360 kilocalories of protein, and 360 kilocalories of fat. Because there are 4 kilocalories of energy in each gram of carbohydrate and protein, dividing the kilocalories by 4, you can eat 120 grams of carbohydrate and 90 grams of protein. Because there are 9 kilocalories in each gram of fat, you can eat 40 grams of fat.

You can create your diet using recipes where you know the grams of carbohydrate, such as the ones in this book. Table 3-2 shows you such a diet.

Table 3-2	A 1,200-Kilocalorie Diet			
Meal	*Recipe*	*Carbs (g)*	*Protein (g)*	*Fat (g)*
Breakfast	Whole-Wheat Waffles (Chapter 6)	30	9	1
Lunch	Goat-Cheese-Stuffed Zucchini (Chapter 11)	17	21	30
Dinner	Horseradish-Crusted Cod (Chapter 12)	73	58	9
Total		**120**	**88**	**40**

All we did in making up this diet was to make sure the carbohydrate total came to about 120 grams. It was purely accidental that the grams of protein and fat worked out so well. If they had not, my next day's diet would have been more of what was missing and less of what was present in too large an amount.

You can see how easy it is to create a diet when the grams of protein, fat, and carbohydrate are listed for you as they are in this book. It is very difficult to do the same thing when you go to a restaurant and have no idea of the contents of the food. At the grocery store, the food label gives you the break-down that you need. That is why it is so important to check the food labels, as explained in Chapter 5, to find out how much carbohydrate, protein, and fat the food actually contains.

The portions on all food labels are based on a 2,000-kilocalorie diet. Not one of the diets in this chapter allows you to eat that many calories. Such a portion may be much too large for a person on a 1,200-kilocalorie diet.

Losing Weight More Slowly at 1,500 Kilocalories

The smaller the deficit of calories between what you need and what you eat, the more slowly you'll lose weight. If your daily needs are 1,700 kilocalories and you eat 1,500, you'll be missing 200 kilocalories each day. Because a pound of fat is 3,500 kilocalories, you'll lose a pound in about 17 days (3,500 divided by 200). You'll lose almost 2 pounds a month, or 24 pounds in a year. You can accomplish this loss by reducing your daily intake by only the equiv-alent of a piece of bread and two teaspoons of margarine. Put that way, losing the weight doesn't seem difficult at all.

Below we use the recipes in this book to make up a 1,500-kilocalorie diet. In this plan, you're eating 600 kilocalories of carbohydrate or 150 grams, 450 kilocalories of protein or 112 grams, and 450 kilocalories of fat or 50 grams.

Table 3-3	A 1,500-Kilocalorie Diet			
Meal	*Recipe*	*Carbs (g)*	*Protein (g)*	*Fat (g)*
Breakfast	Blueberry and Almond Pancakes (Chapter 6)	38	10	2
Lunch	Indian-Inspired Lamb and Legume Chile (Chapter 8)	23	23	14
Dinner	Paillard of Chicken Breast with Fennel and Parmigiano (Chapter 13)	24	51	33
Total		**85**	**84**	**49**

You notice that this plan is 65 grams low on carbohydrate, 28 grams low on protein, and 1 gram low on fat. This allows you to have some fruit with the meal or snacks in between to make up the difference. An apple, half banana, and 12 cherries will provide 45 grams of carbohydrate because each is 15 grams. A tablespoon of cashews and 6 almonds will provide 10 grams of unsaturated fat. Two ounces of ricotta cheese with 5 grams of fat per ounce will provide 10 grams of fat.

As you create your meals, you'll be amazed at how small the portions really are. Four ounces of lean meat isn't much compared to what most people are used to eating at home or in restaurants. Eating proper portions is very important because it will ultimately make the difference between weight gain and weight maintenance or loss. Portion size may also be the difference between controlling your blood glucose and not controlling it. Check out Chapter 1 for more about portion sizes.

Think of the money you will save if — each time you go to a restaurant — your knowledge of portion sizes allows you to take home half of your meal to eat another day.

Maintaining Your Weight at 1,800 Kilocalories

Suppose that you have finally reached a weight (not necessarily your "ideal" weight that we calculate in the section "Figuring Your Daily Caloric Needs") that allows your blood glucose levels to remain between 80 and 140 mg/dl all the time. Now, you want to maintain that weight. You want to eat about 1,800 kilocalories, up another 300 from the previous diet in this chapter. Compared to the 1,200-kilocalorie diet, this may seem like a lot of food.

This plan provides 180 grams of carbohydrate, 135 grams of protein, and 60 grams of fat, maintaining the 40:30:30 division of calories. You can use the recipes to create this diet as well, as shown in Table 3-4.

Exercise for prevention

A study published in the June 2007 edition of *Applied Physiology, Nutrition, and Metabolism* looked at numerous studies of the effect of exercise on the occurrence of diabetes. The study concluded that 30 minutes per day of moderate- or high-level physical activity can effectively and safely prevent type 2 diabetes in all populations.

Table 3-4	An 1,800-Kilocalorie Diet			
Meal	*Recipe*	*Carbs (g)*	*Protein (g)*	*Fat (g)*
Breakfast	Greek Omelet (Chapter 6)	8	20	13
	Two slices wheat toast	30	6	0
Lunch	Creamy Veggie Lover's Soup (Chapter 8)	40	16	8
	3 oz. chicken	0	21	9
Dinner	Spit-Roasted Pork Loin (Chapter 14)	48	55	18
	Crispy Oatmeal Cookies (Chapter 16)	38.5	6	10.5
Total		**168**	**124**	**60**

This time, the plan is short 16 grams of carbohydrates and 11 grams of protein and has the right amount of fat. You can make up the difference with fruits, crackers, and other sources of carbohydrate and protein but not fat.

If you have type 2 diabetes, this plan is an excellent way for you to eat the right amount of calories in the right ratios of energy sources. If you have type 1 diabetes, or you have type 2 and take insulin, you need to know the grams of carbohydrate in each meal in order to determine your insulin needs for that meal.

Checking Out Other Diets

If you go to the diet section of any large bookstore, you'll be overwhelmed by the choices. You'll find diets that recommend protein and no carbohydrate, carbohydrate and no protein, one type of carbohydrate and not another, all rice, all grapefruit, and on and on. How is it possible for all these diets, many of which are exactly the opposite of others on the same shelf, to actually work for you? The answer is they do and they don't. If you follow any diet closely, you'll lose weight. But will the weight stay off? That is the most difficult part (as we're sure you know).

In this section we tell you about the most popular diets presently recommended by this or that brilliant "scientist." Which one do we recommend?

None of them and all of them. If you find that you can get started losing weight successfully with one of these programs, go ahead and do it, but remember that in the end you want to eat a balanced diet that is low in fat and protein and uses carbohydrates that emphasize whole grains and fiber. And remember that you won't be successful without exercise.

Reduction of any source of calories — by reduction of carbohydrates, protein, or fat — has been shown to be equally effective.

The low carbohydrate group

These diets are based on the claim that carbohydrates promote hunger. By reducing or eliminating them, you lose your hunger as you lose your weight. The first of them, the Atkins Diet, promotes any kind of protein, including protein high in fat. Naturally, other diets were developed promoting very little carbohydrate but less fatty protein. Here are your choices:

- ✔ **Atkins Diet:** This plan allows any quantity of meats, shellfish, eggs, and cheese but doesn't permit high-carbohydrate foods like fruits, starchy vegetables, and pasta. Small quantities of the forbidden foods are added in later. The program does recommend exercise but doesn't suggest changes in your eating behavior.

- ✔ **South Beach Diet:** This diet restricts carbohydrates while the recommended proteins are low in fat, unlike the Atkins Diet. Daily exercise is an important component, but the plan doesn't suggest any changes in eating behavior. Over time some carbohydrate is reintroduced into the diet.

- ✔ **Ultimate Weight Solution:** This plan recommends a lot of protein, which naturally results in a reduction in carbohydrate. This program also advises you not to eat foods that are high in fat. Support groups in which you learn how to modify your eating behaviors are very important, and you're supposed to stay in these groups throughout your life. The plan also emphasizes regular exercise, such as walking.

- ✔ **Zone Diet:** In this diet, you have to balance your food intake into exact amounts of carbohydrate, protein, and fat. You're not permitted to eat high-carbohydrate and high-fat food. Regular exercise is recommended, but the plan doesn't suggest changes in your eating behavior. You have to continue with this balance throughout life to maintain your weight loss.

The portion control group

These diets recognize that it's not what you eat but how much you eat that determines your weight. They generally follow the recommendations of the government food guidelines. Here are some examples of portion control diets:

- ✔ **DASH Diet:** Here, the emphasis is on grains, fruits, and vegetables and restricting the amounts of fat. A further modification for those with high blood pressure recommends very little salt. Animal protein, such as meat, fish, and poultry, is limited. An exercise program is suggested but not defined. This diet suggests changes in eating behavior. It is a diet for life (and a very good one).

- ✔ **Jenny Craig:** This diet is balanced in terms of carbohydrates, protein, and fat but pushes its own food products, which can get expensive. You are directed to exercise by the counselor, who is an important (and costly) part of the program as well. To stay on this diet, you need their products lifelong.

- ✔ **Weight Watchers:** This plan uses a point system in which foods are given points according to the amount of fat, fiber, and calories in them. To get to and maintain a certain weight, you're given a daily number of points. As long as you stay within these points, you'll be successful. Therefore, foods that have large amounts of calories will use up your daily points quickly. The program suggests exercise and changes in your lifestyle.

A diet that emphasizes weight training

The Abs Diet is similar to the diets that recommend a balanced approach to eating, with carbohydrates that aren't refined and dairy and meat that are low in fat as the most suggested foods. However, the major emphasis in this diet is on a program called "Total Body Strength Training Workout" to build up the muscles. Changes in eating behavior aren't a large part of the program. To maintain weight loss, you must eat and exercise as the diet prescribes for your entire life.

More extreme diets

These diets require a level of participation that may be difficult for people who have a life. You really need to give your time and energy to staying on the diet. If you go away for a few weeks and stay within their program, you'll have some short-term success. But after you return home, sticking to the program gets difficult. Here are the two major programs currently available:

- ✔ **Dean Ornish Program:** This plan allows fruits, vegetables, and whole grains along with the leanest of meats and poultry. You can't eat processed foods or drink caffeine or alcohol, and you must avoid sugar, salt, and oil. Exercise is recommended as is help with eating behaviors. Meetings are an important part of this program, which you're supposed to follow for life.

✔ **Pritikin Eating Plan:** Whole grains, vegetables, and fruits are essential foods, and the diet allows almost no protein or fat. Exercise is a part of the program as is changing your lifestyle to promote better eating behaviors. You're expected to follow this program for life.

With the exception of the DASH Diet, which is recommended by the U.S. government, none of the diets described in the preceding sections have long-term studies that show, convincingly, that they're better than any other. Each one of them has anecdotal evidence, meaning that one or two or ten people tell you how great they did on this or that diet. But you never hear from those who didn't do so great.

Chapter 4

Eating What You Like

· ·

In This Chapter

▶ Having a plan for eating

▶ Enjoying your favorite ethnic foods

▶ Keeping the right ingredients at hand

▶ Choosing the best tools

▶ Making modifications for better diabetic control

▶ Getting through the holidays

· ·

*H*aving diabetes doesn't mean you have to give up the foods that you grew up with and the foods you love the most. Some parts of every ethnic diet fit well in a diabetic regimen. You can find recipes to prove this premise in Part II of this book. You can also use all kinds of tricks to substitute good-for-you ingredients for those that won't help your diabetes. That's what this chapter is all about. Even foods that seemingly have no business on the plate of a diabetic can be enjoyed if eaten in small portions.

We wish we could eliminate the word "diet" from the diabetic vocabulary. The word implies taking something away or having to suffer somehow in order to follow it. This is not the case at all. You can eat great food and enjoy the taste of every ethnic variety, provided you concentrate on the amount of food and its breakdown into the sources of energy, keeping fats and carbohydrates in control. Perhaps the phrase "nutritional plan" would be better than "diet."

Stop dieting and start eating delicious foods. It may take a lot of willpower, but you can give up dieting if you try hard enough.

Following Your Eating Plan

Creating an eating plan that provides the proper number of kilocalories from carbohydrate, protein, and fat (see Chapter 3) is particularly important when you have diabetes. After you know how much of each you need, you can translate those numbers into recipes and pick out the food that is the delicious end point of all the calculating. Make sure that your choices come from a variety of foods rather than eating the same thing over and over. You will be much more likely to stay on your program if you aren't bored with what you eat.

Before you cook, make sure that the recipes fit into your eating plan. If you have already eaten your carbohydrate portions for the day, make sure that the food you're about to eat has little carbohydrate in it. The same is true for protein and, of course, fat. If you think "moderation" as you make your meal plan, you'll keep to the portions you need to eat and no more.

Seasonal foods should play a primary role in your eating plan for several reasons:

- ✔ Seasonal foods are the freshest foods in the market.
- ✔ They are the least expensive foods.
- ✔ The recipes you can prepare with these fresh foods are some of the most delicious. The recipes in this book show the tremendous influence that fresh ingredients have had on the imaginations of the best chefs in the United States and Canada.

In addition, time is an important factor in your eating plan. You may not have a great deal of time to prepare your food, and some of the recipes in this book may take more time than you can spare. Choose the meals that fit into your schedule. But remember that after you've prepared a recipe a few times, preparation is much faster and easier. Consider the time you spend preparing delicious, healthy food as an investment in your well-being. Take the time to eat properly now so that later you won't have to give up your time being sick.

As a person with diabetes, especially if you have type 1 diabetes, you must figure the timing of your food in your eating plan. You need to eat when your medications will balance your carbohydrates. This process is much easier with the rapid-acting insulins, lispro and glulisine, but if you're still using regular insulin, you'll have to eat about 30 minutes after you take your shot.

Another essential part of your planning is what to do when you feel hungry but shouldn't eat. You can prepare a low-calorie snack for such occasions, or you can provide yourself with some diversion, such as a hobby, a movie, or, best of all, some exercise. Examples of low-calorie snacks are baby carrots, cherry tomatoes, a piece of fruit, and lowfat pudding.

Your diabetes medication may require you to have three meals a day, but if not, having three meals is still important. This approach spreads calories over the day and helps you avoid coming to a meal extremely hungry. Try not to skip breakfast, even though society doesn't encourage taking the time for this meal. Making your own lunch as often as possible gives you control over what you eat. The fast lunches served in restaurants may not provide the lowfat nutrition that you think you're getting. For example, salads are often covered with a lot of oil. It may be the right type of oil, but it still provides a lot of fat calories.

Eating the Best of Ethnic Cuisines

If you become diabetic, you don't have to give up the kinds of food you've always eaten. You can eat the same foods but decrease the portions, particularly if you're obese. People in ethnic groups who are normal in weight are doing two things that you need to do as well: eating smaller portions and keeping physically fit with exercise. Every ethnic choice also has vegetarian foods, which will be mentioned as we describe the foods.

After you receive a diagnosis of diabetes, try to find a dietitian who treats many members of your ethnic group. This person will be best trained to show you how to keep eating what you love, while altering it slightly to fit your needs. The alteration may be no greater than simply reducing the amount of food that you eat each day. Or it may involve changing ingredients so that a high-fat source of energy is replaced by a lowfat energy source with no loss in taste.

Valuing African-American food

African-American food, sometimes called soul food, combines the food preferences and cooking methods of the African slaves with the available ingredients and available fuel found in the United States. Slow cooking with lots of vegetables and meats, eating lots of greens, combining fruits and meats in main dishes, and deep-frying meats and vegetables were cooking traditions brought to the United States. At the time, their foods, which contained too much fat, cholesterol, sugar, and salt, did not hurt the overworked and abused slaves because their daily energy needs were so great. Today, the more sedentary African-American population suffers from one of the highest incidences of obesity and diabetes, not to mention high blood pressure and the consequences of those diseases. As their energy needs fell, African Americans didn't reduce their calorie intake.

The term *soul food* also points to the central place of eating in the African-American population. In the slave quarters, the preparation and sharing of good food helped the slaves to maintain their humanity, helping those even less fortunate than themselves, who might have had no food at all. Because they had no other material possessions, food became the one symbol of wealth that wasn't taken from them. It also served as the focus of the creativity and artistic expression of the female slave.

But people don't have to abandon soul food. African-American cooks at home and chefs in restaurants have learned to use all the healthful ingredients, such as fruits, vegetables, and grains, with much smaller amounts of fat, sugar, and salt. They use spices in place of salt in very creative ways to bring out the taste of their fresh ingredients. The meats are leaner, and they use egg whites instead of the whole egg. They also avoid deep-frying as much as possible.

A new book published in March 2009 called *Vegan Soul Kitchen* by Bryant Terry (Da Capo Press) shows that you can make great soul food without animal protein or dairy.

The psychological implications of food in the African-American population means that changing from less healthy to more healthy food requires a change in mindset. African-American cooks can be just as creative or even more so with healthful ingredients. The use of less fat, less salt, and less sugar is essential, but other ingredients have to take their place. Quantities of food must be modified, and this may be the most difficult change, given the importance of food both as a symbol of wealth and for sharing. People must eat fewer cakes, pies, and cookies and find ways to creatively prepare fruit to take the place of sweet baked goods.

Appreciating Chinese food

When you think of Chinese food, you think rice. But China is such a huge place, and rice can't be grown everywhere. In the north, millet is used to make cereal. About 1500 BC, wheat was introduced from West Asia. Vegetables such as soybeans and cucumbers were added to the rice, and occasionally a little bit of chicken or beef was added. Ginger became a favorite flavoring because it was so readily available.

The Thais gave chicken to China, and pork was already there, while Westerners brought sheep and cattle. The Chinese, mostly peasants, had little fuel and little cooking oil. Consequently, they learned to cut their food into very small pieces so it would cook rapidly, using little oil for their stir-frying.

Around 1000 AD, because Buddhists, who made up a large part of the population, wouldn't eat meat, tofu or bean curd was introduced. The Chinese also learned to make long noodles from wheat and rice.

Chinese cuisine is generally healthful. It includes lots of vegetables, fruits, and seafood, while keeping sugar and desserts to a minimum. People with diabetes need to avoid eating too much rice. Chinese restaurants offer wonderful vegetable dishes, many with tofu as a protein source. You can go into any Chinese restaurant and find numerous dishes that have only vegetables with tofu as a protein source.

When you cook Chinese food, use as little sugar and fat as possible, and steer clear of making deep-fried dishes.

Welcoming French food

French food is always associated with the term "haute cuisine," which means fine food prepared by highly skilled chefs. This kind of cooking derives from Italy and was introduced to France by Catherine de Medici. The French added their own subtle techniques to the methods of the Italians from Florence, adopting their use of truffles and mushrooms and preparing lighter sauces.

The French gave the world the technique of serving a series of dishes, one after the other, instead of a large buffet where people helped themselves to everything at once.

France has several distinct culinary regions:

- ✔ **The north:** Abundant forests provide game, and streams provide fish.
- ✔ **The central area:** The red wines provide the basis for much of the cooking.
- ✔ **The south:** Goose liver, truffles, and Roquefort cheese combine with Mediterranean olive oil, garlic, and tomatoes to produce the distinctive cuisine that is loved throughout the Western world, especially in its new lighter form.

You can go to Paris and find plenty of vegetarian restaurants. French chefs — some of the best in the world — are geniuses at using whatever ingredients are at hand to make delicious meals.

Enjoying Italian food

Italian food reflects the history of Italy. Until 1870, Italy was divided into many different regions, with each one developing its own cuisine. Therefore, there is no one Italian food, but there are some common trends:

✔ The food of northern Italy features more wild game, such as deer and rabbits, along with some farm animals, such as beef, chickens, and goats. Seasonings include garlic, onions, rosemary, and bay leaf.

✔ In the south, much closer to the sea, seafood received much more emphasis. Southerners also developed some of the famous cheeses like ricotta and pecorino. It was here where the Italian staple, the artichoke, was first discovered and cultivated.

The invasions of Arabs from North Africa in southern Italy around 800 AD brought some of the foods that are now most typically thought of as Italian, things like melons, dates, rice, and lemons, but their major contribution was pasta. The Spanish gave the tomato to Italy, but the Italians took it over and made it their own.

Today, northern Italian cooking emphasizes cream and meat sauces. Rice dishes like risotto and polenta made from yellow corn are enjoyed along with gnocchi, a dumpling contributed by Germany.

As you move south, the olive becomes part of many dishes, along with wine for cooking. In southern Italy, the tomato is the basis of most cooking, particularly its use in pasta dishes. The cheeses mentioned earlier also are featured. The closeness of all parts of this region to the sea, as well as to the islands off the western coast, means that fish will be found in many meals.

These mouthwatering dishes aren't denied to the person with diabetes. The Mediterranean diet, with its emphasis on olive oil, has been shown to be healthy for your heart. One of the key changes you may need to make, however, is to reduce the amount of fat in your ingredients. Olive oil is a fat, and as you add more of it to your dishes, the calories climb rapidly. When Italians worked hard in the fields all day or traveled long distances to hunt or fish, they needed those extra calories to sustain them. But when was the last time you lifted a shovel or bagged a deer?

A second important step is reducing the size of your portion of pasta or risotto, whether you eat it at home or in the wonderful Italian restaurants (see Chapter 17 for more about eating healthy at restaurants). None of the recipes give you more than a cup of pasta or ⅔ cup of rice. Compare that with the usual 3 cups of pasta at a restaurant, and you quickly discover what changes you need to make.

On the other hand, the great fresh fruits and vegetables in Italian cooking are just what the doctor ordered, like the tomato, the artichoke, and the beans. These fit perfectly into the new emphasis of the federal food guidelines on fiber and reduction of fat. They also are the reason that Italian food is one of the easiest to convert to vegetarian.

Top off your meal with a glass of Chianti from Tuscany. (Chapter 1 tells you about the benefits of alcohol.) But skip the rich Italian desserts or share a dessert with three other people. We don't think these changes will be a hardship. They take nothing away from the glory of Italian cooking.

Feasting on Mexican food

Mexican food comes from the Mayan Indians of the southeastern part of the country. They were hunters and fisherman, so their main sources of food were wild game, such as rabbit and turkey, and fish. Their diet also included beans and corn. The Aztecs later added chocolate, vanilla, honey, and chili peppers. After Spain conquered the country in 1521, the Spanish diet began to influence Mexican food. The Spanish brought livestock like cows and pigs and taught the Mexicans to make cheese and bread.

The type of Mexican food that has become so popular in the United States, the burrito, is a stuffed wheat tortilla. The Spanish brought in the wheat, so the burrito isn't exactly an indigenous food of Mexico. The Mexican tortilla is made of cornmeal, not wheat.

Mexico has been influenced by other colonial powers, including France, Portugal, all of the surrounding islands in the Caribbean, West Africa, and South America.

As a result of the influences of other countries, Mexican food can be much more complex than the burrito. If you buy a small burrito, you get a fairly good combination of beans, chicken or beef, rice, and salsa, but you may also get your daily dose of salt in this single food. When you make your own, however, you can control the amount of salt.

The ingredients in a burrito, minus the high salt content, can make a nice meal in a hurry. When you make burritos, be sure to avoid cheese and excessive rice and watch out, especially, for the hot pepper. Leave out the chicken or beef, and you can enjoy a delicious vegetarian burrito.

Savoring Thai food

Thai food is a good choice for people with diabetes. It is cooked with little fat because stir-frying is the method of choice. Thai cooking keeps the meat, fish, and poultry to small quantities, thus providing taste rather than bulk, as in a Western diet. The dipping sauces have strong tastes, so they're used in very small quantities, minimizing the salt and sugar in the diet. Vegetables are eaten in larger quantities. At the end of the meal Thais enjoy fruits like mango, pineapple, guava, and papaya, which provide fiber, vitamins, and minerals. Therefore, it's easy to convert to vegetarian eating when you eat Thai food. Just leave out the meat, fish, or poultry.

Thai food, like Italian food, is also the product of many influences. Westerners introduced milk into Thai cooking, and because coconut milk is so readily available, this became a staple of Thai dishes. The Chinese coming down from the north brought stir-frying with them, as well as noodles. Thanks to the Chinese, the five basic flavors of Asian cuisine — bitter, salt, sour, hot, and sweet — were established, and Thai meals use them as their basis for a balance of flavors. Dishes made with soy and ginger are a good example.

India brought curry dishes to Thailand, with coconut milk serving as an antidote to the hot spices in some of those curry dishes. The Thais have put their own delicious stamp on these curries, using a lot of green chili pepper, also given to them originally by Westerners.

Southern Thai food is usually hot and spicy, and fish is a major ingredient because the area is so close to the sea. However, you can always get dishes that aren't so spicy, and the subtle tastes of good Thai cooking have made it tremendously popular in the United States and throughout the world wherever Thais are found. Rice generally is part of the meal.

Most Thai dishes have garlic, a condiment that grows all over Thailand. Coconut milk, actually a combination of the coconut flesh and the liquid inside the coconut, is added to Thai curries and soups. Fish sauce, made by fermenting shrimp, salt, and water together, takes the place of soy sauce in Thai cooking.

In American Thai restaurants, a dish called pad thai has become a favorite entrée. It means "Thai-style stir-fried noodles" and was brought to Thailand by the Chinese. When employment was low in Thailand after World War II, the government promoted noodle shops and stalls as a way of getting people back to work, and pad thai noodles became popular throughout the country. Thai immigrants brought the dish to the United States. It's not exactly representative of the finest Thai cuisine, but it's eaten so frequently in the United States that it must be considered when the diabetic has Thai food, particularly because the sauce often contains a lot of sugar. A small portion of pad thai is fine for the person with diabetes, but leave at least half the serving for another day.

Thai food is so nutritious that there is little about it to warn the person with diabetes. As always, avoid large portions and too much rice. And be careful of the hot spices.

Eating the rest of the world's cuisine

Covering all the world's wonderful cuisines in detail isn't possible in this book. We tried to cover the most popular foods in the English-speaking world, but we could devote an entire book to every type of cuisine. We know that we left out delicious cuisines that many of you love from other countries, such as Greece, India, Guatemala, Costa Rica, Argentina, and Brazil. But we hope that you will still come away with a few general tips about these foods from around the world:

- ✔ You don't have to give up the foods you love because you have diabetes.

- ✔ Food is also love, sharing, social status, wealth (which it represented for slaves), and a lot more.

- ✔ You can avoid the empty calories in fatty, sugary desserts.

Choosing from familiar foods

Esmeralda Cruz, a patient from a region of the Philippines called Pampanga, figured out how to successfully manage her diabetes without giving up the staples of her native cuisine. And good thing — her home is considered by many to be the culinary capital of the country. Esmeralda is a 46-year-old woman with type 2 diabetes, which has been diagnosed for five years. She is 5 feet, 2 inches tall and weighs 156 pounds. Her blood glucose averages 176 mg/dl, and she has a hemoglobin A1c of 8.6 percent.

Esmeralda followed a typical Filipino diet and gained at least 3 to 6 pounds each year for the last four years. She ate a lot of food fried in lard and too much rice for the calories and carbohydrate that is planned for her diet. She also tended not to trim the fat from the meat that she ate.

Her dietitian advised her to make modifications that would help her keep her diabetes in line without sacrificing the foods she loved. She recommended that Esmeralda do the following:

- ✔ Cut off visible fat from her meats
- ✔ Reduce the amount of frying and begin broiling and roasting instead
- ✔ Switch to canola oil in place of lard
- ✔ Reduce the amount of fat she used
- ✔ Eat less rice and choose low-glycemic types, like basmati
- ✔ Add more fish and poultry to her diet

Esmeralda found that the alterations usually didn't affect the food's appeal. For example, one of her dishes, a pork dish called Tortung Babi, was made with three eggs, but reducing the number to two didn't diminish the taste.

After discovering how to modify her diet rather than giving up her native food, Esmeralda began to lose weight. She gradually lost 12 pounds over the next six months, and her blood glucose began to fall to the point that it averaged 132 mg/dl with a hemoglobin A1c of 6.9 percent. Because she made these changes for all members of her family, everyone has benefited.

- ✔ The biggest problem is the large size of the portions. Try sharing or saving the food for another meal instead.

- ✔ A lot of exercise will reverse the damage of just about any dietary indiscretion.

- ✔ You can reduce the fat in your food, and it will still be delicious.

- ✔ You can reduce the salt and lower your blood pressure.

We want you to learn to eat to live — not live to eat. What you put in your mouth has a lot to do with your state of health, no matter where the food comes from.

Stocking Up with the Right Ingredients

Some common ingredients are used in many different recipes. Having them at hand is convenient, saving you needless trips to the market and more exposure to foods you don't need.

Some of the foods that belong in every kitchen or pantry (if you're a vegetarian, make the appropriate substitutions) include the following:

For the freezer:

Chicken breasts	Fruit juice concentrate
Egg substitute	Loaf of bread
Frozen fruit	Soft margarine

For the pantry:

Canned fruit	Oils (olive, canola, peanut)
Canned tomatoes	Onions
Canned tuna, salmon in water	Pasta
Dried fruit, unsugared	Pasta sauce
Evaporated skim milk	Peanut butter
Fat-free salad dressing	Potatoes
Fresh garlic	Red and white cooking wines
Fruit spreads	Reduced-calorie mayonnaise
Grains (rice, couscous)	Reduced-sodium broths
Ketchup	Reduced-sodium soy sauce
Legumes (peas, beans, lentils)	Sugar-free cocoa mix
Mustard	Tomato paste
Nonfat dry milk	Vinegars
Nonstick cooking sprays	Worcestershire sauce

For baking:

Baking powder

Baking soda

Cocoa powder

Cornstarch

Cream of tartar

Dry bread crumbs

Extracts (vanilla, lemon, almond)

Flour (all-purpose, whole-wheat)

Rolled oats

Semisweet chocolate

Sugar-free gelatin

Unflavored gelatin

Sweeteners:

Artificial sweeteners

Honey

Light maple syrup

Molasses

Sugar

Seasonings:

Dried herbs

Fresh herbs and spices

Pepper

Salt

With these ingredients, you're ready for just about any of the recipes in the book. The exceptions are exotic ingredients, such as in ethnic foods, that you can buy in specialty stores as you need them.

Prepare a list of these ingredients and make multiple copies so that you can check off what you need before you go to the market. Leave a little space for the perishables such as fresh fruits, vegetables, milk, meat, fish, and poultry. In the next chapter, we tell you more about the process of shopping for these ingredients.

Using the Right Tools

Just as you wouldn't try to bang in a nail with a shoe (especially with your foot inside), don't try to cook without the right tools. Spending a little more at the beginning pays huge dividends later on. For example, get the best set of knives you can afford. They make all cutting jobs much easier, and they last a long time. Buy good nonstick pans; they make cooking without oils much easier.

Here's the basic equipment that all kitchens should have in order to turn out delicious meals:

Chopping boards

Food processor

Knives

Measuring cups and spoons

Microwave

Mixer with dough hook

Pots and pans

Salad spinner

Scales

Steamer with double boiler

Thermometers (for roasts and turkey)

Making Simple Modifications

You can make all kinds of simple modifications that will reduce calories and reduce the amounts of foods (such as those containing cholesterol) that you are trying to keep in check. You can see that many of the modifications take you in the direction of vegetarianism. You can easily do the following:

- Use skim milk instead of whole milk.
- Use cuts of meat that are low in fat instead of high-fat meats. Lowfat meats include lean beef, lean pork, and skinless white-meat poultry.
- Trim all visible fat off meats and poultry.
- Stay away from packaged luncheon meats, which tend to be high in fat.
- Select foods that are low in sodium and saturated fats (check the label on the food).
- Choose high-fiber foods like whole fruits, vegetables, and grains.
- Enjoy nonfat yogurt instead of sour cream.
- Have dressings, sauces, and gravies served on the side.
- Substitute lentils and beans for meat, fish, and poultry.
- Replace butter with olive oil, herbs, spices, or lemon juice.
- Prepare foods by baking, broiling, and so on — any method other than frying.

Use your imagination to come up with your own unique ways to cut calories and fat.

Taking Holiday Measures

This is a particularly good heading for this section, because the key to getting through a holiday in good diabetic control is to control the portions of everything you eat during the holidays. Eating too much is easy.

If you encounter the "killer B," a buffet table, vow to make only one trip. You'll probably fill your plate with more food than you need, so plan to leave a large portion on the plate. Focus on the foods that you should eat and avoid high-fat and high-sugar foods, particularly desserts. Stick to fruits for high-fiber, low-calorie desserts.

If you're invited to a potluck dinner, make something that you know will work for your nutritional plan. You can certainly find something in this book that fits for you. These recipes have all been taste-tested and are delicious, so you don't have to think that you're bringing something inferior. We suggest that you have a snack before you go to a party so that you don't arrive feeling hungry.

Most important of all, try to forget the all-or-nothing mind-set. If you go off your nutritional plan once or twice, put the lapse behind you and get back to doing the things you know are right for you. The benefits will be immediate in the form of a general feeling of well-being and, of course, long-term in the fact that you won't develop the long-term complications of diabetes.

Chapter 5

How the Supermarket Can Help

In This Chapter

▶ Having a grocery shopping plan

▶ Reading the Nutrition Facts label

▶ Arming yourself to make good choices

*E*very trip to the market is an adventure. This chapter is about coping with the challenge of going grocery shopping without being lured into buying items that aren't good for your diabetes nutritional plan. But it's also about overcoming your natural desire to take home what you know isn't good for you.

You deserve the best, and that holds true for the food you eat as much as anything else. Of course, you could be like the man whose doctor told him that the best thing he could do for himself would be to get on a really good diet, stop chasing women, and stop drinking so much alcohol. The patient replied: "I don't deserve the best. What about second best?" We hope you won't settle for second best.

Going to the Market with a Plan

If you have a hobby, you've probably developed a series of steps by which you can accomplish your hobby in the most efficient manner, whether it's painting pictures or raising tomatoes. If you paint pictures, you certainly wouldn't start painting without deciding on a subject and buying the right paints, brushes, and canvas. If you raise tomatoes, you prepare the soil, add amendments such as manure, and buy the seeds or, more likely, the plants. You use a watering system as well as tomato cages to hold up your crop.

You should plan your excursion to the market in the same careful manner. Decide in advance what you need that complies with your nutritional plan. In Chapter 4, we give you a list of recommendations for the staples you should have at home. You can use those suggestions to make a shopping list to make sure that you purchase what you need. To that list, add the perishables that you'll use immediately, such as meat and poultry or fish, milk and other dairy products, and, of course, fruits and vegetables.

Eat something before you go to the market so that you aren't hungry as you walk down the aisles.

A market is like a huge menu set up to entice you. Most markets are set up in the same way. This setup is not by accident. It's arranged to encourage you to buy. What people buy on the impulse of the moment is often the most calorie-concentrated and expensive food that is least appropriate for them. You'll find that all the perishable food is arranged around the perimeter of the market. The high-calorie foods are in the aisles in the middle of the store. Unless you want to take the long way around, you must go through those aisles to get to the meat, milk, fruit, and vegetables. You pass the loose candies, the cookies, the high-sugar cereals, and all the other no-nos. If you prepare a list and buy only from the list, you won't purchase any of those foods. Walking into the market hungry and without a list is dangerous for your health.

Sometimes the market employs a person who is trained to help people with medical conditions avoid bad choices. Check with your market to find out whether such a person is on staff, and spend some time touring the aisles with him or her. You'll get some valuable insights that will make handling a shopping trip easier.

Some keys to shopping the market most effectively include the following:

- ✔ Shop at the same market each time.

- ✔ Shop as seldom as you can.

- ✔ Go to the market when it is not crowded.

- ✔ Don't walk every aisle.

- ✔ Don't be tempted by free samples. They're usually high in calories to appeal to your taste buds.

- ✔ If you bring your kids (not advisable) to the store, make sure that they aren't hungry.

- ✔ Be especially careful in the checkout lane, where stores force you to run through a gauntlet of goodies — none of which are good for you.

Most markets offer a variety of sections. Each one presents a different challenge and requires a different strategy. You should probably work your way around the market from the bottom of the food pyramid to the top, choosing lots of grains, fewer fruits, vegetables, and dairy and meat products, and fats and sweets least of all. (Check out Chapter 2 for more about the food pyramid.)

The supermarket isn't the only place where you can find good food. Check out your local farmer's market. Most areas have these markets, and many are open all year. And be sure to look into specialty food stores where you can find some of the more exotic ingredients.

The bakery

You can really make a dent in your diet in the bakery section, where all the desserts are on display. These foods usually contain too much fat and carbohydrate; however, you don't have to give up all your "treats." The key is to figure a rich dessert into your meal plan, but only on an occasional basis. Remember to keep the portion small, in any case.

Muffins and pastries are usually high in fat, but in deference to the popular belief that fat makes us fat, stores now sell lowfat muffins and pastries. The problem is that these still contain many calories, so don't overdo it. Try a smaller portion or share your muffin with a friend. A popular choice is angel food cake, but watch out because, even though it's totally fat-free, it's filled with calories. You can enjoy a small portion.

Select breads that have at least 2 grams of fiber per slice and whole-grain breads. Bagels and English muffins should be whole-grain as well. Don't forget that they're usually too large, so plan on eating a serving of half or less. (That goes for any bread.) If you eat too much, you'll consume too many calories.

Produce

Fruits and vegetables are in the produce section. Stores continue to offer the usual apples, pears, and bananas, but today they stock more fruits and vegetables that you may never have seen before. Here is where you can add some real variety to your diet. Try some of these new items, and you may discover that you can substitute them for the cakes, pies, and other concentrated calorie foods that you now eat. For example, you may find that you like some of the new varieties of melons, which are sweet and have a great texture.

The other benefit to trying new fruits and vegetables is that you get a variety of vitamins and minerals from the different sources. Each differently colored vegetable provides different vitamins, so pick out a variety of colors.

To prolong their season, you can freeze some of the fruits, especially the berries, and use them as you need them.

Remember that dried fruits have very concentrated carbohydrate and should be used sparingly.

Root vegetables need no refrigeration but must be kept in a cool, dry place. Most of the other vegetables must go in the refrigerator.

The dairy case

At the dairy case, you can make some very positive diet modifications. Go for the lowest fat content you can eat, but don't neglect the dairy part of the food guide pyramid. That's where you get calcium. Try to find lowfat cheeses, yogurt, and cottage cheese. You can even buy cheeses that aren't lowfat if you use them sparingly. Go for 1 percent or even skim milk if possible.

The deli counter

A deli counter offers luncheon meats and prepared foods. Recent studies show that these processed meats are dangerous to your health. These foods often contain a lot of salt and fat. You probably want to avoid most of the foods in this area (with the exception of prepared chicken, which is often spit-roasted and very tasty). Even the lowfat meats in this section are rich in salt. The pickled foods may also contain a great deal of salt, despite being low in calories and free of fat.

If you choose salads from this area, pick out those that contain oil instead of cream. Don't be afraid to ask a deli employee about the exact ingredients in these prepared foods. In some cases, lower-fat versions are available. People often prefer fatty foods — and the grocery obviously wants people to buy the food — so the market caters to those preferences.

The fresh meat and fish counter

The fresh meat and fish counter provides some good choices for your protein needs. At the meat counter, buy no more than a normal serving for each member of the family. Just because the meat attendant has cut a 12-ounce piece of swordfish doesn't mean that you have to buy the whole thing. You are entitled to get just the piece you want. For convenience, you can get two servings at one time if you know you have the willpower to save the second serving for another meal. Ask the attendant to cut the fish in half so you aren't tempted to eat the whole thing.

Don't forget that lentils and other legumes can provide protein as well.

The same study mentioned above that criticized processed meats found that people who eat meat in general are heavier and have more diabetes than those who don't. Look for lowfat cuts of meat. The best choices for you are top round, sirloin, and flank steak. These tend to be the leanest cuts of meat and are also very tasty. When buying chopped meat (for hamburgers, for example), consider how you plan to cook it. If you like meat cooked well done, you don't always have to choose the package with the lowest fat content, because the fat may be cooked out. Otherwise, look for lower-fat chopped meat.

Try to buy skinless poultry to eliminate a major source of the fat in chicken. You may have to cook it a shorter time, or you can barbecue the chicken using an indirect method (place the coals along the sides of the chicken rather than underneath). The chicken will be much juicier and not dried out.

Try to eat fish at least twice a week because of the positive effect it has on blood fats. Remember that a "fatty" fish such as salmon is good for you but adds extra fat calories.

The fresh meat and fish counter usually offers breaded or battered fish to make your life easier; you only have to put it in the oven. The problem is that the breading or batter often contains too much butter, fat, and salt. Ask the person serving you for a list of the ingredients in the breading or batter. Or better yet, skip the prepared fish and head for the fresh. If you notice a very fishy smell, then the fish is not very fresh.

Frozen foods and diet meals

When the season for your favorite fresh fruits and vegetables is over, the frozen food section may stock these items. However, because markets now often bring in more varieties of fresh food from all over the world year-round, you may not need to turn to frozen products as much.

Food manufacturers are producing a variety of frozen foods, which you can heat in the microwave oven. These meals are often high in fat and salt, however. Be sure to read the food label, which we explain later in this chapter. Avoid frozen foods mixed with cream or cheese sauces.

Diet meals can be a good choice if you want to save time in preparation. The frozen diet meals are low in calories and often low in salt and fat as well. Most diet meals have no more than 350 kilocalories and usually taste good. If you have type 1 diabetes and need to count carbohydrates, they're listed on the box.

Healthy Choice, Lean Cuisine, and Weight Watchers are the three main makers of diet meals, all of which can be counted on for low calories and good taste. Healthy Choice is the lowest in salt. Grocery stores usually have one brand or another on sale, so you can choose the least expensive brand when you shop.

Are frozen diet foods a good choice for you? Many of our patients complain that they lack time to prepare the "right" foods. For those people, prepared diet meals work very well. For the person who likes to involve him or herself in food preparation — for example, people who bought this book for the wonderful recipes — this is not the way to go.

Low-carbohydrate foods are also being made by many of the food manufacturers. See our discussion of the various types of diets in Chapter 3 for ways that these foods can fit in your nutrition plan.

Canned and bottled foods

Canned and bottled foods can be healthful and can help you quickly make recipes calling for ingredients such as tomato sauce. Check the Nutrition Facts label (covered later in this chapter) to determine what kind of liquid a food is canned in. Oil adds a lot of fat calories, so look for the same food canned in water.

Canned vegetables often contain too much salt, so look for low-salt varieties. Canned fruits often contain too much sweetener, so you're better off with fresh if possible.

Watch for this marketing trick: Stores often display higher-priced canned foods at eye level and lower priced products on lower shelves. Also, store brands are often less expensive and just as good as name brands.

Bottled foods include fruit juice drinks, which are high in sugar and low in nutrition. You're better off drinking pure fruit juice rather than a juice drink diluted with other ingredients.

The same principle is true for bottled and canned soda, which has no nutritional value and lots of calories. Substitute water for this expensive and basically worthless food that really doesn't quench your thirst (soft drinks often leave an aftertaste, especially the diet drinks). Try adding lemon or lime to your water or use the flavored calorie-free water drinks.

You can find lowfat or fat-free salad dressing and mayonnaise in this area. Better yet, try using mustard and some of the other condiments to spice up your salads without adding many calories.

The best choices for snacks

You probably frequently feel like eating a little something between meals. Your choice of foods may make the difference between weight gain and weight control, between high blood glucose levels and normal levels. Here are the best selections to choose as you make your way around the supermarket:

- ✔ **Baked chips:** Avoid fried chips, which add lots of fat calories. An ounce of baked chips amounts to 110 kilocalories.

- ✔ **Flavored rice cakes:** These items are filling without calories.

- ✔ **Fruit and fig bars:** These items can satisfy hunger without many kilocalories. A couple of Fig Newmans, for example, will set you back only 120 kilocalories.

- ✔ **Lowfat granola:** Watch out for regular granola, which is high in calories. Depending on the brand, ½ cup of lowfat granola contains 220 to 250 kilocalories.

- ✔ **Plain popcorn:** If you prepare it in an air-popping machine or a microwave oven, it contains only 30 kilocalories per cup and is free of salt and fat.

- ✔ **Raisins and other dried fruit:** Stick to small portions. A quarter of a cup of raisins is only 130 kilocalories.

The preceding list should give you enough choices to satisfy your hunger without wrecking your diabetic control.

Deciphering the Mysterious Food Label

Most packaged foods have a food label known as the Nutrition Facts label, which isn't really mysterious if you know how to interpret it. It was designed to be understood. Figure 5-1 shows a typical food label. The contents of the Nutrition Facts label are regulated by the Food and Drug Administration.

Nutrition Facts
Serving Size 1/2 cup (113g)
Servings Per Container 4

Amount Per Serving	
Calories 120 Calories from Fat 15	
	% Daily Value
Total Fat 1.5g	3%
Saturated Fat 1.0g	5%
Cholesterol 10mg	3%
Sodium 290mg	12%
Total Carbohydrate 15g	5%
Dietary Fiber 0g	
Sugars 14g	
Protein 10g	10%

Figure 5-1:
A Nutrition Facts food label.

The label in Figure 5-1 is from a 1-pound container of cottage cheese with fruit. You can find the following information on the label:

✔ **Serving Size:** The serving size is the portion of the total contents that makes up one serving. Most packaged foods serve more than one person so don't be fooled.

✔ **Servings Per Container:** At ½ cup, this container holds 4 servings.

✔ **Calories:** The number of kilocalories in a serving — in this case, 120 kilocalories.

✔ **Calories from Fat:** The number of fat kilocalories in each serving.

✔ **% Daily Value:** The nutrient amounts appear in grams or milligrams and also as % Daily Value. The % Daily Value refers to the percentage of the daily value for a person on a 2,000-kilocalorie-per-day diet.

✔ **Total Fat:** The total fat is 1.5 grams, of which 1.0 is saturated fat. The fact that there's less than 3 grams of fat allows the producer to refer to this product as *lowfat.*

✔ **Saturated Fat:** The amount of the fat in each serving that is saturated.

✔ **Cholesterol:** This food provides little cholesterol. Therefore, the producer could call it "low cholesterol" because that term applies if the product provides less than 20 milligrams of cholesterol and 2 grams or less of saturated fat per serving (see Chapter 2 for more information).

✔ **Sodium:** At 290 milligrams of sodium, this food provides 12% of the sodium allowed in a 2,000-kilocalorie-a-day diet.

- **Total Carbohydrate:** As a person with diabetes, you need to know the grams of carbohydrate in a serving, both to fit it into your nutritional plan and to determine insulin needs if that is what you take.

- **Dietary Fiber:** This food provides no fiber, so all the carbohydrate is digestible. If fiber were present, you could subtract the fiber grams from the total grams of carbohydrate to get the actual grams from carbohydrate absorbed.

- **Sugars:** The fact that 14 of the 15 grams of carbohydrate come from sugar means that the sugar will be absorbed rapidly.

- **Protein:** As a person with diabetes, you're most concerned with the grams of protein in a portion. The figure for % Daily Value doesn't help you in planning your diet.

- **Vitamins and Minerals:** Usually, the label provides the % Daily Value for vitamin A, vitamin C, calcium, and iron. Some food labels follow that information with a list of ingredients, but this information isn't required as part of the Nutrition Facts label.

Making Good Choices

Thanks to the food labels, you can choose foods that are lower in calories, lower in fat, and have more nutritional value. You can compare foods next to one another and choose the healthier item. For example:

- Smart Balance has only 60 kcal per tablespoon while I Can't Believe It's Not Butter has 90 kcal per tablespoon.

- Uncle Ben's Fast and Natural Whole Grain Instant Brown Rice has 170 kcal per cup while Uncle Ben's Ready Rice Whole Grain Brown has 240 kcal per cup.

- Nature's Own Double Fiber Wheat Bread has 100 kcal per 2 slices while Arnold Double Fiber Whole Wheat Bread has 200 kcal per 2 slices.

- Annie's Naturals Buttermilk Dressing has 60 kcal in 2 tablespoons while Ken's Steak House Thousand Islands Dressing has 140 kcal per 2 tablespoons.

- Campbell's Healthy Request Condensed Chicken Noodle Soup has 60 kcal per cup while Campbell's Condensed Vegetable Soup has 100 kcal per cup.

I could go on and on like this but you get the idea. There are tons of good choices that have fewer calories and often more fiber, vitamins, and minerals than the bad choices. You just need to spend a little time and look at the labels.

Be sure you are comparing one serving to one serving. If you compare one serving to two servings, the larger item is bound to have many more calories.

The best way to verify that your trip to the market has been successful is to evaluate the contents of your grocery sacks. The division of the contents should look similar to the food guide pyramid (see Chapter 2).

Part II
Healthy Recipes That Taste Great

The 5th Wave   By Rich Tennant

"Since discovering Lamar's diabetes, I've used the exchange system when preparing meals. I exchanged my deep fryer for a steam basket, and my candy thermometer for a melon baller."

In this part . . .

You can find delicious recipes from A to Z — apples to zucchini — and everything in between. These chapters take you through your eating day, starting with your breakfast, providing snacks for midmorning and midafternoon, and offering larger meals at lunch and dinner. They end, naturally, with wonderful desserts, which show that you're not doomed to give up what you may consider the best part of the meal.

Chapter 6

The Benefits of Breakfast

A big part of keeping your blood sugar steady is eating regularly. Typically, the longest break without food during a day comes at night. While your body rests and revitalizes itself, your blood glucose level takes a nosedive. Start your day the right way with a healthy balanced breakfast each and every day.

Choose a quick scrambled egg and whole-wheat toast if you're in a hurry. But brush up on the recipes in this chapter for a change of pace. By planning ahead, you can make a delicious breakfast that's anything but boring.

Understanding Diabetic Breakfasts

Breakfast is a critical meal for a diabetic. Getting your day off to a steady, balanced start sets you up for success the rest of the day. Check out Chapter 4 if you need help planning your meals for the day based on your individual needs. The following sections can help you make the right breakfast choices.

Figuring out which fruit is right for you

Fruit doesn't have to be a dirty word for a diabetic. While it's true that fruit is full of natural sugars and your body processes them quickly, you don't have to (and shouldn't) mark them off your list completely.

Whole fruit, rather than juice, is a better choice for diabetics. The fiber and skin in whole fruit slow down the digestion of the fruit, resulting in a more gradual rise in your blood sugar level.

Here's a list of fruits with a lower glycemic index (which I discuss in more detail in Chapter 2):

- ✔ Apples
- ✔ Apricots
- ✔ Blueberries
- ✔ Cherries
- ✔ Grapefruit
- ✔ Kiwis
- ✔ Strawberries

And just for balance, here are a few fruits with a higher glycemic index:

- ✔ Cantaloupe
- ✔ Dates
- ✔ Pineapple
- ✔ Raisins
- ✔ Watermelon

Just because a fruit has a higher glycemic index doesn't mean you can't eat it. Just take it into consideration when you plan when you eat it and what you eat with it.

Putting together protein-packed punches

Eggs aren't the only breakfast protein. In fact, many diabetics must limit their intake of cholesterol, and eggs are an easy target for removal. (Check out "Enjoying Egg-ceptional Dishes," later in this chapter, for smart ways to include eggs at breakfast.) Consider other nontraditional choices when you're making your breakfast changes. Here's a list of protein-rich foods that might make a good addition to your breakfast table:

- ✔ 1 turkey hot dog wrapped in a whole-wheat tortilla
- ✔ 1 ounce boiled shrimp with cocktail sauce
- ✔ 2 tablespoons of peanut butter on whole-wheat toast
- ✔ 1 slice turkey wrapped around lowfat string cheese

✔ 4-ounce grilled chicken breast

✔ ¼ cup cottage cheese with diced grape tomatoes

Starting with Whole-Grain Goodness

When you received your diagnosis of diabetes, maybe you thought your days of eating waffles and pancakes were over. Although starting the morning off with pancakes dripping with butter and maple syrup is probably not in your current eating plan, you can still enjoy relatively sweet treats in the morning, especially if you use whole grains.

Refined grains are processed to remove the bran and the hull, and along with them, up to 90 percent of the nutrients, including vitamins E and B. Whole grains have a lower glycemic index than refined grains. So whole grains are less likely to send your blood glucose soaring and then dipping. The protein, fat, and fiber in whole grains slow their absorption into the bloodstream. In addition, whole grains make you feel fuller and stay fuller longer.

Read labels carefully to ensure that the food you're getting is made from whole grains. Don't just look for "wheat" bread; make sure it says "whole wheat." Some manufactures add caramel color or molasses to refined flour and sell the bread as "wheat bread," potentially confusing hopeful healthy eaters.

🍳 Warm Blueberry Oats

This recipe makes any morning special. It's just as quick as "regular" oatmeal, but adding fresh blueberries gives your antioxidant levels a boost and your taste buds a treat. If fresh blueberries aren't in season, you can substitute frozen. Choose blueberries frozen without additional sugars and thaw them before adding them to your cereal. You can see this dish in the color section.

Preparation time: *5 minutes*

Cooking time: *3 minutes*

Yield: *2 servings*

1 cup rolled oats	*2 teaspoons honey*
2 cups water	*1 cup fresh blueberries*

1 In a microwave-safe bowl, combine the oats and water. Microwave on high for 3 minutes.

2 Remove the bowl from the microwave and stir in the honey and then the blueberries.

Per serving: *Kcalories 218 (From Fat 25); Fat 3g (Saturated 0g); Cholesterol 0mg; Sodium 6mg; Carbohydrate 43g (Dietary Fiber 6g); Protein 7g.*

⊙ Breakfast Polenta with Apples, Walnuts, and Maple Syrup

Polenta is essentially cornmeal that's cooked slowly and flavored with cheese, herbs, and tomatoes as a savory side dish. Tante Marie's cooking school (www.tantemarie.com) in San Francisco developed this breakfast polenta recipe, served with sautéed apples and walnuts.

Preparation time: *15 minutes*

Cooking time: *45 minutes*

Yield: *4 servings*

1 quart water	*2 tart green cooking apples*
1 cup polenta-type cornmeal	*1 tablespoon walnut oil*
½ teaspoon salt	*1 tablespoon sugar*
2 tablespoons soy or yogurt margarine	*¼ cup fresh walnuts*
½ cup nonfat ricotta cheese	*Maple (or apple) syrup to taste*
1 tablespoon maple syrup	

1 Bring the liquid to a boil in a heavy-bottomed pot on the top of the stove. Whisk in the polenta and salt. Cook very slowly over low heat stirring constantly with a wooden spoon until the spoon can stand up, supported in the mixture. This usually takes about 20 minutes. Stir in the margarine, ricotta, and maple syrup. Cover and keep warm. (If you are going to hold it awhile before serving, stir in ½ cup or more water.)

2 Peel, core, and slice the apples in ½-inch slices. Heat walnut oil in a medium-sized sauté pan over medium-high heat. Add the sliced apples; sprinkle with the sugar. Continue to cook the apples, turning occasionally, until the apples are soft when pierced with a fork. Set aside.

3 Meanwhile, heat a separate small sauté pan over medium-high heat. Add the walnuts, tossing until slightly toasted. Remove from heat.

To serve, place a serving of polenta in a bowl, cover with apples, sprinkle with walnuts, and serve with ½ cup nonfat Greek yogurt for extra protein (adds 60 calories).

Per serving: Kcalories 377 (Calories from Fat 128); Fat 14g; (Saturated 2g); Cholesterol 5mg; Sodium 390mg; Carbohydrate 56g (Dietary Fiber 6g); Protein 8g.

Skip the butter because these waffles are delicious without it. If you don't feel like you can go cold turkey, look for a spread, such as Brummel and Brown Yogurt Spread or Smart Balance Buttery Spread, that contains no trans fat.

🍑 *Whole-Wheat Waffles*

This recipe is reason alone to invest in a waffle iron. Look for one with nonstick coating for easy waffle removal. Make sure you let the batter rest for the full 1½ hours before making the waffles. You'll get waffles with a much lighter texture and better flavor.

Preparation time: *90 minutes*

Cooking time: *4 minutes per waffle*

Yield: *4 servings*

1 cup evaporated skim milk	*⅛ teaspoon vanilla extract*
1 teaspoon active dry yeast	*2 packets Splenda*
1 cup whole-wheat flour	*Nonstick cooking spray*
½ teaspoon orange zest	

1 Warm the milk and dissolve the yeast in it. In a bowl, mix the yeast mixture with the flour, orange zest, vanilla, and Splenda. Let sit, covered, at room temperature for 1½ hours.

2 Using a waffle maker coated with nonstick cooking spray, prepare the waffles, following the manufacturer's instructions.

Tip: *Instead of syrup, serve these beauties with Warm Pineapple Salsa. You can find the recipe in Chapter 7.*

Per serving: *Kcalories 157 (From Fat 7); Fat 1g (Saturated 0g); Cholesterol 3mg; Sodium 76mg; Carbohydrate 30g (Dietary Fiber 4g); Protein 9g.*

☞ *Blueberry and Almond Pancakes*

Blueberries are the best source of antioxidants compared with all other fruits. Almonds are also the best nut source of another antioxidant, vitamin E. Enjoy the tasty fruit and crunchy nuts along with this breakfast favorite, shown in the color section.

Preparation time: *10 minutes*

Cooking time: *5 to 7 minutes*

Yield: *4 servings (total 16 pancakes)*

½ cup all-purpose flour

¾ cup whole-wheat flour

2 teaspoons apple juice concentrate

2 teaspoons baking powder

¼ teaspoon salt

1½ teaspoons unsweetened applesauce

1¼ cups lowfat milk

⅛ teaspoon almond extract

3 egg whites, or 6 tablespoons egg substitute

¾ cup fresh blueberries, or frozen berries, thawed

1 tablespoon almond slivers, crushed

Nonstick cooking spray

1 In a bowl, combine the all-purpose flour, whole-wheat flour, apple juice concentrate, baking powder, and salt; set aside.

2 In another bowl, combine the applesauce, milk, almond extract, egg whites, blueberries, and almonds; stir well. Add the flour mixture. Stir until you achieve a fairly smooth batter consistency, approximately 2 minutes. Feel free to leave a few lumps, because overmixing can result in a tougher finished pancake.

3 Coat a large skillet with the cooking spray; place over medium heat until hot. Spoon ¼ cup batter for each pancake. When bubbles form on top of the pancakes, turn them over. Cook until the bottom of each pancake is golden brown.

Per serving: *Kcalories 209 (From Fat 21); Fat 2g (Saturated 1g); Cholesterol 3mg; Sodium 419mg; Carbohydrate 38g (Dietary Fiber 4g); Protein 10g.*

☙ Greek Breakfast Pita

This is a great handheld breakfast for anyone on the go. Look for whole-wheat pitas in the specialty bread or deli section of your grocery store. Use a combination of whole eggs and egg whites to keep the flavor and pump up the portion size but reduce the cholesterol.

Preparation time: *20 minutes*

Cooking time: *8 to 11 minutes*

Yield: *4 servings*

Nonstick cooking spray	*⅛ teaspoon pepper*
4 whole-wheat pitas	*2 medium red potatoes, baked, small diced*
1 tablespoon unsalted butter	*4 whole eggs*
½ small onion, finely chopped	*8 egg whites*
½ cup chopped fresh spinach	*½ cup feta cheese, very small chunks*
⅛ teaspoon garlic powder	

1 Preheat the oven to 350 degrees. Coat a baking sheet with the cooking spray and place the pitas on the baking sheet.

2 Melt the butter in a large, deep skillet over medium heat. Sauté the onions in the butter until tender, 3 to 4 minutes. Add the spinach, garlic powder, and pepper. Sauté for 3 minutes. Add the potatoes. In a bowl, whisk together the eggs and egg whites. Add the egg mixture to the skillet. Cook over medium heat, stirring occasionally, until the eggs are cooked soft, 3 to 4 minutes.

3 Spoon the egg mixture into the pitas. Sprinkle the cheese on top. Bake for 5 to 7 minutes, until the cheese melts.

Tip: *The next time you serve baked potatoes at dinner, make a couple of extra so you have them handy to make this delicious breakfast even speedier.*

Per serving: *Kcalories 433 (From Fat 125); Fat 14g (Saturated 6g); Cholesterol 237mg; Sodium 733mg; Carbohydrate 55g (Dietary Fiber 6g); Protein 24g.*

Stocking Up on Baked Goods

Having diabetes doesn't mean you have to deprive yourself of the ease (and deliciousness!) of grabbing a muffin, biscuit, or slice of quick bread. Plan ahead and keep some of these heart-healthy handfuls on hand for breakfast on the go.

We help you ease into using whole grains in this section by using a blend of all-purpose (white) flour and whole-wheat flour. You can find whole-wheat flour in the baking aisle in just about any grocery store.

⊙ Zucchini Bread

This bread makes a regular appearance in my household. It's full of fiber and vitamins, making it an excellent choice. Don't bother peeling the zucchini before grating it. Just wash it and grate away. Double the recipe and freeze the second loaf. You'll definitely use it!

Preparation time: *12 minutes*

Cooking time: *45 minutes to 1 hour*

Yield: *18 to 20 servings*

Nonstick cooking spray	*1 teaspoon baking soda*
1½ cups whole-wheat flour	*¼ teaspoon baking powder*
1½ cups all-purpose flour	*6 egg whites*
1 cup sugar	*1 cup applesauce*
½ cup chopped pecans	*½ cup buttermilk*
1 teaspoon cinnamon	*2½ cups grated zucchini*

1 Preheat the oven to 350 degrees. Spray 2 loaf pans, 9 x 5 inches or 8 x 5 inches, with nonstick spray.

2 In a large bowl, combine the whole-wheat flour, all-purpose flour, sugar, pecans, cinnamon, baking soda, and baking powder.

3 In another bowl, combine the egg whites, applesauce, and buttermilk. Mix in the zucchini. Then combine with the flour mixture.

4 Pour the mixture into the loaf pans. Bake 45 minutes to 1 hour. Insert a toothpick in the center of the loaf. When it comes out clean, the bread is done. Cool in the pan for 5 minutes and then cool completely on a wire rack.

Per serving: Kcalories 139 (From Fat 22); Fat 3g (Saturated 0g); Cholesterol 0mg; Sodium 92mg; Carbohydrate 26g (Dietary Fiber 2g); Protein 4g.

☜ Sweet Potato Biscuits

Here's a great way to discover sweet potatoes, if you haven't already. They impart a delicate sweetness to these biscuits. Plus, sweet potatoes are another one of those "good for the eye" foods, being full of carotenoids and beta carotene. They also supply a full day's worth of vitamin C, a decent dose of dietary fiber, and delicious flavor to boot. You can see these biscuits in the color section.

Preparation time: *25 minutes*

Cooking time: *12 minutes*

Yield: *6 servings (12 biscuits total)*

1 cup all-purpose flour	*2 tablespoons butter*
1 cup whole-wheat flour	*½ cup buttermilk*
2½ teaspoons baking powder	*⅔ cup mashed cooked sweet potatoes*
¼ teaspoon baking soda	*Nonstick cooking spray*
¼ teaspoon salt	

1 Preheat the oven to 425 degrees. In a bowl, combine the all-purpose flour, whole-wheat flour, baking powder, baking soda, and salt. With a pastry blender or fork, work in the butter until the mixture is coarse (see Figure 6-1).

2 In another bowl, combine the buttermilk and mashed sweet potatoes. Add to the flour mixture and mix until just moistened.

3 Transfer the dough to a lightly floured surface. Knead 2 or 3 times, until smooth (see Figure 6-2). Roll out the dough ½-inch thick. Using a 2-inch biscuit cutter, dipped in flour, cut out 12 rounds.

4 Coat a baking sheet with the cooking spray. Arrange the rounds on the baking sheet. Bake for 12 minutes, until golden brown.

Tip: *Use White Lily brand flour and whole-wheat pastry flour for more-tender biscuits.*

Per serving: *Kcalories 208 (From Fat 41); Fat 5g (Saturated 3g); Cholesterol 11mg; Sodium 333mg; Carbohydrate 37g (Dietary Fiber 4g); Protein 6g.*

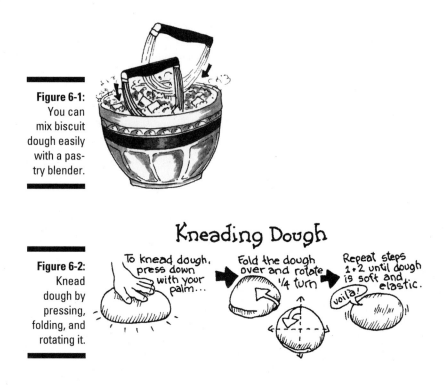

Figure 6-1: You can mix biscuit dough easily with a pastry blender.

Figure 6-2: Knead dough by pressing, folding, and rotating it.

Enjoying Egg-ceptional Dishes

Choosing eggs gives you a protein power punch to start your day. This simple food is an ideal source of protein, containing all essential amino acids. Eggs are also a source of B complex vitamins, vitamin A, vitamin D, vitamin E, selenium, and zinc. However, egg yolks also contain a significant amount of cholesterol. Consequently, low-cholesterol diets restrict the number of eggs allowed each week. People with diabetes should limit their eggs to a couple per week for the same reason.

One great way to enjoy eggs but limit your cholesterol is to enjoy egg whites or use a combination of whole eggs and egg whites. The egg yolk (the yellow center) contains the dreaded cholesterol, so limiting your intake of yolks may be enough to keep egg whites on your list.

Baking egg pies and quiches

These baked breakfast egg dishes are a great way to make delicious, healthy meals for a group. They're a great choice for elegant brunch entertaining or a weekday when you have a little extra time. Alternately, you can make a pie or quiche, cool it completely, and then cut it into individual servings and freeze them for later.

Broccoli and Cheese Pie

Broccoli is one of the best sources of antioxidants out there, meaning it's full of disease-fighting agents. It's great fresh, steamed, baked, or microwaved. If possible, avoid boiling it in liquid that you'll later discard, because you remove too many of its healthy nutrients. Enjoy it in this cheesy crust-free "pie."

Preparation time: *20 minutes*

Cooking time: *30 minutes*

Yield: *4 servings*

Nonstick cooking spray	*1 whole egg, lightly beaten*
1 cup fresh broccoli, small florets	*1 cup skim milk*
½ cup low-sodium chicken broth	*1 cup shredded cheddar cheese*
2 egg whites, lightly beaten	*¼ teaspoon pepper*

1 Preheat the oven to 350 degrees. Coat a 9-inch pie pan with the cooking spray.

2 In a saucepan, cook the broccoli with the chicken broth, uncovered, over medium heat, stirring, until all liquid has evaporated, about 10 minutes. Transfer to a bowl and chill in the refrigerator for 5 minutes.

3 In another bowl, whisk together the egg whites and egg. Add the broccoli, milk, cheese, and pepper.

4 Pour the mixture into the pie pan and bake, uncovered, for 30 minutes, and check with a toothpick for doneness. (The pie may need to bake for up to 45 minutes.) Remove from the oven and cool.

Per serving: Kcalories 171 (From Fat 99); Fat 11g (Saturated 7g); Cholesterol 85mg; Sodium 268mg; Carbohydrate 5g (Dietary Fiber 1g); Protein 13g.

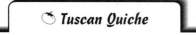

☺ Tuscan Quiche

This vegetarian quiche from Sublime in Ft. Lauderdale, Florida (www.sublime restaurant.com) is high in protein but low in cholesterol thanks to the tofu, soy mozzarella cheese, and nutritional yeast.

Look for nutritional yeast in the bulk section of your local natural food store. It's a complete protein and high in vitamin B-12. With its strong, nutty, cheesy flavor, it's used as a cheese substitute.

This dish can be served either with or without the crust. We provide nutritional information for both presentations.

Preparation time: *30 minutes*

Cooking time: *40 minutes*

Yield: *6 servings*

Filling:	Salt and pepper to taste
24 ounces extra firm tofu	2 tablespoons nutritional yeast
8 ounces vegan soy mozzarella	1 tablespoon granulated onion
1 tablespoon olive oil	1 tablespoon granulated garlic
½ cup chopped fine garlic	**Crust:**
½ cup chopped fine shallots	1 cup whole-wheat pastry flour
1 16-ounce can quartered artichoke hearts (in water)	2 tablespoons soy margarine
	Kosher salt
1 pound blanched chopped spinach	4 tablespoons ice cold water

1 Make the filling. Chop tofu and mozzarella into cubes, place in a food processor, and mix until smooth. Place the mixture in a bowl and chill.

2 Meanwhile, add 2 tablespoons olive oil, garlic, and shallots in a sauté pan. Sauté until ingredients are translucent. Add the artichoke hearts and spinach to the pan and mix well. Season to taste with salt and pepper. Allow this mixture to cool and then add it to the tofu mixture. Add in the dry spices and stir well. Check for seasoning. Place the mixture in the fridge until ready to use.

3 Meanwhile, preheat the oven to 350 degrees. On a cutting board, cut margarine into flour and salt. Quickly add in the water, one tablespoon at a time, until the mixture forms into a solid dough mass. Roll the dough out to a half-inch thick pancake, and then drape it over an oiled 9-inch pie pan, tucking in all the corners. Bake for 15 minutes or until golden brown. Remove from the oven, cool.

4 Place the tofu mixture into the cooked pie shell. Smooth out the mixture and return to the oven for 25 minutes. Remove from the oven.

5 Cool until the center is firm; slice and serve.

Per serving: Kcalories 380 (Calories from Fat 159); Fat 18g (Saturated 2g); Cholesterol 0mg; Sodium 606mg; Carbohydrate 32g (Dietary Fiber 7g); Protein 30g.

Per serving without the crust: Kcalories 295 (Calories from Fat 123); Fat 14g (Saturated 1g); Cholesterol 0mg; Sodium 465mg; Carbohydrate 21g (Dietary Fiber 6g); Protein 28g.

Trying your hand at omelets and frittatas

Omelets and *frittatas* (open-faced omelets) are among the best and easiest ways to get a burst of protein to start your day. In this section, we give you several flavorful recipes to keep your taste buds hopping.

Facing facts about feta cheese

If you haven't tried this terrific Greek cheese, here's your chance. It's a soft, salty cheese that has a tangy bite. It crumbles very easily, and is an easy addition to salads, eggs, or stuffed in olives. The commercially available variety is made from cow's milk and sold in small squares, usually in plastic tubs covered in plastic wrap. You can find it in the gourmet or specialty cheese section of your local grocery.

One of the best things about feta is its strong flavor. A little can go a long way. So if you're looking for flavor but don't want to weigh down your food with lots of cheese and fat, feta's a good choice. Look for flavored feta cheese for a change of pace. You can find it blended with sun-dried tomatoes and basil, and peppercorns.

Greek Omelet

You can be creative here. The essential Greek ingredients are the feta and spinach. But, add any veggies you like — the more the better! Good choices include artichoke hearts, red peppers, onions, zucchini, or asparagus. Just throw them in at Step 2 and cook them until they're tender. Enjoy!

Preparation time: *5 minutes*

Cooking time: *10 minutes*

Yield: *2 servings*

Nonstick cooking spray	*2 whole eggs*
½ cup diced green peppers	*4 egg whites*
½ cup sliced mushrooms	*½ cup crumbled feta cheese*
⅛ teaspoon dried marjoram, crumbled	*1 small plum tomato, seeded and chopped*
1 cup chopped spinach	

1 Coat a large skillet with the cooking spray and place over medium heat. Sauté the peppers, mushrooms, and marjoram until the vegetables are tender, approximately 6 minutes. Add the spinach and cook until wilted, roughly 4 minutes.

2 In a bowl mix together the eggs and egg whites. Pour the egg mixture over the spinach mixture in the skillet. Cook over low heat, stirring occasionally until the eggs are almost cooked. Top with the feta cheese and tomatoes and cover until the eggs are puffy, approximately 5 minutes. Fold the omelet in half and serve.

Per serving: Kcalories 230 (From Fat 120); Fat 13g (Saturated 7g); Cholesterol 246mg; Sodium 607mg; Carbohydrate 8g (Dietary Fiber 2g); Protein 20g.

Vegetable Frittata

Because a frittata is finished in the oven, make sure you choose an oven-safe skillet. This frittata recipe from Tante Marie's cooking school in San Francisco, is full of vegetables, vitamins, and flavor. It makes a great dinner as well, so don't just save it for breakfast.

Preparation time: *25 minutes*

Cooking time: *15 minutes*

Yield: *4 servings*

1 pound broccoli

8 eggs

6 egg whites

1 tablespoon cold water

1 pound spinach

1 tablespoon olive oil

2 large onions

1 large clove garlic

½ teaspoon coarse salt

¼ teaspoon freshly ground black pepper

¼ cup nonfat ricotta cheese

¼ cup soft white cheese, such as goat cheese

¼ cup freshly grated Parmesan cheese

1 Bring a medium-sized pot of water to the boil. Cut the florets of the broccoli into ½-inch pieces; save the stems for another use like soup. When the water is boiling, sprinkle with salt. Add the broccoli florets. Cook rapidly for about 6 minutes, until the broccoli is tender when pierced with a fork. Drain the broccoli in a colander and let cool. Set aside.

2 In a mixing bowl, combine eggs, egg whites, and water. Blend thoroughly. Set aside.

3 Meanwhile, in a 12-inch oven-safe non-stick sauté pan, cook the onions in the olive oil until soft (3 to 5 minutes). Add the garlic and cook another minute. Add the spinach and cook until wilted. Spread the broccoli over the onion and spinach mixture in the sauté pan. Sprinkle with salt and pepper. Mix together ricotta and white cheese, and spread over broccoli. Pour egg mixture over the broccoli.

4 Preheat the broiler.

5 With a rubber spatula, gently move the vegetables around, making sure the egg goes throughout the broccoli mixture on the bottom of the pan. Don't stir the mixture, but gently move the vegetables, allowing the liquid eggs to reach the surface of the pan. Let the mixture cook over medium-high heat so that a crust forms on the bottom of the pan. With a fork, lift the edges of the frittata and tilt the pan to let the runny eggs go underneath.

6 When the whole mixture is set, top with the Parmesan cheese and place under the broiler briefly, likely 3 minutes or so, until the top is golden. Serve in wedges for lunch or supper or cut into squares for hors d'oeuvres.

Per serving: Kcalories 377 (Calories from Fat 162); Fat 18g (Saturated 6g); Cholesterol 438mg; Sodium 784mg; Carbohydrate 22g (Dietary Fiber 6.5g); Protein 28g.

☙ Omelet with Wild Mushrooms

Wild mushrooms are full of delicious earthy flavor. Tante Marie's cooking school in San Francisco developed this recipe with fresh herbs and exotic mushrooms.

Preparation time: *25 minutes*

Cooking time: *15 minutes*

Yield: *4 servings*

8 eggs	*¼ cup fresh chives, minced*
4 egg whites	*¼ cup fresh thyme, minced*
3 tablespoons cold water	*Coarse salt, to taste*
1 tablespoon olive oil, divided	*Freshly ground black pepper, to taste*
4 medium shallots, minced	*¼ cup nonfat ricotta cheese*
8 ounces wild or domestic mushrooms, brushed of dirt and cut in ¼-inch slices or pieces	

1 Crack the eggs and add egg whites into a bowl. Add water, and beat with a fork until the mixture is one color. Set aside.

2 Heat ½ tablespoon olive oil in a small sauté pan, over medium-high heat. Cook the shallots until soft. Add the mushrooms all at once and cook, stirring, until the mushrooms are half wilted. Add the herbs and ricotta cheese. Season to taste with salt and pepper. Continue cooking until the cheese has melted. Remove from the heat.

3 In a medium nonstick sauté pan, heat the remaining ½ tablespoon olive oil over medium-high heat. Pour in the egg mixture, and with a rubber spatula, draw the egg mixture across the pan in one direction and then in the other. You should have a mound of fluffy eggs in the middle of the pan. Let the remaining egg mixture sit and cook for 30 seconds; then, with the rubber spatula, lift the edges of the omelet, and swirl the sauté pan around, to allow the remaining uncooked egg mixture to slide underneath and come into contact with the pan. When all the eggs are lightly cooked, remove the pan from the heat.

4 Cover one half of the open omelet with the mushroom mixture. Then fold over the other half of the omelet. Slide the omelet onto a heated serving plate.

Per serving: *Kcalories 240 (Calories from Fat 123); Fat 14g (Saturated 4g); Cholesterol 428mg; Sodium 375mg; Carbohydrate 9g (Dietary Fiber 1g); Protein 20g.*

⚬ *Artichoke Frittata*

At Eccolo restaurant in Berkeley, California, Christopher Lee created the fluffiest egg frittata you'll ever have. The best part about it? It tastes great. Plus, it's low in saturated fat, high in protein, and great for your blood sugar. You read right — protein is essential for blood sugar control, as you've heard before. This recipe provides a great way to include it at breakfast without all the fat that comes with many high-protein meats.

Preparation time: *25 minutes*

Cooking time: *15 minutes*

Yield: *6 servings*

5 large whole frozen artichoke hearts, thawed	*7 egg whites*
2 teaspoons extra-virgin olive oil	*1 tablespoon unsalted butter*
½ teaspoon plus a few pinches salt	*2 tablespoons finely chopped parsley*
5 eggs	*2 tablespoons finely chopped thyme*

1 Slice the artichoke hearts into ½-inch pieces.

2 Heat a sauté pan over high heat. Lightly coat the bottom with the olive oil. When the oil begins to shimmer, add the artichoke slices, reduce the heat to medium-low, and sauté the artichokes until they're tender, about 10 minutes, stirring occasionally. Season the artichokes with salt as you sauté them. Remove them from the heat.

3 Crack the eggs into a medium bowl. Add the egg whites and season them with a few pinches of salt. Whisk them until they're well blended.

4 For a large frittata, heat a large nonstick pan over medium-high heat and then add ½ tablespoon of butter and allow it to coat the bottom of the pan. Place half of the cooked artichoke slices in the pan and sprinkle them with parsley and thyme. Reduce the heat to low and pour half of the egg mixture over the artichokes. Quickly stir everything together so that the artichokes are evenly distributed. Cook the mixture, without stirring, until the eggs are almost set, approximately 4 minutes, and then flip the frittata over and let it cook for another minute or so. Slide out of the pan and onto a serving plate.

5 Repeat Step 4 to make a second frittata. Cut each frittata into 3 pieces. Serve hot or cold with bread.

Per serving: *Kcalories 119 (From Fat 68); Fat 8g (Saturated 3g); Cholesterol 182mg; Sodium 382mg; Carbohydrate 2g (Dietary Fiber 1g); Protein 10g.*

Chapter 7

Hors d'Oeuvres and First Courses: Off to a Good Start

In This Chapter

▶ Starting your meal off right

▶ Sampling salsas for every occasion

▶ Digging into delectable dips

Appetizers are meant to stimulate your appetite and prepare you for the meal to come. But for a diabetic, they can also help you squeeze in a quick nutritious bite, helping to keep your blood glucose levels stable until the main event. Healthy appetizers are the best way to get you started on a great eating path for the evening.

In this chapter, we give you many great choices for healthy eats, whether you're having a party, an intimate dinner with friends, or a casual game night with the family. Look here for enticing new ways to enjoy simple finger foods as a first course, terrific salsa recipes with tips for creating your own varieties, and a great selection of dips and dippers — no need to skimp on taste. Just remember to choose appropriate portion sizes and pace yourself. You have a whole lot to enjoy.

Enjoying Simple Starters

Casual dining is definitely on the rise. Many social gatherings focus on food, but may not include a traditional sit down meal. Instead many people entertain friends and family with "heavy appetizers." I've collected some recipes that are heavy in satisfaction, but won't weigh you down or blow your whole calorie budget for the day.

If your experience with seafood until now has been fish sticks or broiled halibut, we've got some great ideas for getting you going with seafood appetizers. You can experiment with new flavors without committing yourself to a full seafood entree. But be sure to take a look at Chapter 12 for more taste-tempting seafood recipes.

Most people don't get enough seafood in their diet. Rich in fish oil, omega-3 fatty acids, protein, calcium, and so many other nutrients, seafood is an excellent part of any well-rounded diet. This delectable food is much lower in cholesterol than beef and chicken and has so many varied flavors and textures that you can't get bored with it.

Shellfish, such as scallops and shrimp, are sold by weight and size. When you see shrimp labeled as "26/30," you get between 26 and 30 shrimp per pound. So the higher the number, the smaller the shrimp, and vice versa. You may even see labels that say "U10," which means "under 10," or fewer than 10 shrimp per pound.

Always clean your shrimp properly before cooking them. If you buy your shrimp in a grocery store, the head will most likely be removed. But the shrimp may or may not be deveined, which means the dark "vein" that runs down the back of the shrimp's tail may still be present. Because this veinlike object is actually the shrimp's intestinal track, you should remove it before cooking the shrimp. At your grocery or kitchen supply store (anywhere kitchen gadgets are sold), pick up a tool called a shrimp deveiner and run it along the back end of the shrimp. It cracks the shell and removes the vein in one easy step. Then rinse the shrimp in cool water. Check out Figure 7-1 to see the deveining process.

Cleaning and Deveining Shrimp

Figure 7-1: You can use a special tool to clean and devein shrimp safely and properly.

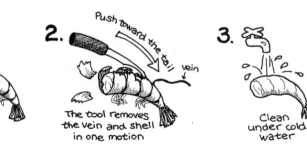

1. Insert deveiner

2. Push toward the tail / vein / The tool removes the vein and shell in one motion

3. Clean under cold water

Shrimp Quesadillas

This recipe puts a nice twist on the classic Mexican dish. Though shellfish is a significant source of cholesterol, it's very low in total and saturated fat — a great alternative to high-fat meats. Just be sure to limit cholesterol intake from animal products the rest of the day.

Preparation time: *15 minutes*

Cooking time: *10 minutes*

Yield: *4 servings*

⅓ cup lowfat sugar-free plain yogurt

2 medium plum tomatoes, seeded and chopped

Nonstick cooking spray

4 10-inch whole-wheat tortillas

1 pound canned baby shrimp, cooked

2 teaspoons fresh cilantro, chopped

1 cup (4 ounces) shredded Monterey Jack cheese

1 In a small bowl, combine the yogurt and tomatoes. Set aside.

2 Coat a large skillet with the cooking spray. Place the skillet over medium heat until hot. Add one tortilla to the pan. Top the tortilla with half of the shrimp, 1 teaspoon of the chopped cilantro, and ½ cup of cheese. Place a second tortilla on top of the mixture. Cook the quesadilla until the cheese begins to melt and the bottom tortilla becomes golden brown. Flip the quesadilla over and continue to cook until the cheese is fully melted and the tortillas are lightly browned. Remove from skillet and place on a cutting board.

3 Repeat Step 2 with the remaining tortillas, shrimp, cilantro, and cheese.

4 Slice each quesadilla into 6 pieces. Place 3 pieces and one-fourth of the tomato mixture on each of 4 plates.

Per serving: Kcalories 364 (From Fat 112); Fat 13g (Saturated 6g); Cholesterol 204mg; Sodium 1,653mg; Carbohydrate 33g (Dietary Fiber 6g); Protein 29g.

⟳ Mushrooms Stuffed with Fennel and Spinach

Classic Stuffed Mushrooms are a great finger food for a cocktail party. The chef from Horizons loves to invent funky stuffing ideas for mushrooms. This version is an ode to spring with a French accent. If you're not familiar with fennel (pictured in Figure 7-2), it has an understated licorice-like flavor. It is delicate and subtle with the added crunch of a fresh vegetable. It's Paris in the springtime!

Preparation time: *15 minutes*

Cooking time: *10 minutes*

Yield: *4 servings*

1 6-ounce bag of cleaned spinach

½ cup chopped fennel

¼ cup chopped onion

1 garlic clove

½ tablespoon Dijon mustard

½ tablespoon vegan mayo

½ teaspoon salt

½ teaspoon pepper

½ teaspoon olive oil

1 teaspoon white wine

1 tablespoon soy or organic Parmesan cheese (optional)

12 large white mushroom caps, stems removed

1 Preheat the oven to 400 degrees.

2 In a food processor, puree all the ingredients, except the mushroom caps, into a coarse paste. Set aside.

3 Place mushroom caps, tops down, in a baking dish. Fill the mushroom caps with the pureed mixture.

4 Bake for 15 minutes or until the mushrooms have softened and the filling is dark green and bubbly.

Per serving: Kcalories 59 (Calories from Fat 18); Fat 2g (Saturated 0g); Cholesterol 0mg; Sodium 421mg; Carbohydrate 10g (Dietary Fiber 3g); Protein 3g.

Figure 7-2:
Crunchy fennel is a great addition to savory stuffed mushrooms.

fennel

Crab Puffs

Crab puffs are the ideal finger food for parties. For this recipe, use the best quality Parmesan cheese you can find — its strong flavor is a terrific complement to the delicate crab and artichoke without adding many calories or much fat. If you're a fan of spicy food, feel free to bump up the horseradish in this recipe for a sinus-clearing experience.

Preparation time: *20 minutes*

Cooking time: *6 to 7 minutes*

Yield: *6 servings (4 pieces each)*

3 tablespoons freshly grated Parmesan cheese

1 can (14 ounces) artichoke hearts, drained and chopped

½ pound snow crabmeat

1 egg white

¼ cup lowfat sour cream

¼ cup lowfat mayonnaise

1 teaspoon fresh squeezed lemon juice

1 teaspoon prepared horseradish

½ teaspoon Worcestershire sauce

1 small garlic clove, minced

3 English muffins, halved

1 Preheat the broiler.

2 In a small bowl, reserve 2 tablespoons of the Parmesan cheese. In a medium bowl, combine the remaining 1 tablespoon Parmesan cheese, the chopped artichokes, crabmeat, egg white, sour cream, mayonnaise, lemon juice, horseradish, Worcestershire sauce, and garlic.

3 Place the English muffin halves on a baking pan and spread the crab mixture equally onto each muffin. Sprinkle the reserved Parmesan cheese on top.

4 Place the pan in the freezer for 10 minutes, or until the crab mixture holds its form.

5 Remove the pan from the freezer and place the pan under the broiler for 6 to 7 minutes, or until the muffin topping is lightly browned and bubbly. Cut each muffin into quarters.

Per serving: *Kcalories 180 (From Fat 47); Fat 5g (Saturated 2g); Cholesterol 41mg; Sodium 536mg; Carbohydrate 20g (Dietary Fiber 1g); Protein 13g.*

Savoring Salsas

We've fallen in love with the Mexican condiment, salsa. Most store-bought versions, however, have too much sugar and vinegar, so they aren't nearly as good as the homemade variety. Why bother with those versions when it's so easy to create your own? Although *salsa* simply means "sauce," we think you'll agree that these salsa recipes taste anything but simple.

Stocking essentials for scrumptious salsas

Add the standard salsa seasonings to any grain or legume for a tasty and nutritious treat anytime. You can flavor cooked brown rice, quinoa, or any cooked beans with any of these tasty additions:

- Cilantro
- Garlic
- Lime juice or lemon juice
- Onions
- Peppers (such as serranos and jalapeños)
- Tomatoes

Check out the following salsa recipes, which use these delicious ingredients.

Use caution when slicing and dicing hot peppers such as jalapeños. Use your knife, not your fingers or fingernails, to remove the super-spicy ribs and seeds, and consider wearing gloves if you have sensitive skin. The pepper oil can get stuck under your nails, making it painful to touch your eyes, nose, or any other moist parts later. And if your skin is exposed to sunlight with residual pepper oil, you can get a nasty burn.

⌒ Mexican Salsa

Chowing down some Mexican salsa is a great way to get a good helping of lycopene, because tomatoes happen to be one of the best sources. *Lycopene,* a great antioxidant that helps fight heart disease, has also been shown to help prevent prostate cancer and maintain eye health. If you're a fan of cilantro like we are, toss in a bit more. Serve the salsa (shown in the color section) with pitas or tortilla chips.

Preparation time: *10 minutes*

Yield: *4 servings*

½ teaspoon lemon juice

½ teaspoon salt

1 pound fresh tomatoes, cored and chopped

½ medium onion, diced

1 tablespoon fresh chopped jalapeño pepper

1 small garlic clove, chopped fine

1 teaspoon fresh chopped cilantro

1 In a mixing bowl, combine the lemon juice and salt. Stir to dissolve the salt.

2 Add the tomatoes and coat them with the juice. Add the onion, jalapeño, garlic, and cilantro and stir.

Tip: *If you like a smooth rather than chunky salsa, toss all the ingredients in a food processor and process the mixture in pulses until it reaches the consistency you desire.*

Per serving: *Kcalories 30 (From Fat 4); Fat 0g (Saturated 0g); Cholesterol 0mg; Sodium 301mg; Carbohydrate 7g (Dietary Fiber 2g); Protein 1g.*

Adding citrus and other fruits to salsas

To give your salsa a fruity twist, don't bother with bottled lemon or lime juice. Fresh is definitely the way to go. Squeezing the juice out is easy to do, and the flavor is far superior.

Here's how to get the most out of your citrus fruit. Check out Figure 7-3 for details.

1. **Roll the fruit on a hard, flat surface, pressing down fairly hard to break up the juice sacs.**

2. **Cut the citrus fruit in half width-wise.**

3. **Holding one half in one hand, stick the tines of a fork into the fruit pulp and squeeze the fruit.**

   Twist the fork as needed to release as much juice as possible.

Juice your fruit over a separate bowl, not into other ingredients. Doing so helps you catch any errant seeds that may try to sneak their way into your delectable dishes.

Lemon and lime aren't the only fruity flavors you can add to your salsas. Check out the following yummy salsas featuring mango and pineapple.

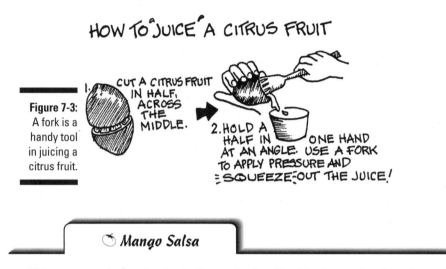

HOW TO "JUICE" A CITRUS FRUIT

1. CUT A CITRUS FRUIT IN HALF, ACROSS THE MIDDLE.

2. HOLD A HALF IN ONE HAND AT AN ANGLE. USE A FORK TO APPLY PRESSURE AND SQUEEZE OUT THE JUICE!

Figure 7-3:
A fork is a handy tool in juicing a citrus fruit.

☉ Mango Salsa

This mango salsa recipe is similar to the familiar Mexican salsa (see the recipe earlier in this chapter) but it offers sweet, firm mango as a perfect partner to the peppers. Feel free to add less mango or more tomato as you experiment with this versatile recipe. With these great ingredients, it's hard to go wrong! Check out a photo of the salsa in the color section.

Preparation time: *15 minutes*

Yield: *4 servings*

1 large ripe mango, peeled, pitted, and chopped

½ small red pepper, seeded and chopped

1 medium tomato, seeded and cubed

1 green onion, green and white parts, chopped

2 tablespoons minced fresh ginger

Juice of 1 lime

3 tablespoons fresh chopped cilantro

In a mixing bowl, combine all the ingredients and mix well. Cover and refrigerate until ready to serve.

Per serving: Kcalories 50 (From Fat 3); Fat 0g (Saturated 0g); Cholesterol 0mg; Sodium 4mg; Carbohydrate 13g (Dietary Fiber 2g); Protein 1g.

⟋ Warm Pineapple Salsa

Fruit salsa can be a terrific sauce for fish, veggies, or pita wedges. Or use it like a jam or syrup to top biscuits, waffles, or pancakes. With cooked fruit salsa, you heat the ingredients until they almost become a glaze. Fruit salsa has a more syrupy consistency than a tomato-based salsa. Experiment and enjoy.

Preparation time: *20 minutes*

Cooking time: *15 minutes*

Yield: *4 servings*

1 tablespoon olive oil	*1 tablespoon cider vinegar*
1 tablespoon slivered almonds	*¼ teaspoon salt*
1 small onion, thinly sliced	*1 tablespoon honey*
2 teaspoons curry powder	*1 tablespoon brown seedless raisins*
16 ounces pineapple tidbits, drained	

1 In a small saucepan, heat the oil over medium heat. Add the almonds and gently toss in the oil.

2 Add the onion and cook until tender and until the almonds are golden brown.

3 Add the curry powder, pineapple, vinegar, salt, honey, and raisins. Bring the mixture to a boil, reduce the heat, and simmer for 10 minutes. Remove the salsa from the heat and serve warm.

Vary It! *Try this recipe with canned mandarin oranges, apricots, or peaches instead of the pineapple, depending on your accompaniments and your taste buds on a given day. But be sure to avoid fruit packed in heavy syrup.*

Per serving: *Kcalories 114 (From Fat 40); Fat 5g (Saturated 1g); Cholesterol 0mg; Sodium 148mg; Carbohydrate 20g (Dietary Fiber 1g); Protein 1g.*

Discovering Delicious Dips

Dips don't have to be fat-laden creamy concoctions that add inches to your waistline and bags to your saddle. With a little creativity, you can create delicious dips that keep you eating healthy and your glucose levels normal.

Whipping up dips with pantry staples

Dips are among the quickest and easiest (not to mention tastiest!) appetizers around. Keep your pantry and fridge stocked with a few dip-making essentials and you'll never be stuck wondering what to whip up when unexpected guests stop by.

Here are our best bets for quick dip-making essentials to keep on hand:

- ✔ **Any of the ingredients listed under "Stocking essentials for scrumptious salsas," earlier in this chapter:** Adding any of the salsa ingredients to any of the items in this list makes for a terrific dip. In fact, one of our favorite quick dips blends a can of black beans (rinsed and drained, of course) with ½ cup of salsa. Whip the mixture in a food processor, and you have an instant party treat.

- ✔ **Beans:** Pureed beans make a great base for a dip, and they're high in fiber and low in fat. Blend them in a food processor and season them with your favorite spices. Look for fat-free, low-sodium canned beans, and try cannellini beans, black beans, pinto beans, black-eyed peas, garbanzo beans, great Northern beans, navy beans, and kidney beans.

  Unless a recipe says otherwise, rinse and drain canned beans before adding them to a dip. Often, the liquid they're canned in is salty or flavored in some way. Rinse and drain and season them your way.

- ✔ **Fancy olives:** Olives impart great flavor and texture to dips. Use some of the olive juice to blend into the dip, too. If olives perk up a martini, just think what they can do for some ho-hum dips!

- ✔ **Fresh herbs:** Fresh herbs make an instant impression on an otherwise bland dip base. Dill, basil, and cilantro are excellent choices for keeping on hand.

- ✔ **Lowfat sour cream:** Use sour cream to add a little body and creamy texture to your dips.

- ✔ **Plain yogurt:** This staple is a natural partner to fresh herbs and a touch of lemon juice. Keep it handy to mix in a soon-to-be bean dip.

- ✔ **Spice blends:** Look for prepackaged, salt-free spice blends. These healthy spices can take the guesswork out of seasoning.

☕ White Bean Dip

Here's a great dip that takes advantage of a well-stocked pantry. Add fresh baby spinach leaves during Step 1 to boost your vitamins and leafy greens quotient. Delicious!

Preparation time: *10 minutes, plus 3 to 4 hours of chilling time*

Cooking time: *5 minutes*

Yield: *4 servings*

Nonstick cooking spray	*½ teaspoon chopped fresh sage*
½ cup chopped onions	*1 teaspoon balsamic vinegar*
2 garlic cloves, minced	*1 tablespoon water*
1 can (15 ounces) cannellini beans, drained and rinsed	*⅛ teaspoon salt*
	⅛ teaspoon pepper

1 Place a medium skillet over medium heat and coat it with nonstick cooking spray. Add the onions and cook until they're soft and translucent, about 1 minute.

2 Add the garlic and continue to cook for about 30 seconds.

3 Place the beans in a food processor and add the cooked onions and garlic, sage, vinegar, water, salt, and pepper. Process until smooth (about 1 to 2 minutes).

4 Transfer the mixture to a bowl, cover it, and refrigerate it for 3 to 4 hours before serving.

Per serving: Kcalories 65 (From Fat 3); Fat 0g (Saturated 1g); Cholesterol 0mg; Sodium 161mg; Carbohydrate 12g (Dietary Fiber 3g); Protein 3g.

Cacit (Cucumber Dip)

Tante Marie's cooking school developed this all-purpose dip. It's similar to a Greek Tzatziki sauce that's often served with gyro sandwiches. It's simple to make, but make sure to leave enough time for the cucumbers to thoroughly drain.

Preparation time: *10 minutes plus 2 hours standing time*

Yield: *4 servings*

1 English cucumber (or 4 small)	*2 tablespoons minced fresh mint*
2 garlic cloves	*1 cup nonfat Greek-style yogurt*
½ teaspoon coarse salt	

1 Cut the cucumber into 1-inch dices. Place the cucumber in a stainless steel colander, and sprinkle with salt. Let the cucumbers drain for 1 to 2 hours, to remove excess liquid.

2 On a cutting board, make a paste of the garlic with the salt. Place garlic mixture in a bowl. Add the cucumbers, mint, and yogurt. Mix well and add salt to taste.

Per serving: Calories 40 (From Fat 0); Fat 0g (Saturated 0g); Cholesterol 0mg; Sodium 313mg; Carbohydrate 4g; Dietary Fiber 1g; Protein 6g.

Tuna Pâté

This pâté is tasty and much lighter than the typical liver-and-oil-based spread that many people are familiar with. Using a food processor makes for quick prep work. Feel free to add more or fewer jalapeños, depending on your taste. Serve this dip with pita or bagel chips or spread it in celery ribs.

Preparation time: *10 minutes, plus 3 to 4 hours of chilling time*

Yield: *6 servings*

¼ small onion

2 teaspoons fresh cilantro

1 tablespoon chopped jalapeño pepper

12 ounces canned tuna, packed in water, drained

½ cup mayonnaise

⅛ teaspoon white pepper

1 In a food processor, combine the onion, cilantro, and jalapeño and pulse until chopped, approximately 1 minute.

2 Add the tuna and process approximately 1 minute.

3 Slowly add the mayonnaise and process until smooth, approximately 30 seconds.

4 Add the pepper and process 1 minute. Check for lumps and process until smooth. Transfer the dip to a serving bowl, chill it for 3 to 4 hours, and serve.

Per serving: Kcalories 195 (From Fat 144); Fat 16g (Saturated 3g); Cholesterol 30mg; Sodium 283mg; Carbohydrate 1g (Dietary Fiber 0g); Protein 11g.

 Truffled Hummus

What could be better than a good hummus? It's a classic, and it makes an easy party food. Making it yourself is only slightly more difficult than opening that plastic container, yet the result yields a freshness of flavor and a creamy texture that can't be beat.

The use of white truffle oil lends itself well to the earthiness of the ground chickpeas. For another take on hummus, make sure to make a stop in Chapter 10 and try the recipe for Southwestern Hummus.

Preparation time: *10 minutes*

Yield: *6 servings*

1 15-ounce can chick peas (drained and rinsed)

1 clove garlic

¼ cup water

1 tablespoon lemon juice

1 tablespoon olive oil

¼ teaspoon salt

1 teaspoon pepper (preferably freshly ground)

1 teaspoon fresh thyme leaves

1 dash ground cumin

1 teaspoon quality truffle oil (or more as desired)

Dash paprika or chili powder (optional)

1 tablespoon fresh parsley, chopped (optional)

1 Blend all ingredients (except paprika and parsley if using) in a food processor until smooth and creamy.

2 Place mixture in serving dish. Garnish with a sprinkle of paprika and parsley if desired.

Tip: *Alternately you could blend the ingredients in Step 1, but omit the truffle oil. Then in Step 2 garnish by drizzling the truffle oil on top. This version creates more of a layered taste.*

Per serving: *Kcalories 70 (Calories from Fat 32); Fat 4g (Saturated 0g); Cholesterol 0mg; Sodium 180mg; Carbohydrate 7g (Dietary Fiber 2g); Protein 2g.*

Choosing healthy dippers

What's a good dip without something to dip into it? Rather than ruining all your hard work of choosing healthy dips by dipping fried chips into them, we offer you the following alternatives to keep you moving in the right direction:

- ✔ **Bagel chips:** Look for these chips in the specialty bread section of your grocery store, but read the label because some are high in fat and sodium. You also can make your own by slicing off slivers of a bagel and then baking them until they're crisp.

- ✔ **Fresh veggies:** Choose broccoli florets, cauliflower florets, carrot sticks, celery sticks, zucchini slices, red pepper spears, endive scoops, or any of your favorites. Any veggie can be a dip delivery system.

- ✔ **Pita wedges:** Make your own by quartering pitas and then baking them until they're crisp.

- ✔ **Whole-wheat crackers:** Kashi makes a line called TLC, Tasty Little Crackers, made with whole-grain flour from seven different grains. Ry-Krisp is a filling and tasty choice as well.

- ✔ **Yucca chips:** This root vegetable has great health benefits. Check out the following recipe.

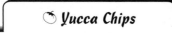 **Yucca Chips**

Yucca is a root vegetable very similar to the potato. It has lots of good fiber and can be substituted for potatoes in soups and stews. Enjoy these chips as a healthy snack instead of potato chips.

Preparation time: *10 minutes*

Cooking time: *45 minutes*

Yield: *4 servings*

⅛ teaspoon salt

⅛ teaspoon pepper

2 large yucca, peeled and cut into wedges

2 tablespoons extra-virgin olive oil

Nonstick cooking spray

1 Preheat the oven to 375 degrees.

2 In a small bowl, combine the salt and pepper. In a large bowl, coat the yucca wedges with the olive oil and then toss them with the salt and pepper.

3 Coat a baking sheet with cooking spray and arrange the wedges on the sheet. Bake about 45 minutes, or until the yucca wedges are cooked through and lightly browned.

Per serving: Kcalories 386 (From Fat 66); Fat 7g (Saturated 1g); Cholesterol 0mg; Sodium 101mg; Carbohydrate 78g (Dietary Fiber 4g); Protein 3g.

Chapter 8

Soup, Beautiful Soup

In This Chapter

▶ Beginning with the basics of soup

▶ Putting stock and other essential supplies to good use

▶ Cutting out the cream, but keeping the flavor

▶ Using cold soups as great transitions and sweet endings

Soups might be the ultimate comfort food. Who doesn't feel better (even with a cold) with a bowl of warm chicken soup? And you can choose a soup for every occasion. No matter what the weather, the state of your health, or who's coming for dinner, we have a soup for you.

In this chapter, we get you started with the basics of making soup, taking you through the steps to make sure your soups turn out just right. We give you the scoop on different types of stocks, provide tips on watching your salt intake, and help you get your pantry stocked for soup making. We give you tips on making healthful, creamy soups full of flavor, but low in fat. And finally, we help you make delicious soups to serve cold on warm summer days.

Understanding Soup-Making Basics

In many soup recipes, the first few steps ask you to sauté some vegetables to bring out their flavor and soften them. Typically, you start by cooking a combination of vegetables, such as onions, carrots, and celery, along with herbs and spices, in a small amount of fat.

You may sauté your veggies in a small amount of lowfat cooking spray oil or butter, or even a bit of fatty smoked meat such as bacon. You may also brown ground meats or cubed meats at this stage. As the ingredients cook, they begin to turn brown and *caramelize,* developing a rich and complex flavor.

Next, you add liquid, perhaps some vegetable broth, chicken or beef broth, milk, wine, or water. First, add just a half-cup or so of liquid to *deglaze* the pot. During this procedure, you can use a wooden spoon and gently dislodge any bits of caramelized vegetables stuck to the bottom of the pot. You want these flavorful morsels to blend in with the other flavors of the soup. Pour in the remaining liquid.

In the final, and longest, steps of cooking, you place all vegetable chunks, beans, grains, or meats, in the simmering liquid and cook to perfection. But not everything cooks at the same rate, so use Table 8-1 to help you decide when to add ingredients.

Table 8-1	Cooking Times for Soup Add-Ins
Ingredient	*Cooking Time*
Beans, dried (presoaked 8 hours)	1½ hours to 2 hours
Beef cubes	2 to 3 hours
Chicken, bone in, pieces	40 minutes
Chicken, boneless	15 to 20 minutes
Fresh vegetables	10 to 15 minutes (45 to purée)
Greens (spinach and others)	3 to 5 minutes
Lentils, dried	15 to 30 minutes
Pasta, dried	8 to 12 minutes
Pearl barley	50 minutes to 1 hour
Potatoes, white or sweet (diced)	30 minutes
Rice, brown and wild	45 to 55 minutes
Rice, white	15 to 20 minutes
Root vegetables (beets, turnips, and so on)	15 to 35 minutes
Seafood, shelled or boneless	5 to 15 minutes

These cooking times are only guidelines, so adjust them as you see fit. Experiment and figure out what works for you.

Soups are a great way to work in your veggies. Use soups as a way to maximize the bounty of summer vegetables at your local farmers' market, especially at the end of the season. Look for these must-have ingredients that have a place in soups, salads, or even quick-cooking pasta sauces:

- ✔ Beets
- ✔ Greens (spinach, cabbage, and bok choy among others)
- ✔ Heirloom tomatoes (look for green zebras, Japanese black trifle, sun sugar, or amana orange, just to name a few)

✔ Herbs (basil, chervil, dill, and cilantro, or whatever you want)

✔ Mushrooms (exotics, such as morels, chanterelle, and wild mushroom blends)

✔ Squash (chayote, acorn, pumpkin, zucchini, and yellow squash)

Stock up on heirloom tomatoes to make the next quick and tasty recipe.

☙ Heirloom Tomato Soup with Fresh Basil

Here is Tante Marie Cooking School's recommendation for making the most of the summer tomato bounty. The recipe was originally inspired by their friend, T. T. They've modified it a bit, to create this incredibly quick and fresh-tasting summer staple.

Preparation time: *20 minutes*

Cooking time: *30 minutes*

Yield: *4 servings*

2 tablespoons extra-virgin olive oil	*5 garlic cloves, peeled and minced*	*Freshly ground black pepper*
5 large fresh heirloom tomatoes, peeled, seeded, and chopped into ½-inch dice	*1 quart good quality low-sodium or vegetable stock, heated*	*30 fresh basil leaves, thinly sliced*
	1 teaspoon coarse salt	*¼ cup freshly grated Parmesan cheese*

1 Heat olive oil in a heavy bottomed skillet over medium heat. Stir in the garlic and let cook gently until it turns slightly golden — be careful not to let the garlic burn.

2 Immediately stir in the tomatoes and gently sauté until slightly thickened, about 5 minutes. Stir in the stock and let simmer another 10 to 15 minutes. Stir in the basil and let the soup simmer gently 2 or 3 minutes more.

3 Serve soup in warmed bowls. Top with Parmesan cheese.

Note: The best way to peel and seed tomatoes is to blanch and shock them, as shown in Figure 11-1 in Chapter 11, to loosen the skin. Start by removing the stem end of the tomato with a small knife. Make an "x" in the opposite end of the tomato with the knife. Drop the tomatoes in gently boiling water for no longer than 10 seconds. Immediately transfer them to a bowl of cold water. Then gently peel off the loosened skins. To seed them, cut the tomatoes in half with the stem end on one side. Over fine mesh strainer fitted onto a bowl or measuring cup, use one hand to scoop out the seeds, while squeezing the tomato half with the other. Don't worry if you don't get out all the seeds. A couple of seeds won't hurt anyone.

Note: T. T. prefers to cook the tomatoes longer than this recipe suggests. She cooks them with the garlic for 15 minutes; then she adds 3 quarts of stock and simmers the soup another 30 minutes. She says it gives it more flavor. You can try it both ways and choose your favorite.

Per serving: Kcalories 167 (Calories from Fat 86); Fat 10g (Saturated 2g); Cholesterol 4mg; Sodium 1,155mg; Carbohydrate 17g (Dietary Fiber 4g); Protein 5g.

Summer Vegetable Stew with Egg

This summer stew boasts a striking presentation — the delicate broth with chunky vegetables topped with a fried egg. Tante Marie's Cooking School worked to develop this nutritional powerhouse that has a good balance of protein and carbohydrates. If you're keeping your veggie drawer well-stocked, you may even have all the ingredients on hand.

Preparation time: 20 minutes

Cooking time: 30 minutes

Yield: 6 servings

3 tablespoons olive oil

2 teaspoons coarse salt, divided

1½ teaspoons ground pepper, divided

2 large onions, halved and sliced

2 large red peppers, cored, seeded, and cut into thin strips

2 large or 6 small eggplants, trimmed and cut in 1-inch pieces

2 large or 6 small green zucchini, trimmed and cut in rounds

12 tomatoes, coarsely chopped

A dash of Tabasco sauce

6 fresh eggs

1 Heat olive oil, ½ teaspoon salt, and the onions in a 10-inch sauté pan over moderately high heat. Cook, stirring from time to time, for about 3 minutes; then stir in the peppers. Continue cooking for another 3 minutes.

2 Toss in the eggplant, season with ½ teaspoon salt and ½ teaspoon pepper, and sauté over moderately high heat for about 3 minutes. Stir in the zucchini with another ½ teaspoon salt and ½ teaspoon pepper and continue cooking over moderately high heat.

3 Stir in the tomatoes. Add another sprinkling of salt and pepper, and add the Tabasco. Let the mixture cook, stirring from time to time, until the tomatoes begin to fall apart.

4 Meanwhile, put a light coating of olive oil in a separate non-stick pan over moderately high heat. When the pan is hot, remove it from the heat, and break the eggs into it, one at a time. Let the eggs cook from the heat of the pan, returning the pan to the heat briefly, and taking it off again, until the whites are set. (The eggs will look like fried eggs, but will not be brown or rubbery on the bottom.) Taste the stew; add additional salt and pepper if necessary. Spoon it into warmed wide bowls, cover each with a pan-fried egg, and serve.

Per serving: Kcalories 285 (Calories from Fat 121); Fat 13g (Saturated 3g); Cholesterol 212mg; Sodium 197mg; Carbohydrate 35g (Dietary Fiber 11g); Protein 12g.

Serving Up Soups with Stocks and Other Essentials

You can begin a soup using water, but making a soup with real depth of flavor calls for stock. Basically, a *stock* is a liquid in which solid ingredients, such as chicken meat and bones, vegetables, and spices, are cooked and then usually strained out. The flavors of these ingredients end up in the final broth.

Look for *stock bases,* the secret ingredient of many a restaurant, near the bouillon and broth in your grocery store. Usually sold in one-pound containers, you can make up to five gallons of stock from a single container. Keeping a container of base in the fridge is more convenient than keeping five gallons of canned broth in your pantry.

Watching out for salt in stock-based soups

Most markets carry various brands of chicken and beef broth that offer good flavor. These products are adequate for making everyday soups and are well worth keeping on hand. Always choose the low-sodium versions to use as stock and then add more salt to your soup as necessary.

If your physician or dietitian has given you any instructions at all about watching your salt, you've probably been told about the high sodium content of canned soup. You may be on a standard 3,000-milligrams-a-day regimen, recommended for most individuals, or a 2,000-milligrams-a-day sodium-restricted diet. Table 8-2 shows some sample amounts of the milligrams of sodium in a single serving of some common soups.

Table 8-2	Canned Soups and Sodium	
Soups	*Serving Size*	*Sodium in Milligrams*
Low Sodium Tomato (Campbell's)	10½ ounces	60
Low Sodium Chicken Broth (Campbell's)	10½ ounces	140
Chicken Broth (Health Valley)	8 ounces	150
Onion Soup Mix (Lipton)	8 ounces (or 1 tablespoon mix)	610
Lentil (Progresso)	8 ounces	750
Tomato (Campbell's)	4 ounces (condensed soup)	760

(continued)

Table 8-2 *(continued)*

Soups	Serving Size	Sodium in Milligrams
Chicken Broth (Campbell's)	4 ounces (condensed soup)	770
Vegetable Beef (Campbell's)	4 ounces (condensed soup)	890
Chicken Noodle Instant Soup (Knorr)	8 ounces	910
Clam Chowder (Campbell's)	4 ounces (condensed soup)	960
Chunky Beef (Campbell's)	10¾ ounces	1,130

For another low-salt stock alternative, you can make a basic vegetable stock by simmering together aromatic vegetables like onion and celery with carrots, which add sweetness, plus some parsley and a bay leaf. You need to cook this mixture for only about 20 minutes.

The classical combination of vegetables (onions, celery, and carrots) is called *mirepoix* (pronounced *meer*-pwa). It's a basic beginning for many soups and stocks. When you're chopping mirepoix for stocks, you can roughly chop the vegetables and even skip the peeling if you prefer. But when getting the veggies ready for soups, take the time to prep them as the recipe suggests.

Add strong-flavored vegetables, like broccoli, cauliflower, and asparagus, with caution, or they'll overpower the other ingredients. Instead, make a basic stock and add strong-flavored vegetables as you need them for a certain soup.

The Potato-Leek Soup recipe takes advantage of low-sodium chicken broth as stock but is still full of great flavor.

Keeping soup supplies in your pantry

Different types of stocks aren't the only items you need to have close by when you're craving soup. Keep the following ingredients in your pantry for an impromptu soup-making session:

- ✔ **Canned evaporated milk:** Use this item in your creamy soup recipes, such as the Creamy Veggie Lover's Soup later in this chapter. Evaporated milk is *not* the same as sweetened condensed milk (a syrupy milk-based concoction with lots of sugar added). Evaporated milk is milk from which 60 percent of the water has been removed. It's concentrated, so it can enhance the flavor of soups and other dishes.

Choose regular evaporated milk rather than evaporated skim milk for soups and sauces. Evaporated skim milk has a tendency to curdle and break when heated. If you still want to save the calories, purée the soup with the skim milk before serving.

✔ **Canned legumes, like beans, lentils, and chickpeas:** They're a great source of fiber and protein, but the dried variety can take some time to prepare. So have the canned variety available to toss in a soup pot in a pinch. Get started using these hearty staples in the Indian-Inspired Lamb and Legume Chili later in this chapter.

Always drain and rinse canned beans and vegetables unless the recipe specifies otherwise. This step removes excess sodium, allowing you to season your soup to your preferred taste.

✔ **Canned tomatoes:** Diced, crushed, whole, or stewed, any of these tomatoes products can make for a quick soup.

✔ **Dried herbs and spices.** Oregano, basil, pepper, salt, dill, and just about anything in your spice cabinet can work into a soup recipe.

✔ **Dried mushrooms:** Rehydrate them in hot water, steep them for about 30 minutes, and then strain the liquid to remove any grit. Roughly chop the mushrooms and add the strained liquid for an extra punch of flavor.

✔ **Garlic:** Garlic adds an amazing flavor to just about anything. You can roast it, sauté it, and purée it; whatever works for your soup. It's great in creamy soups, tomato-based soups, or brothy soups. (Not intended for any visiting vampires eating soup, and don't forget the breath mints.)

✔ **Grains:** Rice, pasta, and barley are great choices to make a soup heartier. Check out Chapter 10 for the full story on cooking with grains.

✔ **Olive oil:** This terrific monounsaturated fat can help make an already nutritious soup heart healthy, too. Keep some on hand at all times.

✔ **Onions:** These fragrant bulbs add their terrific flavor and aroma to anything you cook.

✔ **Potatoes:** These starchy veggies cook up quickly and can add body to your soups. Choose them for puréed soups as they help thicken soups almost instantly, like in the Potato-Leek Soup earlier in this chapter.

✔ **Salt-free seasoning mixes:** If you have trouble with high blood pressure, you probably need to steer clear of salt as much as possible. Salt-free seasoning blends can give you many delicious flavor combinations and take the guesswork out of seasoning your soups.

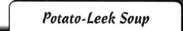

Potato-Leek Soup

This soup is great basic comfort food. Leeks (which look sort of like overgrown green onions) must be sliced and then soaked and washed thoroughly to remove dirt and sand deep down in the bulb. Check out Figure 8-1 to see how to cut up a leek. Swish sliced leeks around in a bowl of cold water. Soak them for a few minutes until the dirt and grit settle to the bottom of the bowl. Lift the leeks out of the water and drain on a paper towel. Repeat the procedure again with fresh water.

Preparation time: *20 minutes*

Cooking time: *25 minutes*

Yield: *4 servings*

Nonstick cooking spray

1 large leek, chopped and rinsed (don't use the dark green part of leek)

2 cups potatoes, peeled and cut into ¼-inch cubes

2 cups low-sodium chicken broth

¼ teaspoon pepper

⅛ teaspoon salt

1 Coat a large pot with cooking spray and place over medium heat until hot. Add the leeks. Sauté until soft and translucent.

2 Add the potatoes and chicken broth. Bring to a boil and simmer for 10 to 15 minutes, until the potatoes are cooked. Add the pepper and salt. Continue to simmer for 2 minutes. Remove from the heat.

3 Place half of contents of the pot into a blender, cover, and process until smooth.

4 Carefully pour the blender mixture back into the pot with the remaining broth and potatoes. Stir together with a wire whisk. Bring back to a simmer.

Per serving: Kcalories 87 (From Fat 8); Fat 1g (Saturated 0g); Cholesterol 2mg; Sodium 134mg; Carbohydrate 17g (Dietary Fiber 2g); Protein 3g.

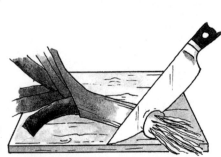

Figure 8-1: Cutting up a leek.

ON A CUTTING BOARD, USING A CHEF'S KNIFE, CUT OFF THE ROOT ENDS OF THE LEEKS.

SLICE THE LEEK LENGTHWISE, WITH THE TIP OF THE KNIFE.

The U.S. Department of Agriculture's Dietary Guidelines for Americans suggest at least five servings of fruits and vegetables every day to ensure adequate intake of vitamins, minerals, and fiber. Enjoying a bowl of vegetable soup such as the following recipe is a delicious way to meet your quota.

Classic: Hearty Vegetable Soup

When you prepare vegetable soup, first add the items that require longer cooking (such as beets and carrots) and later add quick-cooking ingredients (such as spinach and tomatoes). You'll have all your vegetables just where you want them, done to perfection when your soup is finished. However, this procedure does require your time and attention. Another way to make sure that all the vegetables finish cooking about the same time is to cut the longer-cooking ones (such as potatoes) into smaller pieces and the faster-cooking types (such as squash) into larger chunks.

Preparation time: *15 minutes*

Cooking time: *30 minutes*

Yield: *4 servings*

Nonstick cooking spray	1 cup diced fresh yucca	⅛ teaspoon thyme
½ cup diced onions	½ cup diced fresh tomatoes	½ teaspoon oregano
½ cup diced celery	½ cup diced zucchini	2 cups low-sodium chicken broth
½ cup diced carrots	1 bay leaf	⅛ teaspoon white pepper

1 Choose a large pot with a tightly fitting lid. Coat the pot with the nonstick spray and cook, stirring constantly, the onions, celery, and carrots until the onions are translucent — about 5 to 7 minutes. You can spray the pot with additional cooking spray or add a little stock or water if the vegetables begin to stick or burn. Add the yucca, tomatoes, zucchini, bay leaf, thyme, oregano, chicken broth, and white pepper and stir to combine.

2 Bring the vegetable soup to a boil over high heat, uncovered, and then simmer, covered, for 20 minutes.

3 Remove the bay leaf and serve immediately as a light lunch or mini meal.

Note: *Adding salt is optional, but it does increase the sodium level.*

Per serving: *Kcalories 124 (From Fat 10); Fat 1g (Saturated 1g); Cholesterol 2mg; Sodium 85mg; Carbohydrate 26g (Dietary Fiber 3g); Protein 3g.*

Modifying classic favorites with an international kick

Soups are part of every cuisine. And virtually any soup can get a little ethnic flavor by changing the spices and seasonings (all of which are found in most kitchens). In the next recipe, the garam masala, a traditional Indian spice blend, gives this chili a taste of India. You can find this tasty spice blend in the spice section of most grocery stores now. If you want to change the flavors to match another culture's cuisine, change the seasonings.

Try these few ideas to substitute for the garam masala, changing the flavor, but keeping the basic recipe.

- ✔ Chinese five-spice powder, ground ginger, and a touch of sesame oil stirred in at the end of cooking, for a Chinese-inspired chili
- ✔ Chili powder and cayenne, for a traditional southwestern chili
- ✔ Cinnamon, for a Cincinnati-style chili
- ✔ Basil, marjoram, oregano, thyme, and rosemary, for a taste of Italy
- ✔ Thyme, cinnamon, ginger, allspice, cloves, garlic, and onions, for a little Jamaican jerk flavor
- ✔ Cumin, coriander seed, and cloves, for a taste of North Africa

Indian-Inspired Lamb and Legume Chili

This recipe, from food writer Heather Dismore, is an easy one-pot meal that's full of good nutritional benefits. The beans are a wonderful source of dietary fiber, and in this recipe, they meet about a third of your daily fiber needs. Increased fiber can help with blood sugar control as well as enhance satiety, keeping you fuller for longer. Lamb is a good source of iron and vitamin B12, which can both help prevent and improve anemia. Lamb tends to be a high-fat meat, however, so be sure to drain the fat during the cooking process.

Preparation time: *10 minutes*

Cooking time: *2½ hours (largely unattended)*

Yield: *8 servings*

1½ pounds lean ground lamb

1 cup chopped red onion

3 garlic cloves, minced

2 cans (14½ ounces each) no-salt-added diced tomatoes, undrained

1 cup dry red wine

1 tablespoon chili powder

1½ teaspoons ground coriander

1½ teaspoons garam masala

¼ cup serrano chiles, seeded and minced (about 2 chiles)

1 can (15 ounces) black beans, drained and rinsed

1 can (15 ounces) lentils, drained and rinsed

1 can (15 ounces) chickpeas, drained and rinsed

1 Combine the lamb, onion, and garlic in a large stockpot. Cook over medium heat until the lamb is browned and crumbled, about 5 minutes. Stir as needed. Drain in a colander to remove excess fat. Return drained meat mixture to the stockpot.

2 Stir in the tomatoes, wine, chili powder, coriander, garam masala, and chiles. Bring to a boil. Cover, reduce heat, and cook 2 hours, stirring occasionally.

3 Stir in the black beans, lentils, and chickpeas. Simmer an additional 30 minutes. Serve immediately.

Per serving: *Kcalories 311 (From Fat 126); Fat 14g (Saturated 6g); Cholesterol 61mg; Sodium 248mg; Carbohydrate 23g (Dietary Fiber 9g); Protein 23g.*

Creating Creamy Concoctions

Who doesn't love a delicious creamy soup? But as you probably know, putting cream in soups adds calories *and* saturated fat, neither of which are very good for a diabetic diet. If you can't get enough of creamy soups, we have some good news. You can have a great creamy texture — without the stuff you don't need.

One great way to get the creamy texture without the bad stuff is to substitute 2 percent milk for cream in your favorite soups. It gives you plenty of the creaminess and mouth feel you expect because it does have some fat and body, but it cuts the fat grams and calories. Try this great alternative in the following soup recipe.

⏱ Cauliflower-Parmesan Soup

This recipe comes from Rathbun's in Atlanta (see Appendix A). This soup is warm, hearty, and perfect for a cool day. We substitute 2 percent milk, which has just enough fat to prevent curdling, in place of cream. The 2 percent milk has reduced this soup's fat content by nearly 50 percent. Remember to always try to use a lowfat version of dairy products.

This dish is reminiscent of a creamy potato soup, with far fewer calories and starch. Cauliflower, a cruciferous vegetable high in vitamin C and fiber, can be a great substitute for potatoes in many traditional recipes. Try using cauliflower next time you are about to whip up a batch of mashed potatoes. You may be pleasantly surprised not only with the taste but also with the modest effect this dish has on your blood sugar.

Preparation time: *15 minutes*

Cooking time: *40 to 45 minutes*

Yield: *4 servings*

1 head cauliflower cut into chunks	*2 tablespoons lemon juice*
2 shallots, chopped	*2 tablespoons honey*
3 cups 2 percent milk	*½ teaspoon kosher salt*
½ cup grated Parmesan cheese	*½ tablespoon pepper*

1 In a large pot, place the cauliflower, shallots, and milk and bring to a boil. Reduce heat to a simmer until the cauliflower is tender, about 35 minutes.

2 Transfer to a blender and purée until smooth (always be extra careful when blending hot liquids), or use a rotary beater to achieve a smooth consistency. While the soup is blending, add the cheese and process until smooth. Finish by adding the lemon juice, honey, salt, and pepper.

Per serving: *Kcalories 216 (From Fat 59); Fat 7g (Saturated 4g); Cholesterol 23mg; Sodium 324mg; Carbohydrate 28g (Dietary Fiber 3g); Protein 14g.*

Top your soup with beautiful garnishes to make a simple weeknight supper as delicious for your eyes as it is to your tummy. A few of our favorite fresh garnishes include the following:

- Chiffonade basil (see Chapter 9 for an explanation of chiffonade)
- Diced red pepper
- Finely grated lemon zest
- Grated or shaved Parmesan cheese and minced parsley
- Julienned radishes, jicama (see Figure 8-2), or daikon radish
- A dollop of light sour cream and cilantro
- Minced olives
- Thinly sliced green onions

Figure 8-2:
Jicama is a crunchy vegetable with a thin brown skin and white flesh.

Garnish this next creamy soup with Parmesan cheese and minced parsley to add to both the freshness and richness.

☺ Creamy Veggie Lover's Soup

How could you go wrong with veggies? Heather Dismore contributes this soup full of nutritional benefits. And it's super tasty too. One serving provides more than 100 percent of your daily vitamin C needs, more than half of your vitamin A needs, and more than 25 percent of your potassium, calcium, and vitamin D needs — also great for bone health! It's also a tremendous source of beta carotene and lycopene. Enjoy this dish by itself — the calorie, carbohydrate, protein, and fat contents are just enough for a light meal.

Preparation time: *20 minutes*

Cooking time: *30 minutes*

Yield: *4 servings*

2 tablespoons olive oil	¼ teaspoon ground thyme
⅓ cup minced onion	¼ teaspoon pepper
⅓ cup thinly sliced carrots	2 cans (about 14 ounces each) fat-free reduced-sodium beef broth
⅓ cup thinly sliced celery	
2 teaspoons minced garlic	1 can (6 ounces) tomato paste
3 cups sliced fresh mushrooms	1 cup evaporated skim milk
1 cup diced red pepper	2 cups cooked mini penne pasta
1 teaspoon ground sage	¼ cup Parmesan cheese (optional)
	2 tablespoons minced fresh parsley (optional)

1 Heat the oil in a large saucepan over medium heat until hot. Add the onions, carrots, celery, and garlic. Cook 3 to 4 minutes, until the vegetables begin to "sweat," or begin to give off a bit of liquid.

2 Add the mushrooms, red pepper, sage, thyme, and pepper. Cook and stir for 5 minutes or until the vegetables are crisp yet tender.

3 Add the beef broth and tomato paste; bring to a boil over medium-high heat. Cook 15 minutes.

4 Place half the soup in container of a food processor and purée (always use caution when processing hot liquids). With the food processor running, slowly pour in the evaporated skim milk.

5 Return the soup-milk mixture to the soup pot. Stir to combine. Add the cooked pasta and heat through. Serve immediately with the Parmesan cheese and parsley, if desired.

Per serving: Kcalories 281 (From Fat 69); Fat 8g (Saturated 1g); Cholesterol 40mg; Sodium 489mg; Carbohydrate 40g (Dietary Fiber 4g); Protein 16g.

Choosing Chilled Soups

Chilled soups are great appetizers, light lunches, or even desserts. You can choose any taste (sweet, spicy, savory) or ethnic flavor profile (Latin, Polish, French, you name it), and there's probably a chilled soup to match. Because you serve them cold, they're great to serve all summer long.

Don't feel like you need to wait for a special occasion to serve these chilled soups. They're so easy that you can serve them any time.

Cooling off with veggies

Get started with chilled soups by trying this easy Chilled Cucumber Soup. Spice it up as you see fit. Substitute fresh mint or cilantro for the dill to change the flavor.

☕ *Classic: Chilled Cucumber Soup*

Make cucumber soup even more refreshing by adding naturally tart yogurt. Yogurt, plus the nonfat sour cream in this recipe, makes this soup a substantial and satisfying starter course for lunch or dinner. Or add a punch of lemon zest to create a tangy palate cleanser between courses.

Preparation time: *20 minutes*

Cooking time: *15 minutes*

Yield: *4 servings*

Nonstick cooking spray

1 large or 2 small cucumbers, peeled, seeded, and cut into ¼-inch slices (2 cups)

2 shallots, minced

¼ cup white wine

2 cups low-sodium chicken broth

¼ teaspoon pepper

⅛ teaspoon salt

½ cup nonfat sour cream

½ cup plain nonfat yogurt

4 fresh dill weed sprigs

1 Coat a large skillet with the cooking spray and place over medium heat until hot. Sauté the cucumber and shallots, tossing or stirring frequently until soft and translucent (about 5 minutes).

2 Stir in the wine and chicken broth. Bring to a boil and simmer for 10 minutes. Add the pepper and salt. Continue to simmer for 2 minutes. Remove from heat.

3 Place the contents of the skillet in an electric blender or a food processor, cover, and process until smooth.

4 Pour the mixture into a bowl. Let cool slightly. With a wire whisk, stir in the sour cream and yogurt. Cover and chill. Garnish with the dill weed sprigs.

Per serving: Kcalories 66 (From Fat 8); Fat 1g (Saturated 0g); Cholesterol 3mg; Sodium 186mg; Carbohydrate 10g (Dietary Fiber 1g); Protein 5g.

☜ Live Cucumber and Avocado Soup

Candle 79 in New York features this quick, refreshing soup on warm days. Created by Chef Angel Ramos, it's low in calories and high in fiber for its portion size. It's a zesty starter to a vegetarian feast, or a terrific first course followed by grilled fish.

Preparation time: *10 minutes*

Cooking time: *0 minutes*

Yield: *4 servings*

4 cucumbers, roughly chopped

2 avocados, peeled and pits removed

½ jalapeño, seeds removed

¼ bunch cilantro

1 sprig mint, stems removed

Juice from ½ lime

½ teaspoon salt

1 small radish, julienned and chopped

Sweet corn kernels cut from 1 ear

½ red bell pepper, julienned and chopped

1 In a high-speed blender combine cucumbers, avocados, jalapeño, cilantro, mint leaves, lime juice, and salt. Blend on high until all ingredients have been well puréed, about 1-2 minutes.

2 Place a fine mesh strainer over a 1-2 quart container. Drain the avocado mixture through the strainer, working it through with a spatula if necessary. Taste and reseason with salt and pepper if desired.

3 Ladle a serving of the cucumber and avocado soup into a bowl. Place the julienne of radish and red pepper, and some sweet corn kernels on top to garnish. Enjoy!

Per serving: Kcalories 190 (Calories from Fat 118); Fat 13g (Saturated 3g); Cholesterol 0mg; Sodium 300mg; Carbohydrate 19g (Dietary Fiber 10g); Protein 5g.

Focusing on fruit

Fruit soups are among the most popular chilled soups, probably because people often eat fruit cold. So puréeing it first and then eating it isn't a stretch. Fruit soup recipes aren't always that simple, but they're not much tougher. Try cooking fruit soups with that classic blend of strawberries and rhubarb in this next recipe. Watermelon is the star of the other recipe in this section.

☼ Rhubarb Soup with Fresh Strawberries

When most people think of rhubarb, not much comes to mind, except for rhubarb pie — and for most people, even that thought rarely occurs! Chef Didier Labbe from the Clementine restaurant in San Francisco (see Appendix A) has offered a chilled rhubarb soup recipe for your cooking pleasure. (See the soup in the color section.) This one is a keeper — not only because it's delicious, interesting, and different, but also because it packs in more than 100 percent of the recommended daily allowance of vitamin C in just one serving! The original recipe calls for sugar to sweeten things up, but we substitute Splenda, and you'd never know the difference.

Preparation time: *15 minutes*

Cooking time: *20 minutes*

Yield: *2 servings*

1 pound rhubarb, peeled and cut into ½-inch-thick slices

¼ cup Splenda

1 pound strawberries, cleaned and sliced

1 cup water

Juice of ½ lemon

6 mint leaves, julienned

1 In a large mixing bowl, combine the rhubarb and Splenda and mix well. Set the bowl aside.

2 In a saucepan, combine the strawberries, water, and lemon juice. Cover and boil for 5 to 6 minutes. Using a colander, strain the strawberries to obtain just the juice. Discard the pulp.

3 Pour the strawberry juice back into the saucepan and add the rhubarb-and-Splenda mixture. Boil for 10 to 15 minutes. Remove the pan from heat and store the soup in the refrigerator until it's cold. Serve the soup chilled with the mint leaves as a garnish.

Tip: *Because rhubarb is seasonal, you may need to use the frozen kind, which already comes in pieces.*

Per serving: *Kcalories 117 (From Fat 10); Fat 1g (Saturated 0g); Cholesterol 0mg; Sodium 10mg; Carbohydrate 27g (Dietary Fiber 8g); Protein 3g.*

☙ *Watermelon Gazpacho*

Kyle Ketchum, from Lark in Detroit, Michigan (see Appendix A), delights with this warm weather treat. Just when the dog days of summer really start getting to you, try this refreshing gazpacho. (*Gazpacho* is a fancy word for a cold, uncooked soup.) This one takes advantage of the watermelon, one of the season's most popular fruits and a surprising twist on the usual summertime snack. Not only is this soup cool and invigorating, but it's also full of good nutrition. Watermelons are a great source of the antioxidants lycopene, beta carotene, and vitamin C, as well as vitamin A. This soup is quite low in calories, a good thing for your waistline. But before you go for a second scoop, remember that fruit has sugar and should be eaten in moderate amounts.

Preparation time: *45 minutes, plus 1 hour of chilling time*

Yield: *4 servings*

1 cup thinly sliced cucumbers

¼ teaspoon kosher salt

6 cups cubed and seeded watermelon (from about a 3-pound seedless watermelon)

½ cup cranberry juice

½ cup small diced red bell pepper

½ cup small diced red onion

½ cup small diced celery

¼ cup finely chopped parsley

1 tablespoon sherry vinegar

2 tablespoons lime juice

8 each fresh mint leaves, chiffonade (see Chapter 9 for an explanation of chiffonade)

1 In a small bowl, toss the cucumbers with the salt.

2 In a blender, add the watermelon and cranberry juice. Pulse until just blended. (Overblending causes the watermelon to froth and lose its color.) Pour through a sieve into a bowl and press on the pulp to extract all the juice. Discard the pulp.

3 Add the bell pepper, onion, celery, parsley, vinegar, and lime juice to the watermelon juice. Cover and refrigerate for 1 hour to chill and allow the flavors to blend together.

4 Rinse the cucumbers and pat dry.

5 Ladle the soup into chilled bowls (or martini glasses) and garnish with the cucumber slices and mint.

Per serving: *Kcalories 116 (From Fat 11); Fat 1g (Saturated 0g); Cholesterol 0mg; Sodium 140mg; Carbohydrate 27g (Dietary Fiber 3g); Protein 2g.*

Chapter 9

Taking Salads Seriously

Salads are among the most flexible items in a diabetic diet. They're chock-full of delicious and nutritious veggies with complex carbohydrates that help people with diabetes manage their glucose levels. Depending on what you add to them, dress them with, or pair them with, they can be a snack, meal, appetizer, or even a terrific last course. Stuff them in a pita pocket for a quick sandwich. Fill up a portable plastic container with them for an easy brown-bag lunch. Or toss them with a light vinaigrette for an easy meal.

In this chapter, we show you how to make the most from your salad choices. We give you excellent ideas for veggie-only salads and tips for whipping up great homemade dressings to match your nutritional needs. We show you how to add fruit to your salads for a sweet, refreshing twist. And finally, we offer recipes for entree-style, protein-packed salads, a perfect meal solution for just about any nutritional quandary.

Feasting on Great Salad Greens

Whether greens are an important part of the salad you're making or added just for garnish, using special and novel greens makes your salad stand out. Skip the pale green iceberg lettuce and buy some darker green lettuces like romaine and leaf lettuce instead (see Figure 9-1 for a sampling). The greener the leaf, the more nutrients it contains, especially magnesium, a mineral important for heart and bone health.

Figure 9-1:
A sampling of tasty greens to try for your next salad.

Picking fresh greens at the store

When you go shopping, consider picking up some of these types of greens:

- ✔ Arugula
- ✔ Boston butter lettuce
- ✔ Endive
- ✔ Escarole
- ✔ Frisée
- ✔ Mizuna
- ✔ Radicchio
- ✔ Red leaf lettuce
- ✔ Romaine
- ✔ Spinach
- ✔ Swiss chard
- ✔ Watercress

Store your salad greens in the vegetable bin of your fridge. Store romaine and radicchio with the head intact because the outer leaves keep the inner leaves moist. However, loose-leaf lettuce, like arugula and spinach, has a shorter shelf life. To store this type of lettuce, remove the leaves and wash and drain them. Gather and wrap them in a clean, damp paper towel or two and then store in a plastic bag. The leaves will stay fresh for a couple days, but not much longer.

☺ Grilled Romaine Caesar Salad

This delicious recipe is Vegetate's (Washington D.C.) take on a classic Caesar salad; they replace the anchovies with toasted, ground *nori* (seaweed sheets often used for making sushi rolls) and instead of eggs, they use silken tofu, a high protein, cholesterol free improvement.

Preparation time: *10 minutes*

Chill time: *30 minutes*

Cook time: *5 minutes*

Yield: *4 servings*

½ sheet toasted nori

1 package silken tofu

2 tablespoons olive oil

1½ ounces lemon juice

2 cloves garlic

1 teaspoon vegan Worcestershire sauce

Salt and pepper to taste

6 romaine hearts

Grilled bread or croutons (garnish)

1 Grind nori sheet in blender or food processor to a fine powder. Add remaining ingredients (except romaine hearts and garnish) and puree until smooth. Refrigerate dressing for 30 minutes.

2 Meanwhile, wash romaine hearts and slice off ends. Cut each romaine heart in half. Drizzle each half with olive oil and season with salt and pepper.

3 Place each romaine heart face down on hot grill (or grill pan) for 45 seconds or until lightly charred. Remove and serve on chilled plate with drizzled Caesar dressing. Garnish with grilled bread or croutons.

Per serving: Kcalories 104 (Calories from Fat 62); Fat 7g (Saturated 1g); Cholesterol 0mg; Sodium 134mg; Carbohydrate 5g (Dietary Fiber 1g); Protein 6g.

☺ Watercress Salad

During the summer months, take advantage of all the fresh, seasonal produce that is available. Forget about using iceberg lettuce, which offers nearly nothing in the way of good nutrition. Watercress, on the other hand, is a deep green leafy lettuce that has lots of vitamin A and beta carotene, which is great for eye health. This green leafy vegetable also happens to give you nearly one-fourth of your daily need of calcium, so eat 'em up for your bones.

We limit the amount of Gorgonzola cheese in this dish, courtesy of Derek's Bistro in Pasadena, California (see Appendix A), in order to keep the calorie and fat levels at an appropriate level. Gorgonzola, however, is a great cheese to use because it lends lots of good flavor in a small amount. Try sticking with sharper cheeses like this one, Parmesan, or cheddar instead of the milder ones — you'll need less and get more flavor!

Preparation time: *30 minutes*

Yield: *4 servings*

Vinaigrette dressing:	**Salad:**
½ onion, finely chopped	*2 small Granny Smith apples*
1 teaspoon chopped fresh thyme	*8 cups watercress, rinsed, destemmed and patted dry (purchase ready-to-use watercress if time is limited)*
1 teaspoon chopped fresh oregano	
¼ cup canola oil	*4 ounces Gorgonzola blue cheese, crumbled*
¼ cup sherry vinegar	*½ cup roasted pecans (see the tip at the end of the recipe)*
Salt and pepper	

1 To prepare the vinaigrette, place the onion, thyme, and oregano into a large bowl. Add the canola oil and sherry vinegar. Whisk the mixture together until everything is well combined. Add salt and pepper to taste.

2 Prepare the apples just before ready to serve to maintain their freshness and color. Leaving the skin on, slice the apples in half and core them. Julienne (slice into long strips) the cored apples.

3 Place the watercress in a large bowl and add the dressing. (You may not need all the dressing, so add carefully to taste.) Dish onto four plates and sprinkle the blue cheese and pecans over the greens. Arrange the apples on top and serve.

Tip: *To prepare the roasted pecans, preheat the oven to 350 degrees. Place a piece of parchment paper on a baking sheet and spread out the pecans in one even layer. Sprinkle with 1 teaspoon sugar. Bake for 10 minutes and then remove from the baking sheet. Set aside to cool.*

Per serving (with 2 tablespoons vinaigrette): *Kcalories 368 (From Fat 288); Fat 32g (Saturated 8g); Cholesterol 25mg; Sodium 559mg; Carbohydrate 16g (Dietary Fiber 4g); Protein 9g.*

☞ *Fresh Mushroom Salad*

This dish from Barbetta in New York City (see Appendix A) truly glorifies the mushroom — and the praise is well-deserved. Mushrooms are a popular and versatile vegetable with numerous health benefits. They're a great source of dietary fiber as well as many of the B vitamins, which can help support good energy levels.

Restaurant owner Laura Maioglio says that this salad, traditionally of Piemonte, Italy, is made with wild porcini mushrooms and white truffles. If you can't obtain fresh porcini, cultivated cremini mushrooms still give you a delicious salad. During truffle season at Barbetta, the salad is served with white truffles hunted by the restaurant's own truffle hounds! Drizzled on top of the mushrooms is the quite luxurious porcini olive oil in which porcini mushrooms steep their flavor into the oil as they sit together. Making your own olive oil can save you money because it costs a bundle in the specialty food stores!

Preparation time: *20 minutes, plus several days for steeping the olive oil*

Yield: *4 servings*

1 ounce dried porcini mushrooms	1 bunch oak leaf lettuce
1 quart extra-virgin olive oil	Juice of 1 lemon
10 ounces fresh porcini mushrooms	Salt and pepper
1 bunch Lolla Rossa lettuce (or substitute red leaf lettuce)	

1 Prepare your own porcini olive oil by steeping the dried porcini mushrooms in the olive oil. Let stand a few days for the oil to acquire the flavor of the mushrooms. Save the oil you don't need in this recipe for future use to give any number of dishes a fabulous taste.

2 Put 8 mushrooms aside and slice the remaining mushrooms very thin.

3 On 4 medium-size plates, place a few leaves of Lolla Rossa over a few oak leaf lettuce leaves. Place 1 whole mushroom on either side of the lettuce leaves to look as if the mushrooms are growing between the lettuce leaves. Place the sliced mushrooms in the remaining space on the plate.

4 Drizzle the porcini olive oil and lemon juice over the mushrooms and lettuce, and salt and pepper to taste.

Tip: *Drizzle your extra porcini olive oil on steamed or roasted veggies, add a touch of it to risotto during the final stages of cooking, or use it to give a punch of flavor to a marinade.*

Per serving (with 2 tablespoons porcini olive oil): Kcalories 286 (From Fat 248); Fat 28g (Saturated 4g); Cholesterol 0mg; Sodium 175mg; Carbohydrate 9g (Dietary Fiber 3g); Protein 4g.

Boning up on bagged salad blends

Fortunately, produce manufacturers are taking convenience foods to a healthy level for a change. Look in your produce section for prewashed, ready-to-use salad greens and blends. You can open a bag and have a delicious meal in a matter of minutes. For super easy and quick salads, pick up prewashed salad blends like these:

- **American blend:** This familiar blend usually includes iceberg lettuce, carrot shreds, radish slices, and red cabbage.

- **European blend:** It's a great mix to try if your salad experience stops at iceberg lettuce. It includes mild green leaf lettuce, romaine, iceberg, curly endive, and a bit of radicchio. It goes well with just about any dressing, toasted nuts, and any kind of cheese, including blue cheese and goat cheese.

- **Italian blend:** This blend is terrific for simple protein-based salads, light Caesar dressing, or a traditional Italian vinaigrette. It usually consists of a blend of romaine and radicchio.

- **Spring mix:** This tasty mixture is a staple at most fine restaurants. It's usually a blend of baby greens that include baby spinach, radicchio, and frisée. It may also be called mesclun, spring greens, or field greens. It makes a gorgeous garnish or bed for serving fresh fish or steak.

Different manufacturers call different mixes by different trademarked names. Many blends also include other veggies, like radishes, carrots, and even snow peas. All blends should include a description or listing of the greens (and other tasty veggies) included in their package, so find what suits your fancy and get munching!

Although these salad greens blends are great, many manufacturers also sell salad kits, which include the salad greens, dressing, cheese, and croutons. Watch the fat and unnecessary calories that these convenience kits can provide. And remember, you don't have to eat it just because it comes in the kit. Feel free to toss that full-fat Caesar dressing in the trash.

Growing your own greens

Growing fresh baby greens is incredibly simple, no matter where you live. Their shallow root systems make them ideal for indoor gardening. All you need is a shallow bowl or planter, high-quality potting soil, lettuce seeds, and a nice sunny window.

Here's how you do it:

1. **Fill a shallow container that has good drainage with high-quality potting soil.**

2. **Gently press seeds into the soil.**

   Because you'll be harvesting your baby greens when they're, well, babies, you don't need to space out the seeds. Go ahead and just sprinkle them around rather than make nice neat rows.

3. **Water your seeds.**

   Keep the seeds moist but not soggy. Light but frequent watering produces the best leafy greens.

4. **Set the container in a sunny window.**

   Most greens *germinate*, or sprout seeds, within a few weeks. Feel free to start harvesting when the greens are a few inches tall. Just trim off what you need with kitchen shears.

 To keep a constant supply of greens on hand, sow a second container two weeks later. Use a mixture of different seeds to create your own spring mix. For more information on growing lettuce or other vegetables in containers, check out *Container Gardening For Dummies,* by Bill Marken and the editors of the National Gardening Association, published by Wiley.

Creating sensational homemade dressings

Until very recently, bottled salad dressings didn't offer much in the way of flavor unless they were full of fat, salt, sugar, and other no-nos for a diabetic diet. Some of the newer light dressings have improved flavor, are less detrimental to your health, and are convenient. But there's really no substitute for making dressings yourself. And believe it or not, the process is pretty simple.

To make basic diabetic-friendly vinaigrette, follow these steps:

1. **Measure equal parts oil (usually extra-virgin olive oil), acid (like balsamic vinegar or lemon juice), and stock (like low-sodium chicken stock) and whisk them together.**

2. **Blend desired herbs and seasonings into the dressing and whisk some more.**

 To add a truly professional touch, combine all your ingredients (except the oil) in a food processor or blender. With the appliance running, slowly pour the oil into the other ingredients. The dressing will *emulsify,* or blend, really well.

☜ Truffle Vinaigrette

Chef Vitaly Paley from Paley's Place in Portland, Oregon (see Appendix A), uses truffles in this vinaigrette to create a truly luxurious, distinct flavor. Truffles are similar to mushrooms in that they're actually a fungus — but don't let that fool you; they're simply wonderful. You can find truffles at most fine food stores — they're worth searching for. You can drizzle this vinaigrette atop steamed vegetables or mixed greens. It contains no cholesterol and only a trace of saturated fat — olive oil is one of those heart-healthy sources of monounsaturated fat and can be beneficial for lowering cholesterol levels.

Preparation time: *5 minutes*

Yield: *18 to 20 servings (2 tablespoons per serving)*

1 to 2 ounces truffles, cleaned and finely chopped	⅓ cup balsamic vinegar
	1 cup olive oil
1 small shallot, peeled and finely chopped	Salt and pepper to taste
3 to 4 thyme sprigs, picked and chopped	Drizzle of truffle oil

Combine all the ingredients in a bowl and whisk them together well, or combine all the ingredients in a jar with a lid and shake vigorously.

Per serving (2 tablespoons): *Kcalories 105 (From Fat 99); Fat 11g (Saturated 2g); Cholesterol 0mg; Sodium 31mg; Carbohydrate 2g (Dietary Fiber 1g); Protein 0g.*

Often, a simple dressing is best. Steeping herbs, garlic, and dried mushrooms in oil gives you an excellent base to make your own tasty dressings. Add a little acid, like lemon juice or vinegar, and you're on your way.

Going Beyond Greens with Tomatoes

For many people, salad and lettuce are synonymous. While salad greens are amazingly nutritious, it's fun to try your hand at other salads that highlight other terrific vegetables, like tomatoes and cucumbers. Flavor them up with other extras, such as toasted nuts and freshly made dressings, and you have a great alternative to a traditional salad. For another great salad without greens, check out the Olive and Lentil Salad in Chapter 10.

Getting nutty with salads

Nuts have an undeserved reputation for being fattening. Not so! In moderation, nuts are an excellent source of fiber and monounsaturated fat, the good fat. Plus, they provide you with long-lasting protein that helps to stabilize your blood sugar.

Here's a list of seeds and nuts to try in your next salad:

✔ Almonds

✔ Cashews

✔ Pecans

✔ Pine nuts

✔ Sunflower seeds

✔ Walnuts

Whenever possible, toast nuts before adding them to any dish. The toasting process really brings out the flavor of the nuts, making them much more satisfying to eat. Simply place them in a sauté pan over medium-high heat, shaking them occasionally to ensure they don't burn. They're done when they become fragrant and slightly darker in color.

☺ Summer Tomato Salad

Although summertime is great for vibrantly red, juicy, sweet tomatoes, you can enjoy them year-round — and should! Tomatoes are packed with lycopene and beta carotene, two antioxidants known for their disease-fighting capabilities. This dish, courtesy of Paley's Place in Portland, Oregon (see Appendix A) and shown in the color section, is low in saturated fat and contains no cholesterol but still remains intense in flavor from the fresh basil and garlic. In all your cooking, try using fresh herbs and spices for flavoring instead of high-fat spreads and salt.

Preparation time: *10 minutes*

Yield: *4 servings*

4 medium tomatoes, diced small

1 garlic clove, minced

6 leaves basil, chiffonade (the sidebar "Flavoring salads with fresh herbs," earlier in this chapter, explains chiffonade)

2 tablespoons olive oil

1 tablespoon balsamic vinegar

Salt and pepper to taste

Combine all the ingredients in a large bowl and serve the salad at room temperature.

Tip: *Try a combination of tomatoes in this salad to add color and flavor. Look for Green Zebras, yellow teardrops, pear tomatoes, grape tomatoes, and everyone's first favorite tomato, the cherry. So many choices, so little time!*

Per serving: Kcalories 99 (From Fat 65); Fat 7g (Saturated 1g); Cholesterol 0mg; Sodium 152mg; Carbohydrate 8g (Dietary Fiber 1g); Protein 1g.

Flavoring salads with fresh herbs

Fresh herbs are an excellent addition to almost anything, especially salad. Their robust flavors can help you cut down the need for adding fat and salt to your foods. You can mince herbs, but some recipes, such as the one for Summer Tomato Salad in this chapter, call for herbs to be *chiffonade.* Chiffonade literally means "made of rags," and it pretty well describes what the final product looks like. Leafy lettuce or herbs are rolled together tightly and then thinly sliced width-wise to form long, stringy strips.

Here are a few descriptions of our favorite salad herbs.

- **Basil:** Technically a member of the mint family, this herb has a sweet peppery flavor that's the cornerstone of most pestos. Look for basil varieties like lemon basil and cinnamon basil to spice up your everyday salads.

- **Cilantro:** Use the tender stems and leaves of this herb to give a pungent push to any Latin- or Asian-inspired dishes. It pairs extremely well with citrus flavors.

- **Dill:** The feathery leaves of this pungent herb are the main ingredient in many a salad dressing and fish sauce. It's great paired with citrus.

- **Mint:** Sometimes thought of as only the dessert garnish, mint is used worldwide in both sweet and savory dishes. It's an incredibly aromatic herb that can lend its fragrance and flavor to salad dressings, dips, condiments, and beverages.

- **Parsley:** Whether you prefer flat-leaf or curly parsley, this herb is recognizable to most people. The best way to describe its flavor is fresh. Some people use it as a natural breath freshener. Chop it up and throw it into your salad along with your greens to brighten your salad's flavor.

Adding Fresh Fruit to Your Salad

Everyone knows how refreshing fruit salad can taste, made with three or four of the season's best crops. But in a diabetic diet, fruit, which is full of natural and easily absorbed sugars, needs to be enjoyed in moderation. How can you still include the juicy pleasures of fruit in a diabetic diet? By creating meals with small amounts of fruit and combining it with other foods, as in the following Fig, Mozzarella, and Mizuna Salad. Figs, mozzarella, and olive oil combine to balance the fat, protein, and carbohydrates.

Fig, Mozzarella, and Mizuna Salad with Thai Basil

Tante Marie's cooking school provides this recipe that's a great combination of sweet and savory. The quick and elegant presentation makes this salad a natural for entertaining.

Mizuna is a Japanese mustard green. Its leaves are shaped much like dandelion leaves, but are more subtle and delicate, with a jagged edge, and a mild earthy flavor. It's a great lettuce to grow yourself, so if you can't find it in a gourmet grocery store near you, consider growing your own with the instructions later in this chapter.

Preparation time: *15 minutes*

Yield: *4 servings*

8 green figs	*⅓ cup fruity extra-virgin olive oil*
12 small balls of fresh mozzarella	*1 teaspoon coarse salt*
1 bunch or 12 ounces mizuna or arugula	*Freshly ground black pepper, to taste*
1 bunch or 4 ounces Thai basil or purple mint	

1 Wash the figs and remove the little stems with a paring knife. Remove the mozzarella balls from their liquid. Wash the greens; drain thoroughly. Remove basil (or mint if using) leaves from the stems. Wash the herbs; pat the leaves dry.

2 Place the greens and herbs in a medium bowl and toss with the olive oil.

3 Pile the greens mixture in the middle of four dinner plates. Using your thumbs, gently pull figs in half and lay them open-side up around the greens mixture on the plates. Arrange 3 balls of cheese around the greens pile on each plate well.

4 Sprinkle each plate with a little extra olive oil, a few drops of lemon juice, and a sprinkle of coarse salt. Grind fresh pepper to taste over each salad.

Per serving: Kcalories 428 (Calories from Fat 286); Fat 32g (Saturated 11g); Cholesterol 47mg; Sodium 824mg; Carbohydrate 25g (Dietary Fiber 6g); Protein 15g.

Blood Orange, Beet, and Avocado Salad

In this recipe I recommend using pale colored beets because the deep red beets I used when testing the recipe turned everything dark red. This recipe is a mixture of some of our favorite fruits and vegetables.

Preparation time: *25 minutes*

Cooking time: *1 hour or more*

Yield: *6 servings*

1 head red lettuce (or a small bag of mesclun)

4 blood oranges

1 bunch yellow beets

2 avocados

¼ cup shelled pistachios or toasted pine nuts

Coarse salt

1½ tablespoons red wine vinegar

3 tablespoons good quality extra virgin olive oil

freshly ground black pepper, to taste

1 Preheat oven to 400 degrees.

2 Cut the leaves and roots from the beets. Rub them with olive oil and wrap each in foil. Bake beets until soft when pierced with a fork, at least 1 hour. When the beets are cool enough to handle, remove the skins and cut the beets into wedges.

3 Meanwhile, wash and dry the lettuce and place it in a large bowl.

4 Cut both ends off the oranges, lay them on a cut side, and with a knife, remove the rind in 1-inch strips around the orange, cutting down to the flesh. Squeeze any excess juice from the cuttings over the lettuce. Cut the skinned oranges into rounds.

5 Cut each avocado in half, and cut the flesh of each half into slices.

6 Arrange the blood orange slices, the avocado slices, and the beets over the lettuce. Sprinkle with pistachios or pine nuts.

7 When ready to serve, mix a scant half teaspoon of salt in the bowl of a spoon with the vinegar. Toss vinegar mixture over the salad, then add the olive oil and pepper to taste. Toss salad gently so that all the ingredients are lightly coated with dressing. Arrange salad on individual salad plates.

Per serving: *Kcalories 245 (Calories from Fat 159); Fat 18g (Saturated 3g); Cholesterol 0mg; Sodium 159mg; Carbohydrate 21g (Dietary Fiber 9g); Protein 5g.*

Enjoying Entrée Salads

For many of us, salads have become the main attraction. These days you can even get a very decent entrée salad at your local fast food restaurant. Eating salad has never been easier. To continue that push toward easy healthful eating, we offer you the tasty entrée salads in this section.

Surveying simple seafood salads

Most seafood is naturally delicious, so it really doesn't take much effort to turn it into something special. A little bit of seasoning, a light dressing, and some tasty greens, and you have yourself a meal. Marinate sea scallops in a little olive oil and lemon juice and broil them. Or steam your favorite white fish with herbs and seasonings and then serve it on a bed of greens. Just about any seafood item can take the main stage in your mostly salad meal. For more terrific seafood recipes, make sure to stop by Chapter 12.

Shrimp Salad

The shrimp and mayo in this salad provide enough fat and protein to really stick with you to get you through to your next meal. Enjoy the extra crunch of the red and yellow bell peppers. Choose your favorite mixed greens. See "Feasting on Great Salad Greens," earlier in this chapter, for more information on salad greens.

Preparation time: *15 minutes*

Yield: *4 servings*

1 pound medium shrimp, cooked	¼ cup lowfat mayonnaise
¼ cup chopped red pepper	1 teaspoon Dijon mustard
¼ cup chopped yellow pepper	1 teaspoon lemon juice
1 tablespoon chopped fresh cilantro	¼ teaspoon white pepper
¼ cup chopped fresh chives	4 cups fresh mixed salad greens

1 In a bowl, combine the shrimp, red and yellow peppers, half of the cilantro, and chives.

2 In another bowl, whisk together the mayonnaise, mustard, lemon juice, and white pepper. Spoon over the shrimp mixture and toss together.

3 Arrange the salad greens on 4 large plates. Top the greens with equal portions of the shrimp mixture.

4 Sprinkle with the remaining cilantro.

Per serving: *Kcalories 154 (From Fat 23); Fat 3g (Saturated 0g); Cholesterol 221mg; Sodium 440mg; Carbohydrate 7g (Dietary Fiber 2g); Protein 25g.*

The typical Asian diet is getting a lot of attention in the media as being a healthy one. In general, Asian populations tend to have less incidence of heart disease, cancer, and diabetes. Their diets tend to focus on seafood as the main protein; plant-based foods, like soy products and rice, rather than dairy products; and tons of vegetables. The following recipe gives you a chance to sample the flavors of this healthful cuisine.

Teriyaki Salmon Salad

Salmon, nature's wonder food, is full of those omega-3 fatty acids, one of the good fats. Including them in the diet can help delay signs of aging and wrinkles, treat arthritis and skin eruptions, and prevent cancer, heart disease and Alzheimer's. Yes, omega-3s can do all that!

Preparation time: *15 minutes*

Cooking time: *10 to 12 minutes*

Yield: *2 servings*

1 tablespoon Dijon mustard

1 tablespoon dry white cooking wine

1 tablespoon low-sodium teriyaki sauce

1 teaspoon low-sodium soy sauce

1 teaspoon honey

1 teaspoon lemon juice

½ teaspoon garlic powder

¼ teaspoon white pepper

2 skinless salmon fillets, 6 ounces each

2 cups field salad greens

¼ small red onion, thinly sliced

1 Preheat the oven to 350 degrees. In a medium bowl, combine the mustard, wine, teriyaki sauce, soy sauce, honey, lemon juice, garlic powder, and white pepper. Place the salmon in the bowl and coat thoroughly.

2 Place the salmon in a baking dish, pour the remaining liquid over the salmon, and place the dish in the oven. Bake for 10 to 12 minutes.

3 Arrange 1 cup of greens on each plate and place a salmon fillet on top. Sprinkle the red onion over the plate.

Per serving: *Kcalories 256 (From Fat 65); Fat 7g (Saturated 1g); Cholesterol 97mg; Sodium 559mg; Carbohydrate 8g (Dietary Fiber 2g); Protein 39g.*

Punching up your salad with protein

Pairing salads and protein is a natural fit for a diabetic diet. Most of the meal is actually made up of the healthy veggies, accented by a small but satisfying portion of protein, the ideal ratio in a diabetic diet.

Canned legumes, like chickpeas (also known as garbanzo beans) and kidney beans, are an excellent and inexpensive way to make sure you're getting enough protein. Plus these protein powerhouses are cholesterol free, making them an all-around excellent choice.

 *Chickpea Salad*

This great, all-purpose salad can be stuffed in a pita pocket with mixed greens for a quick well-rounded meal. Vary it by adding different vegetables, like tomatoes, or different spices, like cumin or curry powder. Make it your own.

Preparation time: *10 minutes*

Yield: *2 servings*

1½ cups canned chickpeas, drained and rinsed

¼ cup celery, chopped

¼ cup red pepper, chopped

¼ cup red onion, chopped

⅛ teaspoon salt

⅛ teaspoon white pepper

2 tablespoons lowfat mayonnaise

Pita bread or mixed greens

1 In a bowl, coarsely mash the chickpeas. Add the celery, red pepper, onion, salt, pepper, and mayonnaise and toss well.

2 Serve over pita bread or mixed greens.

Per serving (without pita or greens): *Kcalories 206 (From Fat 30); Fat 3g (Saturated 0g); Cholesterol 0mg; Sodium 641mg; Carbohydrate 35g (Dietary Fiber 9g); Protein 10g.*

Crunchy Chicken Stir-Fry Salad

Here's a great way to enjoy a chicken salad that's not the same old greens-topped-with-grilled-chicken-breast thing. It's loaded with interesting veggies (like bok choy and snap peas) and other tasty tidbits (like almonds) that give a terrific flavor and texture.

Preparation time: *15 minutes*

Cooking time: *25 minutes*

Yield: *2 servings*

1 tablespoon sesame oil

12 ounces boneless, skinless chicken breasts, sliced into strips

½ cup baby carrots

¼ teaspoon garlic powder

⅛ teaspoon onion powder

⅛ teaspoon white pepper

¼ teaspoon sesame seeds

½ cup broccoli florets

¼ cup celery, small sliced diagonally

½ cup snap peas

1 tablespoon low-sodium teriyaki sauce

1 teaspoon low-sodium soy sauce

½ cup low-sodium chicken broth

1 cup blanched and roughly chopped Chinese bok choy (see Chapter 11 for info about blanching)

2 tablespoons slivered almonds

1 Heat a large skillet over medium-high heat. Add the oil. Add the chicken strips, carrots, and garlic powder. Sauté until the chicken is lightly browned (about 7 minutes). Add the onion powder, white pepper, sesame seeds, broccoli, and celery. Cook and continue stirring until the vegetables are soft.

2 Lower the heat and add the snap peas, teriyaki sauce, soy sauce, and chicken broth. Continue stirring. Simmer until the liquid has reduced slightly.

3 Divide the bok choy between two plates. Spoon the chicken mixture over the bok choy. Sprinkle the almonds on top.

Per serving: Kcalories 352 (From Fat 136); Fat 15g (Saturated 3g); Cholesterol 95mg; Sodium 403mg; Carbohydrate 12g (Dietary Fiber 5g); Protein 40g.

Using leftovers to your advantage

"Leftovers" doesn't have to be a dirty word. In fact, think of them as a life simplification strategy. When you're marinating and grilling chicken for dinner, double your recipe and reserve the extra for quick salads later in the week. Stop by the grocery on your way home and get a fresh bag of greens, and your healthful dinner is in the bag.

Here's a list of great leftovers that can make an excellent next-day salad:

- ✔ Broiled sirloin steak
- ✔ Grilled chicken breast
- ✔ Cocktail shrimp
- ✔ Roasted turkey breast
- ✔ Pan-seared beef tenderloin
- ✔ Roasted pork tenderloin

Classic: Oriental Beef and Noodle Salad

If you have a craving for Chinese take-out, satisfy your hunger with this healthy, lowfat version, full of Asian flavor. Using a minimum of meat with lots of vegetables is typical of Chinese cooking. Although this style of cooking evolved by necessity, due to a scarcity of eat, the result of this hardship was the creation of an exceptionally healthy cuisine. A good example is this beef and noodle salad, made with lean meat and a minimum of cooking oil.

Preparation time: *15 minutes*

Cooking time: *15 minutes*

Yield: *4 servings*

8 ounces thin spaghetti

4 teaspoons sesame oil

Nonstick cooking spray

1 pound boneless top sirloin steak, trimmed of fat, cut 1-inch thick, and cut into slices about ¼-inch thick

2 teaspoons low-sodium soy sauce

2 teaspoons red wine vinegar

1 teaspoon Dijon mustard

¼ teaspoon ground ginger

1 clove garlic, minced

⅛ teaspoon white pepper

2 tablespoons thinly sliced green onion

2 tablespoons finely chopped red bell pepper

2 teaspoons chopped fresh cilantro

1 Bring a large pot of water to boil. Salt the boiling water and cook the spaghetti according to package directions, typically 5 to 6 minutes. Drain, rinse under cold running water, and drain again. Transfer to a large bowl and toss with the sesame oil and set aside.

2 Coat a large cast-iron or nonstick skillet with the cooking spray and place over medium-high heat until hot. Add the steak slices and cook until medium rare, about 1 minute per side. Add the steak to the bowl with the pasta.

3 In a small bowl, whisk together the soy sauce, vinegar, mustard, ginger, garlic, and white pepper. Add the green onions and red pepper and toss well. Add to the bowl with the spaghetti and steak and toss well.

4 Divide among four serving plates, sprinkle with the cilantro, and serve.

Per serving: *Kcalories 435 (From Fat 122); Fat 14g (Saturated 4g); Cholesterol 71mg; Sodium 186mg; Carbohydrate 44g (Dietary Fiber 2g); Protein 34g.*

Chapter 10

Stocking Up on Grains and Legumes

Diabetics must watch their intake of carbohydrates because they directly impact blood sugar levels. One big source of carbohydrates is grains. Grains form a part of the food guide pyramid, the guide to healthy eating from the United States Department of Agriculture (USDA). (See Chapter 2 for more about the pyramid.) Talk to your doctor and dietitian about the best choice for your health situation.

In this chapter, we show you how to include rice and other grains in recipes and dishes to brighten up any meal. We provide recipes and information on using pasta as part of your daily regimen. And finally, we give you the inside scoop on using legumes in so many ways that you're bound to find something new and tasty.

Relishing Rice and Other Grains

Grains are truly the food that changed the world. Cultivated by early farmers, they helped my ancestors become settled, non-nomadic peoples, building stable civilizations the world over. We owe a lot to these little packets of nutrition, like rice and quinoa.

Eating rice the right way

Rice is a worldwide staple, but it often gets a bad reputation because so many people eat the bland, processed white rice slathered with fat-heavy sauces. Instead, try less processed, flavored rice that can stand on its own or can be enhanced by a few simple seasonings or cooking techniques. And always remember to eat in moderation.

Here are a few rice varieties that may be new to you with ideas on how to use them:

- **Arborio:** It's an Italian short- to medium-grained rice used in making risotto. The rice gives off starches as it cooks to add to the creaminess of this popular Italian dish. Try it for yourself in the recipe for Risotto alle Erbe Made with Extra-Virgin Olive Oil in this section.

- **Basmati:** Its name means "queen of fragrance" for its distinct nutty aroma during cooking. Its fragrance is enhanced as it's aged after harvesting. True basmati rice is grown in the foothills of the Himalayas, but a few new basmati-like varieties are grown in the United States under the names Texmati and Kasmati.

- **Brown:** This rice has the whole rice grain intact, with only the inedible outer husk removed. Because it has the bran coating intact, it's higher in fiber but has a shorter shelf life (around six months). Use it in any recipe that calls for white rice, but give it a bit more time to cook (about 45 minutes). To get started with it, try the Middle Eastern Brown Rice Pilaf in this section.

- **Jasmine:** Aromatic long-grain rice from Thailand, this rice is highly prized but less expensive than basmati. Try it out in the Black Bean Pie recipe later in this chapter.

- **Long-grain:** A broad category of rice, long-grain rice has long, evenly shaped pieces that tend to be drier and less starchy than short-grained varieties. Long-grain rice separates easily after cooking. Basmati, jasmine, and wild rice are all long-grain rices.

- **Medium-grain:** As the name implies, medium-grain rice is longer than short-grain rice and shorter than long-grain rice.

- **Short-grain:** This rice has short, almost round grains and a higher starch content than long-grain rice, giving it a sticky, clumpy consistency after cooking.

- **Wild rice:** This "rice" is actually the grain of a wild marsh grass. It has a chewy texture and nutty flavor. It's often combined with other rice.

Middle Eastern Brown Rice Pilaf

Sometimes people complain that brown rice never seems to taste right or it just never achieves a good consistency. Here is a dish, contributed by food writer and *For Dummies* author Heather Dismore, that uses this whole grain and incorporates many other textures and flavors that will leave you loving brown rice forever! This is a good lesson in creativity and risk taking! Seek out new and different recipes that change the flavors until you find one you like. If you hesitate to try brown rice again, try this recipe before you swear off this healthy food forever.

Preparation time: *10 minutes*

Cooking time: *1 hour*

Yield: *6 servings*

2 tablespoons olive oil	*¾ cup uncooked brown rice*
1½ cups chopped onion	*2 cups chicken broth*
1 clove garlic, minced	*¼ cup chopped fresh green onions*
2 carrots, sliced	*Salt and pepper*
2 cups fresh sliced mushrooms	

1 Heat the olive oil in a deep skillet with a tight-fitting lid over medium heat. Sauté the onions, stirring frequently until they soften. Add the garlic and carrots and continue stirring for 5 minutes. Add the mushrooms and rice and cook until the mushrooms soften, about 7 to 8 minutes.

2 Add the chicken broth. Bring to a boil. Cover and reduce the heat. Continue cooking until all the liquid is absorbed, approximately 45 to 50 minutes. Fluff with a fork. Toss with the green onions. Season with salt and pepper to taste.

Per serving: Kcalories 174 (From Fat 60); Fat 7g (Saturated 1g); Cholesterol 2mg; Sodium 547mg; Carbohydrate 25g (Dietary Fiber 3g); Protein 4g.

☎ Risotto alle Erbe Made with Extra-Virgin Olive Oil

Here is a wonderful risotto dish offered to us from Barbetta restaurant in New York (see Appendix A). Important to note is the importance of stirring the risotto constantly! This is not a moment for TV watching or telephone answering! The risotto at the end should be smooth and flowing, and once done, you must eat it immediately. This saying in Italy tells the story: "You must wait for risotto, but risotto cannot wait for you."

Making risotto with olive oil was first introduced by Barbetta Restaurant and certainly is a healthy change from the traditional method, which calls for butter. Essentially, risotto is made from Italian rice, and for people with diabetes, rice has falsely been accused of being "bad" food. Too many carbs, and for that matter, too much of anything is "bad," but this risotto dish, served in moderation, can certainly be part of a balanced, healthy diet. It's absolutely delicious and worth every bite. Pair the risotto with some protein, such as fish or poultry, and fiber, from nonstarchy veggies, to keep your blood sugars on an even keel.

Preparation time: *45 minutes*

Cooking time: *20 minutes*

Yield: *6 servings (1 cup each)*

1 bunch fresh sage	1 teaspoon salt
1 bunch fresh rosemary	Pinch of pepper
1 bunch fresh parsley	1 cup Italian rice, Carnaroti or arborio
1 bunch fresh basil	1 cup dry white wine
1½ quarts water	½ cup grated Parmigiano cheese
5 tablespoons extra-virgin olive oil, divided	Salt and pepper
½ medium onion, finely chopped	

1 From the fresh sage, rosemary, parsley, and basil, chop enough in equal parts (roughly 3 tablespoons) of each type of herb to make ¾ cup. Set aside.

2 Using butcher's twine, tie together one stem each of sage, rosemary, parsley, and basil (once tied together, the herbs resemble a bouquet of flowers). Place the bouquet in a saucepan with the 1½ quarts of water. Bring to a boil. Remove from heat. Allow the bouquet to steep for 30 minutes. Strain and keep warm. This will serve as your herb stock. Bring stock back to a low simmer before adding to risotto in Step 5.

3 In a 3-quart saucepan, heat 3 tablespoons of oil over medium heat.

4 Add the chopped onions, salt, and pepper. Cook for 1 minute. Add the rice, wine, and chopped herbs. Immediately stir and continue to stir every 15 seconds until the risotto absorbs the wine. Keep the heat medium to high.

5 When the wine has evaporated, begin to add simmering stock ½ cup at time, stirring continuously. Add a bit of salt and pepper depending on your taste. Once ½ cup of the stock is absorbed and the rice looks dry, add another ½ cup. Repeat until you've added roughly 3 to 4 cups of the herb stock, and the rice is soft but *al dente,* or firm to the bite. If the rice tastes hard and starchy, continue adding stock. This step takes about 25 to 30 minutes total. ***Note:*** You must continue to stir the risotto during this stage of cooking. Stirring helps to bring out the starchy creaminess in the rice and ensures the proper texture and consistency.

6 Once the risotto is cooked, its consistency should resemble thick oatmeal. Remove the pot from the heat. Add the grated Parmigiano cheese and the remaining 2 tablespoons of oil. Stir very well. Allow to rest 2 minutes. Stir once more before serving. Season with salt and pepper to taste.

Per serving: Kcalories 278 (From Fat 128); Fat 14g (Saturated 3g); Cholesterol 5mg; Sodium 516mg; Carbohydrate 31g (Dietary Fiber 1g); Protein 7g.

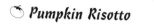 Pumpkin Risotto

This recipe for Pumpkin Risotto, from Tante Marie's Cooking School in San Francisco, is a celebration of the fall produce harvest. It calls for pumpkin, but you can substitute butternut, acorn, or other firm-fleshed squash for twist.

We've listed nutritional information for 6 entrée servings, but you could instead create 12 side-dish portions to serve as a side with Thanksgiving dinner, replacing mashed potatoes or another starchy side dish. One added healthy benefit: Because this risotto is so delicious, you won't need the gravy that bland starches beg for.

Preparation time: *10 minutes*

Cooking time: *45 minutes*

Yield: *6 servings*

6 to 7 cups of low-sodium vegetable broth	½ cup dry white wine
¼ cup olive oil	1 tablespoon minced fresh sage
1 ¾ cups Arborio rice	½ teaspoon salt
1½ cups peeled, seeded and diced fresh pumpkin	¼ teaspoon freshly ground black pepper
	¼ cup freshly grated Parmesan cheese

1 In a medium-large saucepan, heat the vegetable broth to a simmer over medium heat. Maintain simmer throughout the other steps.

2 In a separate 3-quart heavy saucepan or skillet, heat the olive oil over medium heat. Toss in the rice and diced pumpkin and stir with a wooden spoon until the rice is coated with the oil.

3 Add the white wine to the rice mixture and stir constantly until all the wine has been absorbed. Ladle ½ cup of hot broth into the pan and stir until it is absorbed. Continue with rest of the broth, adding ½ cup at a time and letting each addition be absorbed completely by the rice before adding more liquid.

   Remember: *The constant stirring allows the rice to release its starch into the cooking liquid, resulting in the characteristic risotto creaminess.*

4 When the rice is creamy and cooked through but still firm, or al dente, (roughly about 25 to 30 minutes stirring time), stir in the sage, salt, pepper and Parmesan cheese. Serve immediately.

Per serving: *Kcalories 350 (Calories from Fat 106); Fat 12g (Saturated 2g); Cholesterol 3mg; Sodium 866mg; Carbohydrate 53g (Dietary Fiber 4g); Protein 8g.*

Kicking it up with quinoa

Quinoa (pronounced kēn wäh) is considered by some to be the most nutritious of all the whole grains (see Figure 10-1). This ancient superfood is becoming more popular, showing up on the menus of gourmet restaurants nationwide. Quinoa is high in protein and fiber, provides 25 percent of your daily iron needs, and is a tremendous source of magnesium, potassium, and phosphorus. It is more nutritious than white rice and in most dishes can be substituted for the more popular grain.

Most mainstream grocery stores carry it these days, but if you have trouble tracking it down, try your local health food store. Whenever possible, opt for the grain itself, rather than a processed boxed quinoa pilaf. As with other grains, the less processed the better.

Always rinse quinoa thoroughly before cooking it. Don't be tempted to skip this step. Even if your quinoa is processed, which removes much of the *saponin*, or protective outer covering, the dust still remains. It can add a nasty bitter flavor to your finished dish. Don't risk it. Place the quinoa in a fine mesh strainer. Run cold water through the grains until the water runs clear. Drain the water off, stir the grains around a bit, and then re-rinse to ensure you've removed all the bitter outer coating.

Figure 10-1:
Quinoa is a terrific source of protein, fiber, vitamins, and minerals.

Moroccan Quinoa

Moroccan spices, like turmeric, ginger, and cinnamon, combine with almonds and dried fruits to give this quinoa a delicious North African flavor. Heather Dismore contributed this recipe to keep your taste buds perky and your blood sugar stable. It's a great way to get started with quinoa if you haven't already discovered this amazing grain.

Preparation time: *20 minutes*

Cooking time: *40 minutes*

Yield: *4 servings*

1 cup quinoa, drained and rinsed thoroughly

1 cup water

1 cup low-sodium chicken broth

2 teaspoons olive oil

1 cup diced red onion

½ teaspoon cumin

¼ teaspoon turmeric

½ teaspoon cinnamon

¼ teaspoon ground ginger

¼ cup slivered almonds, toasted

¼ cup raisins

Salt to taste

Fresh mint (optional)

1 Place the rinsed quinoa, water, and chicken broth in a 1½-quart saucepan and bring to a boil. Reduce to a simmer, cover, and cook until all the water is absorbed (about 15 minutes). Fluff with a fork. Set aside.

2 While the quinoa is cooking, heat the oil in a nonstick skillet. Sauté the onions until they begin to caramelize. Add the cumin, turmeric, cinnamon, and ginger, cooking until fragrant. Stir in the almonds and raisins until heated.

3 Add the hot quinoa to the skillet. Toss to combine. Heat until the mixture is heated through. Adjust salt if needed. Serve garnished with fresh mint, if desired.

Per serving: *Kcalories 274 (From Fat 79); Fat 9g (Saturated 1g); Cholesterol 1mg; Sodium 186mg; Carbohydrate 43g (Dietary Fiber 5g); Protein 9g.*

Quinoa and Black Bean Salad over Chilled Avocado Soup

This simple salad from Millennium Restaurant in San Francisco is a vegetarian dream. With its elegant presentation, it makes a great light entrée during the summer. Make it for guests or for yourself when you want a gorgeous dish with a lot of flavor, but not a lot of calories.

No need to mince the garlic or peppers for the avocado soup. Just plop them into the blender as-is.

Preparation time: 30 minutes

Cooking time: 20 minutes, plus 2 hours cooling time

Yield: 4 servings

Avocado Soup:

2 ripe avocados, peeled and seeded

½ yellow onion, diced

1 clove garlic, peeled

½ serrano or jalapeno pepper, or more to taste

3 tablespoons cilantro leaves

½ teaspoon dried oregano

2 cups water

Juice of 2 limes

Salt to taste

Quinoa Black Bean Salad:

1 cup quinoa, drained and rinsed thoroughly

2 cups water

2 15-ounce cans black beans, drained and rinsed

½ red onion, small diced

1 cup cherry tomatoes, sliced in half

2 tablespoons minced cilantro

2 tablespoons minced fresh parsley

½ teaspoon dried oregano (or 1 teaspoon fresh oregano minced)

½ teaspoon smoked paprika

Juice of 1 lime

Salt and black pepper to taste

1 Place the ingredients for the avocado soup (except salt) into a blender. Blend until smooth. Season to taste with salt. Refrigerate until needed, at least 2 hours.

2 Place the rinsed quinoa and water in a 1½-quart saucepan and bring to a boil. Reduce to a simmer, cover, and cook until all of the water is absorbed (about 15 minutes). Fluff with a fork. Set aside. Allow to cool to room temperature, about an hour.

3 Mix remaining ingredients together in a mixing bowl. Adjust salt and pepper to taste.

4 To serve, pack 1 cup of the quinoa salad into a ring mold in the center of a pasta bowl. If you don't have a ring mold handy, just mound the salad in the center of the bowl. Gently pour 3 ounces of the avocado soup around the salad.

Tip: Top with avocado slices, if desired. Slice them just before serving to help them keep their bright color and avoid browning.

Per serving: *Kcalories 416 (Calories from Fat 160); Fat 18g (Saturated 3g); Cholesterol 0mg; Sodium 314mg; Carbohydrate 56g (Dietary Fiber 16g); Protein 15g.*

Quinoa and Spiced Adzuki Beans

Vegetate, voted Best Vegetarian Restaurant for Washington D.C., contributes this version of rice and beans. The quinoa contributes a full protein serving, while the adzuki beans are not only tasty but are known in many Asian cultures to have medicinal effects. The Chinese believe that adzuki beans strengthen the heart, aid blood circulation, improve fatigue, and help keep the digestive system healthy. With their abundance of iron, they're a particularly good choice for meeting the nutritional needs of women.

Preparation time: *15 minutes*

Cooking time: *2 hours, mostly unattended*

Yield: *4 servings*

1 cup dried adzuki beans	*1 dried chili*
7 cups water, divided	*1 small bay leaf*
1 small onion, quartered	*½ teaspoon smoked paprika*
6 slices fresh ginger root	*salt and pepper to taste*
3 garlic cloves	*1 cup quinoa, drained and rinsed thoroughly*
2 tablespoons olive oil	

1 Place all ingredients (except quinoa and 2 cups of water) in a large saucepan and bring to a boil. Reduce heat to low, cover and simmer 1½ to 2 hours, or until beans are just tender. Remove and discard onion, bay leaf, ginger, garlic, and chili. Add salt and pepper to taste and simmer 2 to 3 minutes longer.

2 Meanwhile, place the rinsed quinoa and remaining 2 cups water in a 1½-quart saucepan and bring to a boil. Reduce to a simmer, cover, and cook until all the water is absorbed (about 15 minutes). Fluff with a fork.

3 To serve, place ½ cup of quinoa in each bowl. Top with bean mixture.

Per serving: *Kcalories 322(Calories from Fat 25); Fat 3g (Saturated 0g); Cholesterol 0mg; Sodium 157mg; Carbohydrate 61g (Dietary Fiber 9g); Protein 15g.*

☙ Roasted Root Vegetables and Quinoa

From Candle Café, the organic vegan eatery in New York City, comes this earthy and satisfying vegetarian dish. If you need a protein boost, consider adding a portion of grilled chicken or shrimp to this already complete meal.

Preparation time: *30 minutes*

Cooking time: *45 minutes*

Yield: *4 servings*

2 medium carrots, peeled and cut into 2-inch pieces

2 parsnips, peeled and cut into small chunks

2 beets, peeled and cut into small chunks

1 yam, peeled and cut into small chunks

1 garlic clove, sliced

1 tablespoon extra-virgin olive oil

1 tablespoon soy sauce or tamari

Pinch of dried basil

Pinch of dried oregano

Pinch of dried thyme

Pinch of freshly ground black pepper

Salt and pepper to taste

3 cups water

1½ cups quinoa, rinsed and drained

1 Preheat oven to 325 degrees.

2 In a large mixing bowl, place the carrots, parsnips, beets, yam, and garlic. Add remaining ingredients (except water and quinoa) to the bowl. Toss well to combine. Transfer vegetable mixture to a shallow baking sheet and bake for 45 minutes, or until tender. Add salt and pepper to taste.

3 Meanwhile, place the rinsed quinoa and water in a 1½-quart saucepan and bring to a boil. Reduce to a simmer, cover, and cook until all the water is absorbed (about 15 minutes). Fluff with a fork.

4 To serve, mound 1 cup of quinoa in the center of plate. Ring with ¼ of the vegetables.

Per serving: Kcalories 418 (Calories from Fat 67); Fat 7g (Saturated 1g); Cholesterol 0mg; Sodium 308mg; Carbohydrate 79g (Dietary Fiber 11g); Protein 12g.

Trying out barley

Barley is a whole grain that is a delicious side dish to serve with meats and poultry. Try the following recipe to include some barley in your diet.

Classic: Barley Pilaf

Barley that still retains the bran takes a long time to cook, so manufacturers *pearl* the barley, which means they remove the bran. Pearled barley is the kind you usually find in supermarkets. Look for barley with grains that are oval, not round, a sign that the bran is mostly intact. In comparison with rice and wheat, barley has significantly less effect on blood glucose. Barley is also tasty added to soups.

Preparation time: *10 minutes*

Cooking time: *50 minutes*

Yield: *6 servings*

1 piece smoked ham hock, 6 ounces	*4 cups water*
2 stalks celery, cut into 2-inch lengths	*1 tablespoon safflower oil*
2 bay leaves	*1 medium onion, chopped*
½ teaspoon dried sage	*1 cup pearled barley*
Pepper	

1 In a large pot, put the ham hock, celery, bay leaves, sage, pepper to taste, and water. Over high heat, bring to a boil, lower the heat to medium, and cook, uncovered, for 20 minutes. Volume of the broth will reduce by about 1 cup.

2 In a medium pot, heat the safflower oil over medium heat. Cook the onion, stirring occasionally, until soft, about 5 minutes. Add the barley and cook, stirring for 1 minute.

3 When the ham hock stock is prepared, pour the broth through a sieve into the barley. Bring to a boil.

4 Turn the heat to low, cover the pot, and cook the barley until tender and all the liquid is absorbed, about 30 minutes. If the barley is not quite done, add 1 or 2 tablespoons water and continue to cook. If the barley is cooked but liquid remains, turn off heat and let the barley rest in the covered pot while the grain continues to absorb the liquid.

Per serving: Kcalories 146 (From Fat 24); Fat 3g (Saturated 0g); Cholesterol 0mg; Sodium 20mg; Carbohydrate 28g (Dietary Fiber 6g); Protein 4g.

Preparing Perfect Pasta

Pasta comes in many shapes and sizes (see Figure 10-2 for a sampling). Here are some guidelines to help you decide what works for your recipe:

✔ For lighter, brothy sauces and pestos, choose delicate, long pasta, like vermicelli, spaghetti, linguine, or angel hair.

✔ For meatier, chunkier sauces or pasta salads, choose shorter shapes with ridges or holes, like cavatelli, penne, farfalle, and wagon wheels. The smaller pieces make it easier to grab pasta and sauce with every bite. And the ridges and holes in the pasta grab bits and chunks of your sauce.

✔ For heavier and creamier sauces, choose flat, ribbonlike pasta, such as fettuccine.

Most pasta is made from semolina flour, not refined white flour. It's a complex carbohydrate, rather than a simple carbohydrate, meaning that it gives your body more lasting energy and a more gradual release of sugar. A ½ cup serving of cooked pasta contains 99 calories, less than half a gram of fat, and less than 5 milligrams of sodium, and it costs you only 1 starch exchange.

Here are a few other benefits of choosing pasta.

✔ It has a relatively low glycemic index of 41. For more about the glycemic index and how it can help you manage your blood glucose levels, check out Chapter 2.

✔ It's a quick food to prepare. You can get this filling side dish ready in about 10 minutes.

✔ It goes with just about anything. Pasta is so versatile. You can toss it with chicken broth and fresh herbs, or fresh veggies and a little bit of olive oil. If you can cook it, you can serve it with pasta.

  • Create Chinese flavored dishes with a splash of sesame oil, crunchy water chestnuts, bok choy, and cilantro. Add thinly sliced beef for a full meal.

  • Mix up a Mediterranean delight by adding tomatoes, garlic, and fresh basil. Throw in some pine nuts and seafood for a lowfat, tasty weeknight supper.

  • Invent your own Latin lunch, by including grilled onions, chicken breast, chiles, and chayote squash.

  • Introduce flavors from the Caribbean by tossing pasta with shrimp, flaked coconut, jerk seasonings, and vegetable stock.

  • Work in some Vietnamese inspired cuisine, by adding it to vegetable broth, chopped chiles, cilantro, and lean pork.

✔ It's very filling. A ½ cup serving may not seem like much, but a little can go a long way, especially if you bulk up the fiber content of your dish with fresh veggies. Or opt for 2 starch servings, and have a full cup of pasta and enjoy it as a main course.

Figure 10-2:
Pasta comes in many shapes and sizes.

☞ Classic: Butterfly Pasta with Sun-Dried Tomatoes and Artichoke Hearts

The few ingredients that this simple recipe calls for complement each other perfectly, as you can see from the photo in the color section. The dish is a certified crowd pleaser, full of color and flavor and ideal for entertaining. The pasta is best served at room temperature, so you can make it hours in advance, freeing you for the last-minute details of throwing a party.

Preparation time: *15 minutes (plus overnight marinating time)*

Cooking time: *10 minutes*

Yield: *4 servings*

2 ounces sun-dried tomatoes, chopped

½ cup extra-virgin olive oil

3 cloves garlic, minced

½ cup finely chopped basil leaves, plus extra whole leaves for garnish

1 jar (15 ounces) marinated artichoke hearts, drained

8 ounces butterfly pasta

Salt and pepper (optional)

Grated Parmesan cheese (optional)

1 In a shallow bowl, combine the tomatoes, olive oil, garlic, and basil. Let rest overnight to allow the tomatoes to rehydrate.

2 Transfer the tomato mixture to a large bowl and add the artichoke hearts. Lightly toss together.

3 Bring a large pot of water to boil and cook the pasta according to the directions on the package until the pasta is al dente, cooked but not soft. Drain and add to the tomato artichoke mixture. Adjust seasoning with salt and pepper.

4 Serve at room temperature, garnished with whole basil leaves and Parmesan cheese on the side, if desired.

Per serving: *Kcalories 550 (From Fat 289); Fat 32g (Saturated 4g); Cholesterol 0mg; Sodium 566mg; Carbohydrate 59g (Dietary Fiber 6g); Protein 13g.*

Classic: Seafood Farfalle Salad

It's no surprise that in Italy, a country with many port cities, many pasta dishes include fish. The Italians have even figured out how to use the black ink of octopus in one special pasta dish. This recipe is much tamer, however. It's a low-calorie but quite satisfying combination of seafood and pasta. Using farfalle, pasta shaped like a butterfly or a bow tie, adds eye appeal. If you have access to a specialty Italian food market, you may even be able to find farfallini, the smallest butterflies, or farfallone, the largest.

Preparation time: *25 minutes*

Cooking time: *20 to 25 minutes*

Yield: *4 servings*

8 ounces farfalle pasta	*1 clove garlic, minced*
Nonstick cooking spray	*2 teaspoons chopped fresh parsley*
½ pound bay scallops	*⅛ teaspoon black pepper*
½ pound cooked baby shrimp	*½ cup plum tomatoes, peeled, seeded, and diced*
½ teaspoons white wine vinegar	
1 tablespoon extra-virgin olive oil	*1 small cucumber, peeled, seeded, and diced*
1 teaspoon freshly squeezed lemon juice	*2 tablespoons seeded and finely chopped green bell pepper*
1 teaspoon dried thyme leaves	

1 Bring a large pot of water to a boil. Salt the boiling water and cook the farfalle according to package directions. Drain, rinse under cold running water, and drain again. Set aside.

2 Meanwhile, coat a medium nonstick skillet with cooking spray or 2 teaspoons of canola oil and place over medium heat until hot. Add the scallops and shrimp, a few at a time, and sauté, turning them as they brown, allowing 1½ to 2 minutes per side; remove them to a bowl as they finish.

3 In a large bowl, whisk together the vinegar, olive oil, lemon juice, thyme, garlic, parsley, and pepper. Add the tomatoes, cucumber, and green pepper and mix thoroughly. Combine the pasta, scallops (and their released juices), and shrimp. Toss the pasta mixture with the dressing mixture.

Per serving: Kcalories 350 (From Fat 61); Fat 7g (Saturated 1g); Cholesterol 82mg; Sodium 167mg; Carbohydrate 47g (Dietary Fiber 3g); Protein 26g.

Although most of the pasta you'll find in your local grocery is made from semolina flour, you can find pasta made from a variety of different flours, including these:

✔ **Brown rice:** This pasta is a great alternative for people allergic to wheat. Check the label, but most brown rice pasta is both wheat and gluten free. They may also be dairy-free and organic. Try this delicious pasta in the following recipe.

✔ **Soy:** Pasta made with soy flour tends to be higher in protein and lower in carbohydrate than semolina pasta, but always read the label to make sure you're making the right choice for your needs.

✔ **Whole wheat:** If you're looking for a higher fiber pasta, whole-wheat pasta may be what you're looking for. It's characterized by a more robust flavor than its semolina counterpart.

☺ *Classic: Kasha and Brown Rice Pasta*

Sometimes simple food, such as this delicious combination of kasha and pasta, tastes the best. Kasha is buckwheat *groats* (hulled and crushed buckwheat). The flavors are mellow and nutty with just a hint of mushroom, a step beyond blandness but still quiet comfort food. This mixture is meant to be a background dish, served with savory foods such as a chicken roasted with herbs or slow-cooked flank steak prepared with onion and dried fruits. This merger of whole grains and pasta is especially favored in Eastern European and Russian cooking.

Preparation time: *10 minutes*

Cooking time: *25 minutes*

Yield: *6 servings*

2 teaspoons safflower oil	*2 cups boiling vegetable broth or water*
1 medium onion, chopped	*Pepper*
1 egg, slightly beaten	*Sea salt (optional)*
1 cup kasha (buckwheat groats)	*4 cups water*
½ cup sliced button mushrooms	*1½ cups brown rice rotini (Lundberg brand)*

1 In a heavy medium saucepan, heat the oil and sauté the onion until translucent, 5 to 7 minutes.

2 Beat the egg in a small bowl. Add the kasha and mix together, coating each grain with the egg. Add to the onions. Cook the kasha while stirring until the grains are dry and separated.

3 Add the mushrooms, broth, pepper, and sea salt, if desired. Cover the skillet and simmer until all the liquid is absorbed, about 15 minutes.

4 In the meantime, bring the 4 cups water to a boil in a large pot. Add the rotini and cook for 6 minutes, or until tender but still firm. Drain and, if necessary, keep warm while the kasha finishes cooking.

5 When the kasha is fully cooked, fluff with a fork and stir in the rotini.

Per serving: *Kcalories 187 (From Fat 32); Fat 4g (Saturated 1g); Cholesterol 35mg; Sodium 348mg; Carbohydrate 34g (Dietary Fiber 3g); Protein 6g.*

Letting Legumes into Your Diet

Legumes (pronounced LAY-gooms) are the protein-packed staple of a vegetarian diet, but you don't have to swear off meat to enjoy them. The family of grains includes thousands of plant species, including beans, soybeans, lentils, peas, and the beloved peanut.

It's tough to find a more perfect all-round food than legumes. They're rich in protein, low in fat (what fat they do have is the good fat), high in dietary fiber, and rich in complex carbohydrates and vitamins. Besides being healthy, they're inexpensive, very versatile, and easy to use. They store well when dried, and have a shelf life of a full year.

Because legumes are also high in carbohydrate, a person with diabetes still needs to be mindful of portion sizes here. The benefits that the fiber and protein provide, however, make them a more optimal choice than the usual carbs like bread, pasta, or rice.

Red-Wine-Braised Lentils

This recipe, courtesy of Poggio in Sausalito, California (see Appendix A), is an easy accompaniment to any poultry or meat dish. The hearty lentils are flavored by the slow-cooked method of braising in which they begin to achieve the flavor of the red wine. Lentils are a complex carbohydrate full of fiber, as well as a good source of protein.

Preparation time: *10 minutes*

Cooking time: *1 hour and 20 minutes*

Yield: *6 servings*

1 tablespoon butter

2 tablespoons olive oil

1 cup diced onions

½ cup chopped celery

½ cup diced carrots

Salt and pepper

½ teaspoon thyme leaves

2 ounces diced prosciutto

⅛ cup dried porcini mushrooms, reconstituted and sliced (see the tip at the end of the recipe)

1½ cups red wine

2 cups dried brown lentils

1 bay leaf

5 cups low-sodium chicken broth

1 In a medium saucepan, heat the butter and olive oil. Sauté the onions, celery, and carrots, until they begin to *sweat*, or give off a bit of liquid. Season the vegetables with salt and pepper to taste and cover the pot. Cook until the vegetables are soft, approximately 10 minutes.

2 Add the thyme, prosciutto, and dried porcini mushrooms. Add the wine and reduce by one-third. Add the lentils, bay leaf, and chicken broth and simmer for about 1 hour, until the lentils are soft.

3 Remove the bay leaf. Adjust the salt and pepper if needed. This dish may be refrigerated for up to 3 days, until ready to use.

Tip: *To reconstitute the dried porcini mushrooms, place them in ¼ cup hot water for 30 minutes, chop them, and strain the liquid. If you want, you can use the liquid as part of the cooking liquid. Just substitute the mushroom broth for ¼ cup of the chicken broth in Step 2.*

Per serving: Kcalories 348 (From Fat 88); Fat 10g (Saturated 3g); Cholesterol 17mg; Sodium 387mg; Carbohydrate 44g (Dietary Fiber 16g); Protein 23g.

Lentils are quick cooking legumes, so you don't need to soak them before cooking like you do with dried beans. If you're extra conscientious, feel free to pick over the lentils, as you would with dried beans. Rinse them well to remove any dirt or other debris. Then sort through them a handful at a time, looking for dirt clods, stones, and other foreign particles. Try them in soups, saucy Indian curries, or this terrific "salad."

Olive and Lentil Salad

This dish, from Heather Dismore, is considered a "salad," but don't let that word fool you! This dish is unlike many salads — it's hearty and will keep you full and satisfied for a long time. This olive and lentil mix has a ton of fiber and protein (from the lentils) and enough heart-healthy monounsaturated fats (from the olives) that will digest slowly and therefore keep you feeling full for longer. It has only a moderate amount of carbohydrates, so your blood sugars won't be hugely affected here. This one-pot meal offers you a significant amount of iron, calcium, folate, and vitamins A, C, and B6.

Preparation time: *30 minutes*

Cooking time: *40 minutes*

Yield: *6 servings*

Salad:

1 cup dry lentils

2 bay leaves

1 sprig fresh thyme

1 carrot, finely chopped

1 stalk celery, finely chopped

2 tablespoons minced shallots

1 tablespoon minced garlic

2 Roma tomatoes, seeded and sliced thinly

½ yellow bell pepper, diced

1 jar (8 ounces) green olives, roughly chopped (reserve juice for the dressing)

2 tablespoons roughly chopped fresh oregano

Salt and pepper

4 ounces goat cheese, crumbled

Dressing:

¼ cup red wine vinegar

2 tablespoons green olive juice

1 tablespoon minced shallot

3 teaspoons Dijon mustard

1 teaspoon salt

1 teaspoon pepper

¼ cup olive oil

1 In a 2-quart saucepan, combine the lentils, bay leaves, thyme, carrots, celery, shallots, and garlic. Cover with 2 inches of water. Bring to a low boil and cook until the lentils are just tender, about 40 minutes. Drain and set aside to cool.

2 After the lentils have cooled, add the tomatoes, peppers, olives, and oregano. Mix thoroughly. Salt and pepper to taste. Gently stir in the goat cheese.

3 In a blender, combine the vinegar, olive juice, shallot, mustard, salt, and pepper. Remove the knob from the lid of the blender. With the blender running, slowly pour in the olive oil to emulsify the dressing. Adjust seasonings as necessary. Pour over the salad and toss gently to coat.

Per serving: *Kcalories 343 (From Fat 192); Fat 21g (Saturated 5g); Cholesterol 15mg; Sodium 1,326mg; Carbohydrate 28g (Dietary Fiber 8g); Protein 14g.*

"Beans, beans, they're good for your heart." Well, this in fact is very true. Beans offer a tremendous amount of fiber, more specifically soluble fiber — the type that can lower your LDL, or "bad" cholesterol. Because they're plant based, they have no cholesterol.

☝ White Beans and Spinach

Beans are part of the standard diet of almost every culture, and the Italians are no exception. Heather Dismore contributed this recipe that uses the cannellini beans, an Italian staple, paired with nutritious vitamin-A-rich spinach. Use canned beans and pre-washed spinach to make this nutritious powerhouse as easy to make as it is to enjoy.

Preparation time: *10 minutes*

Cooking time: *20 minutes*

Yield: *4 servings*

1 tablespoon olive oil

½ cup diced onions

3 cloves garlic, peeled and sliced thinly

1 cup sliced cremini mushrooms

¼ cup white wine

1 tablespoon Dijon mustard

Half a 10-ounce bag of triple-washed spinach

1 can (15 ounces) white beans (like navy, cannellini, or great Northern), rinsed and drained

2 tablespoons fresh minced oregano

Salt and pepper

1 Heat the olive oil in a skillet over medium-high heat. Add the onions and sauté until translucent. Add the garlic and mushrooms. Cook until just fragrant. Add the white wine and mustard. Scrape up any browned bits that may be stuck to the skillet.

2 Add the spinach and cover. Steam the spinach for 3 to 4 minutes, or until wilted but still bright green. Add the white beans. Continue to cook until heated through. Add the oregano and salt and pepper to taste. Adjust seasonings as necessary.

Per serving: *Kcalories 122 (From Fat 37); Fat 4g (Saturated 1g); Cholesterol 0mg; Sodium 385mg; Carbohydrate 18g (Dietary Fiber 5g); Protein 5g.*

You can find many canned legumes in your grocery store. They're a bit more expensive than the dried variety, but they can help you create a well-balanced nutritious meal quickly. Keep a few cans in your cupboard for quick and satisfying meals, like this Black Bean Pie, that will keep you full and keep your blood sugar stable.

TIP

When using canned anything, like beans or veggies, whenever possible, drain and rinse the food before cooking to get rid of excess sodium. But before you toss out the liquid, remember to double-check the recipe. Some recipes, like the one for Black Bean Pie here, use the liquid in the recipe.

🍅 Black Bean Pie

This recipe is a great way to get most of the basic food groups covered. The beans, peppers, and cilantro can stop a craving for Mexican food dead in its tracks. Serve it up with a crisp green salad to round out your meal plan.

Preparation time: *45 minutes*

Cooking time: *20 minutes*

Yield: *6 servings*

1 can (14 ounces) black beans	*1 tablespoon chopped fresh cilantro*
½ cup jasmine rice, uncooked	*1 teaspoon garlic powder*
1 9-inch frozen pie shell	*1 teaspoon cumin, ground*
Nonstick cooking spray	*1 teaspoon chili powder*
½ cup diced onion	*½ teaspoon cayenne pepper*
¼ cup diced red bell pepper	*2 tablespoons cornstarch*
¼ cup diced green bell pepper	*¾ cup shredded cheddar cheese*

1 Preheat the oven to 350 degrees. Drain the black beans and reserve the juice. Set aside.

2 Cook the jasmine rice according to package directions. Set aside. While the rice is cooking, bake the pie shell until slightly browned, approximately 5 to 7 minutes. Set aside.

3 Heat a medium skillet over medium-high heat. Once it's heated, spray with the cooking spray. Add the onions and red and green peppers. Sauté until the vegetables are crisp-tender, approximately 5 to 7 minutes. Set aside.

4 In a bowl, combine the beans, rice, onion mixture, cilantro, garlic powder, cumin, chili powder, and cayenne pepper. In another bowl, combine the reserved black bean juice with the cornstarch to make a paste. Mix the paste into the black bean mixture.

5 Spread the black bean mixture in the pie shell. Cover with the cheese. Bake for 15 to 20 minutes, until the cheese starts to brown. Let set for 15 minutes before serving.

Per serving: *Kcalories 303 (From Fat 112); Fat 12g (Saturated 5g); Cholesterol 15mg; Sodium 435mg; Carbohydrate 37g (Dietary Fiber 5g); Protein 10g.*

◌ Southwestern Hummus

Hummus is a classic Mediterranean and Middle Eastern dish, but this rendition, from Heather Dismore (and shown in the color section), is spicy and southwestern. This creamy spread (with little fat!) makes for a surprisingly healthy appetizer — great served with whole-wheat pita bread wedges, baked tortilla chips, or raw vegetables. (If you're looking for other delicious dipper ideas to pair with this tasty spread, check out Chapter 7.) The main ingredients here are garbanzo beans, or chickpeas, which are an excellent vegetarian source of protein, as well as dietary fiber — two great reasons why hummus makes for a perfect snack also. Protein and fiber are essential for good blood sugar control, so keep a bowl of hummus on hand when you're looking for something light, quick, and easy.

Preparation time: *10 minutes*

Yield: *4 servings*

1½ tablespoons minced garlic

2 cans (15 ounces each) garbanzo beans, drained and rinsed

¼ cup salsa

2 tablespoons fresh lime juice

1 teaspoon cumin

½ teaspoon chili powder

1 teaspoon cayenne (more or less as you prefer)

1 tablespoon olive oil

⅓ cup roughly chopped cilantro

Salt and pepper

Garnishes (optional):

1 tablespoon light sour cream

2 tablespoons diced avocado

1 tablespoon minced cilantro

1 tablespoon minced black olives

1 Place the garlic, beans, salsa, lime juice, cumin, chili powder, cayenne pepper, olive oil, cilantro, and salt and pepper to taste in a food processor. Adjust seasonings to taste. Place in a covered bowl. Chill in the refrigerator for 2 to 3 hours to allow flavors to meld, or blend thoroughly.

2 When ready to serve, spread the hummus in the bottom of a medium-sized serving bowl, and top with the garnishes in the following order: light sour cream, avocado, cilantro, and black olives.

Per serving: *Kcalories 170 (From Fat 48); Fat 5g (Saturated 1g); Cholesterol 0mg; Sodium 477mg; Carbohydrate 24g (Dietary Fiber 6g); Protein 7g.*

Chapter 11

Adding Veggies to Your Meals

In This Chapter

▶ Giving old favorites a fresh taste

▶ Making "noodles" from firm vegetables

▶ Mixing up tasty mushroom dishes

▶ Dressing up vegetables for special occasions

▶ Enjoying vegetarian entrees

*O*ur bodies thrive on the fantastic phyto-chemicals, must-have vitamins and nutrients, and fabulous fiber found in vegetables, but most people don't eat enough of them. Yet there are so many ways you can eat them: in soups, in salads, puréed in sauces, on the side, or as the main event. Whether you eat them cooked or raw, using fresh or frozen products, you can improve your health today by increasing the amount of vegetables you eat.

In this chapter, we help you update common vegetables in exciting new ways. We focus on using mushrooms in delicious ways. We help you create some special-occasion recipes to impress your guests. And finally, we show you how to enjoy delicious vegetarian entrees.

Adding a New Twist to Old Favorites (and Not-So-Favorites)

Most people have a vegetable that has haunted them since childhood. Whether you had the misfortune to taste flavorless collard greens at a family reunion when you were nine or were forced to sit in front of a plate of luke-warm boiled carrots you just couldn't choke down, you probably have one you just don't like. Well, hopefully, we're about to change that.

In this section, we give you delicious recipes using traditional vegetables that you can find in the kitchens of most people but that you may not be fond of — yet. But never fear — after trying a few, you'll have a whole new appreciation for them.

Including delicious extras

The following recipes focus on adding tasty flavors such as rice vinegar, herbs, and cheese to old stand-by vegetables like collard greens, broccoli, and zucchini. Try them the next time you want to add some zing to your veggies.

🍅 Vegetate Collard Greens

Vegetate, the award winning vegetarian restaurant in Washington D.C., provided this recipe for sautéed collard greens. By slicing the collard greens thinly, you can reduce the cooking time, so the greens retain their nutritional value, freshness, and color. Try this cooking technique with any local greens.

Preparation time: *10 minutes*

Cooking time: *10 minutes*

Yield: *4 servings*

1 bunch collard greens (washed and de-stemmed)	*1 tablespoon minced shallot*
	Salt and pepper to taste
1 tablespoon grapeseed oil	*1 teaspoon red chili flakes*
1 tablespoon minced garlic	*1 tablespoon rice vinegar*

1 Stack 4 to 5 collard green leaves and roll into cigar shape. Slice about 1-inch-thick slices with sharp knife to create ribbons of collard greens. Continue until all leaves are sliced.

2 Add grapeseed oil to sauté pan over medium to high heat. Sweat garlic and shallots for about 1 minute (do not burn) and add collard green ribbons. Toss the greens with tongs. Add salt, pepper, and chili flake. Collards should be shiny and starting to lightly brown on edges. Add rice vinegar and toss. Serve immediately.

Per serving: Kcalories 56 (Calories from Fat 34); Fat 4g (Saturated 0g); Cholesterol 0mg; Sodium 159mg; Carbohydrate 5g (Dietary Fiber 3g); Protein 2g.

Broccoli is one of the most nutritious veggies out there. If you still can't seem to acquire a liking for it though, look no further. Prepare the following elegant recipe for your family or guests, and everyone will be so pleasantly surprised — especially when you tell them the rich, savory sauce has barely any fat.

☙ *Broccoli with Creamy Lemon Sauce*

Who doesn't love broccoli and cheese? And for most of us, the more cheese the better! And what's even better, you can enjoy this one (courtesy of food writer Heather Dismore) guilt-free. This creamy sauce is made with mainly lowfat ingredients instead of the full-fat dairy products that usually go into rich sauces. Just be sure not to add any more salt. The cottage cheese and Parmesan already contribute enough for flavor.

Preparation time: *10 minutes*

Cooking time: *35 minutes*

Yield: *6 servings*

⅔ cup lowfat cottage cheese

¼ cup evaporated skim milk

2 tablespoons grated Parmesan cheese

1 teaspoon lemon juice

⅛ teaspoon ground turmeric

White pepper

3 cups hot cooked broccoli florets

1 In a blender, combine the cottage cheese, milk, Parmesan cheese, lemon juice, turmeric, and white pepper to taste and purée until the mixture achieves a thin consistency, about 30 seconds.

2 Heat the sauce in a skillet, stirring occasionally, until heated through, but do not boil.

3 Serve the sauce over the warm broccoli.

Per serving: *Kcalories 45 (From Fat 8); Fat 1g (Saturated 1g); Cholesterol 3mg; Sodium 155mg; Carbohydrate 4g (Dietary Fiber 1g); Protein 6g.*

Zucchini and Parmigiano-Reggiano Salad

This recipe is sure to become a favorite in your household. Chef Kevin Rathbun of Rathbun's in Atlanta (see Appendix A) uses simple, quality ingredients like Parmigiano-Reggiano (the original and best Parmesan cheese in the world), extra-virgin olive oil, and fresh lemon juice to give this dish rich flavors with very little effort.

Preparation time: *15 minutes*

Yield: *4 servings*

3 medium zucchini, peeled and sliced	*1 teaspoon sea salt*
½ cup Parmigiano-Reggiano, shaved thin	*½ teaspoon pepper*
1 tablespoon lemon juice	*2 tablespoons chopped lemon verbena*
4 tablespoons extra-virgin olive oil	

Place the zucchini in a bowl and shave the Parmigiano-Reggiano in the bowl. Add the lemon juice, olive oil, salt, pepper, and verbena. Toss to incorporate the ingredients and serve.

Tip: *Lemon verbena is a potent herb, with a strong lemon flavor. Look for it in specialty food markets. Alternatively, look for it at your local nursery and grow your own. If you can't find it, you can always pick another herb (like tarragon or basil). The substitution will change the flavor but will still be delicious.*

Per serving: *Kcalories 188 (From Fat 151); Fat 17g (Saturated 4g); Cholesterol 8mg; Sodium 766mg; Carbohydrate 5g (Dietary Fiber 2g); Protein 6g.*

Chunky Zucchini-Tomato Curry

This veggie dish is delicious, perfect as a side or as a dip or on top of crisp crostini. It's full of Indian-inspired spices and remains modestly low in calories and fat. No added salt is needed as the spices already offer plenty of flavor. Heather Dismore offers this unique way to serve up simple veggies like zucchini and tomatoes. Be creative with spices like the ones used here to make vegetables that you and your guests will love.

Preparation time: *10 minutes*

Cooking time: *20 minutes*

Yield: *4 servings*

2 tablespoons olive oil

1 medium red onion, finely diced

2 teaspoons grated fresh ginger

4 cloves garlic, minced

1 teaspoon ground coriander

2 teaspoons curry powder

1 cup canned crushed tomatoes

1 pound zucchini, quartered lengthwise and large diced

1 Heat the olive oil in a large nonstick skillet. Sauté the onion, ginger, and garlic for about 5 minutes, or until the onions are translucent. Add the coriander and curry powder. Continue cooking 1 minute.

2 Stir in the tomatoes and zucchini. Simmer approximately 10 minutes, or until the zucchini is tender.

Per serving: Kcalories 97 (From Fat 64); Fat 8g (Saturated 1g); Cholesterol 0mg; Sodium 38mg; Carbohydrate 8g (Dietary Fiber 3g); Protein 2g.

Enhancing natural flavors with dry steaming

Dry steaming refers to cooking vegetables in their own natural juices rather than adding additional moisture. In the case of carrots, they have a medium to high moisture content, so when you heat them in a closed environment (like in a pot with a tight-fitting lid), they use the liquid that they give off during the cooking process to create steam and facilitate the cooking process. So the food is essentially steamed without adding any water. You get a similar effect when you microwave vegetables without adding water.

Don't microwave vegetables, or anything else, in a completely closed container. Always provide a vent of some sort for steam to escape.

☜ Dry-Steamed Dilled Carrots

Here's a tasty twist on a veggie favorite. Heather Dismore uses fresh herbs here to give these carrots a new and interesting flavor. Carrots are one of the best sources of vitamin A, antioxidants, lutein, and beta carotene. These are the nutrients best known for eye health. The orange fruits and vegetables are all good sources of these antioxidants, so get them in whenever you can!

Preparation time: *10 minutes*

Cooking time: *35 to 40 minutes*

Yield: *12 servings*

2 tablespoons butter	¼ cup minced fresh dill
1 pound baby carrots	Salt and pepper

1 Melt the butter in a deep skillet with a tight-fitting lid. Add the carrots. Cook over medium to medium-low heat for approximately 35 to 40 minutes. Shake the skillet occasionally during cooking, without removing the lid.

2 Remove the lid after 35 to 40 minutes and check to confirm that carrots are tender. Allow any excess moisture to evaporate from the skillet. Toss the carrots with the dill. Salt and pepper to taste.

Per serving: Kcalories 31 (From Fat 19); Fat 2g (Saturated 1g); Cholesterol 5mg; Sodium 62mg; Carbohydrate 3g (Dietary Fiber 1g); Protein 0g.

Blanching vegetables for optimum taste and nutrition

Blanching is a terrific technique for cooking vegetables without losing many of the vitamins that make them so healthy for you. It's also surprisingly simple. You immerse vegetables in boiling water, leave them in the water for a short period of time, and then *shock* them, or immerse them in ice-cold water to stop the cooking. This technique helps to prevent the vegetables from getting mushy. Check out Figure 11-1 to see the basic steps.

Here are the detailed steps to follow for blanching vegetables.

1. **Bring salted water to vigorous boil in a 2-quart saucepan.**

2. **While the water is working up to a boil, prepare the ice bath.**

Fill a medium-sized mixing bowl one-half to three-fourths full with ice. Add water to just cover the ice.

3. **Blanch the vegetables.**

Place the trimmed vegetables, in batches if necessary, in the boiling water. Cook the vegetables until they're crisp tender.

You want to keep a constant boil, but adding too many veggies at a time can slow down the process.

4. **Shock the vegetables.**

Remove the vegetables with a slotted spoon and immediately place them in the ice bath. Remove them from the ice bath after the vegetables are completely cooled, usually 1 to 2 minutes.

To check for doneness, remove a single vegetable piece with a slotted spoon; submerge it in the ice bath until it's cool enough to place in your mouth. Then actually taste it to check the texture. Do this step quickly so that if the veggies are ready, the rest of them in the boiling water won't overcook while you're testing.

5. **Reheat the vegetables and season as desired.**

Figure 11-1: Blanch vegetables in boiling water and then place them in an ice-cold water bath to stop the cooking.

Blanching times vary based on the vegetable and the size of the pieces, but check out Table 11-1 for approximate times for reference.

Table 11-1 Approximate Blanching Times for Vegetables

Vegetable	*Size*	*Approximate Time*
Asparagus	Spears	3 to 4 minutes
Broccoli	Florets, bite sized	3 minutes
Brussels sprouts	Whole	3 to 5 minutes
Cabbage	Leaves	5 to 10 minutes
Carrots, baby	Whole	5 minutes
Carrots	Diced or strips	2 minutes
Cauliflower	Florets, bite sized	3 minutes
Corn	Cob	4 minutes
Eggplant	Slices	3 minutes
Green beans	Whole	3 minutes
Greens like spinach	Leaves	2 minutes
Mushrooms	Whole or caps	5 minutes
Okra	Pod	3 to 5 minutes
Peas, shelled	Whole	1½ minutes
Peas	Pod	2 to 3 minutes
Summer squash	Bite-sized chunks	3 minutes
Tomatoes	Whole, for peeling	1 minute
Zucchini	Bite-sized chunks	3 minutes

Give blanching a try with several of the recipes in this book, including the following recipe for Haricot Vert and the Yellow Tomato Sauce later in this chapter.

Haricot Vert

Haricot vert (pronounced ah-ree-co VEHR) is a fancy French word that literally means "green beans" and refers to (surprise!) green beans, or what we sometimes call string beans. If you find true French haricot vert in a gourmet market, use them in this recipe. They're a bit smaller and thinner than common string beans, but the flavor is very similar. But if you can't find them, feel free to substitute fresh string beans. Canned beans won't work because they're already cooked beyond tender. The Baricelli Inn in Cleveland (see Appendix A) contributed this classic and simple recipe. Enjoy this elegant vegetable with any hearty entrée.

From top: Southwestern Hummus (Chapter 10); Mexican Salsa (Chapter 7); Mango Salsa (Chapter 7)

Summer Vegetable Stew with Egg (Chapter 8); Heirloom Tomato Soup with Fresh Basil (Chapter 8)

Shrimp Quesadillas (Chapter 7) with Warm Pineapple Salsa (Chapter 7); Quick Chicken Tostadas (Chapter 15)

From top: Portobello Mushroom Sandwich (Chapter 11); Oriental Beef and Noodle Salad (Chapter 9)

Beer-Braised Pork and Crisp-Herb Cabbage with Apple-Tarragon Dipping Sauce (Chapter 14)

Cranberry-Raspberry Granita (Chapter 16); Chocolate-Almond Biscotti (Chapter 16);

Preparation time: *10 minutes*

Cooking time: *10 minutes*

Yield: *6 servings*

6 cups string beans

2 tablespoons butter

Salt and pepper

Cut off the ends of the beans and blanch in boiling water for 1 minute (see the instructions earlier in this section); remove and place them in a cold water bath with ice. Drain and reheat in a skillet with the butter and salt and pepper to taste.

Tip: *Serve these tasty veggies with Veal Tenderloin with Chanterelle Mushrooms in Chapter 14, also from the Baricelli Inn.*

Per serving: *Kcalories 71 (From Fat 37); Fat 4g (Saturated 2g); Cholesterol 10mg; Sodium 101mg; Carbohydrate 9g (Dietary Fiber 4g); Protein 2g.*

Using Vegetables in Place of Pasta

Pasta gets a lot of bad press these days, but the biggest problem with it is the portion size that most people typically eat. For healthy ways to include pasta and other grains in your diabetic diet, check out Chapter 10.

When you're craving the rich delicious Italian sauces but don't want the carbs of traditional pasta, veggies make a terrific substitute. Make "noodles" from strings of cucumber or slices of zucchini. Get started with this great Zucchini and Cucumber Linguine with Clams.

A *mandoline* is a handy tool to have around your kitchen. Take a look at it in Figure 11-2. It's a manual slicing device that quickly makes consistently sized cuts of foods. You can use it to julienne or make even ¼-inch strips of cucumber (as in the next recipe). You can make paper-thin strips of sweet potatoes for making your own baked chips or thick lemon wheels for water. Consider getting one to ease the prep work of making your own veggie noodles. Look for a mandoline at your local cooking supply store or gourmet shop.

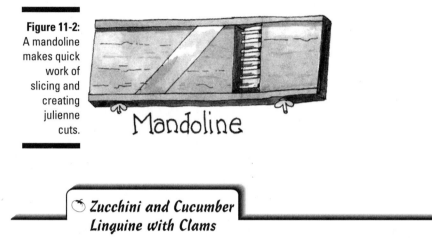

Figure 11-2:
A mandoline
makes quick
work of
slicing and
creating
julienne
cuts.

Mandoline

🍑 *Zucchini and Cucumber Linguine with Clams*

David Burke, executive chef at DavidBurke and Donatella in New York City (see Appendix A), offers this shellfish lover's delight. After steeping in the delicious wine and clam sauce, the zucchini and cucumbers actually begin to taste much like linguine, without the calories and carbohydrate. You're sure to impress your guests when you serve this light appetizer at your next dinner party. Because this dish is low in calories, they'll even have plenty of room left for the main course.

Clams are chock-full of vitamin B12 and iron. If you're cutting back on fat by avoiding red meat, you can feel confident that you won't be missing out on these essential nutrients, which are abundant in carnivorous diets. By the way, when purchasing clams and other shellfish, be sure the shells are closed. The open ones can be contaminated and cause severe food-borne illness.

Preparation time: *20 minutes*

Cooking time: *20 minutes*

Yield: *4 servings*

2 tablespoons olive oil	*1 tablespoon butter*
2 tablespoons chopped garlic	*Salt and pepper*
2 tablespoons chopped shallots	*1 teaspoon red pepper flakes*
¼ cup minced red peppers	*1 large seedless cucumber, cut into long julienne strips to resemble noodles (use a mandoline or a sharp knife)*
18 to 24 Manila or littleneck clams	
1½ cups white wine	
2 lemons (juice and zest)	*1 large zucchini, julienned*
	¼ cup chopped parsley

1 Heat the olive oil in a sauté pan. Add the garlic, shallots, and red peppers and sauté until golden, approximately 10 minutes. Add the clams, white wine, and lemon juice. Cover and bring to a boil. Continue to cook until the clams open, approximately 5 minutes.

2 When the clams open, add the butter, salt and pepper to taste, and the red pepper flakes. Remove the clams. Toss in the cucumber and zucchini noodles and heat until they are warm and wilted, approximately 7 minutes.

3 Divide among 4 bowls and top each with the clams and the remaining juice. Garnish with the chopped parsley and lemon zest.

Per serving: Kcalories 171 (From Fat 95); Fat 11g (Saturated 3g); Cholesterol 28mg; Sodium 188mg; Carbohydrate 10g (Dietary Fiber 3g); Protein 11g.

Making the Most of Mushrooms

If you haven't taken a tour of the produce department lately, you might be surprised by the variety of mushrooms out there (some can be seen in Figure 11-3), each with a distinct look and flavor. In this section, chefs from several award-winning vegetarian restaurants have supplied some creative ways to get the most flavor out of their favorite fungi.

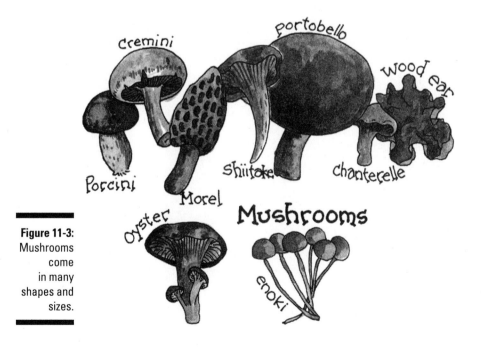

Figure 11-3: Mushrooms come in many shapes and sizes.

☝ *Mushroom Garlic Medley*

Horizons contributed this delicious homage to mushrooms and garlic. Additionally, it's full of other vegetables like snow peas and red and green peppers, giving you tons of phytochemicals and antioxidants.

This dish has a hint of sweetness from fruit and agave nectar. For details about the health benefits of agave nectar, see Chapter 16.

Preparation time: *15 minutes*

Cooking time: *15 minutes*

Yield: *6 servings*

¼ cup abalone mushrooms (sliced thinly)	⅓ cup snow peas
½ cup oyster mushrooms (sliced thinly)	¼ cup red pepper (sliced into long strips)
1 ½ cups shitake mushrooms (sliced thinly)	¼ cup green pepper (sliced into long strips)
2 ½ cups button mushrooms (sliced thinly)	⅓ cup garlic (sliced thinly)
1 cup broccoli (separate the individual heads)	1 tablespoon olive oil
¼ cup carrots (sliced thinly)	¼ cup enoki mushrooms
½ cup zucchini (sliced thinly)	

1 Blanch the mushrooms and vegetables (except for the enoki mushrooms). Take a look at the section "Blanching vegetables for optimum taste and nutrition," earlier in this chapter for help. Drain well. Set aside.

2 In a wok, heat olive oil over medium-high heat and sauté the sliced garlic until golden brown. Add blanched mushrooms and vegetables, and Sweet and Savory Sauce (see the next recipe) to the wok and sauté together with the garlic for 4 to 5 minutes.

3 Meanwhile, separate the enoki mushrooms into separate stalks. Cut the base of each mushroom bunch and then pull each stalk to separate it. Set aside.

4 Place the mushroom mixture in a heated serving dish. Garnish with enoki mushrooms.

Sweet and Savory Sauce

½ cup pears (diced)	3 ounces sake
½ cup apples (diced)	1 tablespoon agave nectar
½ cup oranges (diced)	½ tablespoon sesame oil
¼ cup onions (diced)	1 ½ teaspoons mushroom powder
¼ cup radishes (diced)	½ tablespoon reduced-sodium soy sauce
2 tablespoons ginger paste	1 teaspoon black pepper
2 tablespoons sesame seed	1 tablespoon potato powder
½ cup plus 3 tablespoons water, divided	

1 Combine diced pears, apples, oranges, onions, radishes, ginger paste, sesame seeds, and ½ cup water in a mixer. Mix on low speed until mixture blended.

2 Place mixture into a pot. Add sake, agave nectar, sesame oil, mushroom powder, soy sauce, and black pepper.

3 In a separate bowl, mix potato powder with 3 tablespoons water. Add the potato powder mixture to the pot. Let the sauce simmer for 5 minutes over low flame, stirring continuously.

Per serving: Kcalories 128 (Calories from Fat 47); Fat 5g (Saturated 1g); Cholesterol 10mg; Sodium 61mg; Carbohydrate 19g (Dietary Fiber 4g); Protein 4g.

○ *Portobello Mushroom Sandwich*

The portobello mushroom has ingratiated itself to people everywhere. Its thick, beefy caps make it the perfect choice to star in this substatntial vegetarian sandwich, developed by Tante Marie's Cooking School in San Francisco.

Preparation time: 10 minutes

Cooking time: 5 minutes

Yield: 4 servings

4 medium-sized portobello mushrooms

8 tablespoons extra virgin olive oil

Salt and pepper to taste

Chopped fresh herbs such as thyme, parsley, or chives

8 pieces whole-grain bread, toasted

1 With a brush or damp cloth, remove any dirt from the mushrooms. Remove the stem and save for another use. Place the mushrooms in a wide bowl and coat on all sides with the olive oil. Sprinkle generously with salt and pepper and the chopped fresh herbs.

2 Preheat a broiler, or start a charcoal fire. When hot, place the mushrooms on the grill over the fire. Grill for about 1 minute on each side. The mushrooms should be juicy but not shrunken.

3 Cut the buns in half lengthwise or cut the bread to look like hamburger buns. Place the grilled mushrooms on the buns and serve warm.

Tip: Look for 100 percent whole-wheat hamburger buns to make this dish even easier to prepare.

Per serving: Kcalories 397 (Calories from Fat 261); Fat 29g (Saturated 4g); Cholesterol 0mg; Sodium 406g; Carbohydrate 29g (Dietary Fiber 5g); Protein 7g.

☜ *Organic Tofu and Shitake Mushrooms*

HanGawi, the award winning vegetarian Korean restaurant in New York (www.hangawirestaurant.com), developed this wonderful combination of sautéed organic tofu with shitake mushrooms served with vegetarian "oyster" sauce. You can find the more exotic ingredients (like the soybean powder, vegetarian oyster sauce, and agave nectar) at your local natural food store.

Preparation time: *30 minutes*

Cooking time: *3 minutes*

Yield: *4 servings*

24 ounces organic firm tofu	*1 tablespoon olive oil*
¼ cup organic soybean powder	*12 pieces medium-size fresh shitake mushrooms*

Vegetarian Oyster Sauce

2½ ounces vegetarian oyster sauce	*½ teaspoon sesame oil*
2 tablespoons agave nectar	*Dash of black pepper*
1 tablespoon water	*2 sesame leaves (chopped into small pieces), basil leaves can be used if sesame leaves are not available*
1 teaspoon tomato ketchup	
1 teaspoon sesame seeds	

1 Cut tofu into rectangles with approximate dimensions of 3½ inches by 4 inches with ½-inch thickness. Coat the pieces with soybean powder.

2 Over medium-high heat, heat olive oil in a sauté pan. Fry the tofu with olive oil until the pieces are golden brown.

3 Meanwhile, In a separate pan, pan-fry the shitake mushrooms. Set aside.

4 Mix all the ingredients for the sauce in a pot and heat for about 2 minutes over low flame.

5 Put a piece of shitake mushroom on top of each of the tofu pieces. Pour the sauce over the tofu and shitake mushrooms and serve.

Per serving: Kcalories 344 (Calories from Fat 144); Fat 16g (Saturated 2g); Cholesterol 0mg; Sodium 490mg; Carbohydrate 22g (Dietary Fiber 7g); Protein 36g.

Giving Veggies the Gourmet Treatment

Vegetables are ripe for dressing up with the full gourmet treatment. They're flavorful on their own, but they take most seasonings, spices, and cooking techniques very well. You really can't mess them up unless you overcook them. Experiment with your favorite recipes by using the techniques in this chapter. Also, try a few that you haven't tried before just to broaden your vegetable horizon.

🍅 Pickled Vegetables

Have your favorite veggies, but pickle them. Be creative! Try this with any vegetables you like. Eccolo restaurant in Berkeley, California (see Appendix A), serves these pickled vegetables as a side to many dishes. It's a tasty way to satisfy hunger pains without sending those blood sugars through the roof. You can see this dish in the color section.

Preparation time: *30 minutes*

Cooking time: *3 minutes*

Yield: *20 servings, or 3 pounds of pickles*

1 tablespoon yellow mustard seed	*3 sprigs thyme*
1 teaspoon fennel seed	*1 cup sugar*
1 teaspoon black peppercorns	*3 tablespoons salt*
4 dried pepperoncini	*3 pounds vegetables (such as carrots, cauliflower, cherry peppers, fennel, onions, or turnips), cleaned and cut into bite-sized pieces*
2 bay leaves	
3 cups water	
1 cup white wine vinegar	

1 Combine the mustard seed, fennel seed, peppercorns, pepperoncini, bay leaves, water, vinegar, thyme, sugar, and salt in a large pot and bring to a boil. Add the vegetables and simmer for about 3 minutes.

2 Turn off the heat, but leave the vegetables in the pickling solution. The residual heat will cook them through.

3 Discard the pickling juice and store in the refrigerator for up to 5 days.

Tip: Serve these pickles with sandwiches or fried fish or just snack on them on their own.

Per serving: *Kcalories 28 (From Fat 0); Fat 0g (Saturated 0g); Cholesterol 0mg; Sodium 283mg; Carbohydrate 7g (Dietary Fiber 2g); Protein 1g.*

Zucchini is a terrific all-around vegetable. You can eat it raw, stew it, bake it in muffins, grill it, steam it, blanch it, or melt cheese on it. It makes excellent "noodles" (check out the Zucchini and Cucumber Linguine with Clams recipe earlier in this chapter). To get an idea of just how versatile this veggie is (and how much you can dress it up), check out the following recipe.

☀ Goat-Cheese-Stuffed Zucchini with Yellow Tomato Sauce

Kyle Ketchum, from Lark in Detroit, Michigan (see Appendix A), has prepared this dish, which can make for a lovely appetizer, a side entree, or even a small meal. The distinct flavors of garlic, lemon, tomato, and savory goat cheese meld into one phenomenal flavor. They each stand strong alone, however, and are sure to come alive with every moment in your mouth. This vibrant dish is high in protein and quite low in carbohydrate, making it suitable for people managing their blood sugars. Keep in mind, however, that goat cheese is quite rich and high in saturated fat. Be sure to enjoy these zucchinis in moderation.

Try this yellow tomato sauce as indicated here or atop any favorite vegetable.

Preparation time: *40 minutes*

Cooking time: *25 to 30 minutes*

Yield: *6 servings*

6 medium green zucchini	*¼ cup basil chiffonade (see the tip at the end of this recipe)*
1 pound chèvre goat cheese (room temperature)	
	Salt and pepper
¼ cup bread crumbs	*1 tablespoon olive oil*
Zest of 1 lemon	

1 Preheat the oven to 350 degrees. Wash the zucchini and pat dry. Cut the ends off the zucchini and then cut each zucchini in half to create 2 pieces of equal length. Use a paring knife or melon baller to core out the center of the zucchini.

2 Put the goat cheese in a bowl and add the bread crumbs, lemon zest, and basil. Season with salt and pepper to taste. Mix well and taste for seasoning. Spoon the cheese mixture into the zucchini shells.

3 Drizzle the olive oil on the zucchini, season with salt and pepper to taste, and place on a baking sheet. Bake until the cheese begins to bubble and the bread crumbs start to brown, about 30 minutes.

4 Remove the zucchini from the oven, drizzle the Yellow Tomato Sauce (see the next recipe) on top of them, and return to the oven for 1 to 2 minutes.

Tip: Chiffonade literally means "made of rags," and it pretty well describes what the final product looks like. Leafy lettuce or herbs are rolled together tightly and then thinly sliced width-wise to form long, stringy strips.

Yellow Tomato Sauce

4 ripened yellow tomatoes (substitute red tomatoes if yellow ones aren't available)

¼ cup minced garlic

2 tablespoons olive oil

Salt and pepper

1 Core the tomatoes, blanch in salted water for 10 seconds, and then shock in an ice water bath. Take a look at Figure 11-1, earlier in this chapter, to see how this technique works. Allow the tomatoes to chill for a few minutes and then remove from the water and peel the skin. Cut the tomatoes in half and squeeze out the pulp and seeds.

2 Place the tomatoes in a blender, add the garlic, and blend. With the blender on high, drizzle in the olive oil until the sauce achieves a smooth, even consistency, approximately 3 to 5 minutes. Season with salt and pepper to taste.

Per serving: Kcalories 411 (From Fat 272); Fat 30g (Saturated 17g); Cholesterol 60mg; Sodium 661mg; Carbohydrate 17g (Dietary Fiber 4g); Protein 21g.

Many of you may love Chinese food, but sometimes your favorite dishes are loaded with sweeteners and other starches that limit the frequency that you can enjoy them. The next time you get a craving for stir-fry, try out this flavorful dish, which doesn't have any added sugars.

☁ Asian Vegetable Stir-Fry

With this stir-fry, be creative and use any vegetables that you like. The health benefits here don't get any better! All these vegetables in combination are rich in countless vitamin and minerals, notably vitamins A, C, B6, folate, calcium, and potassium. This stir-fry from Heather Dismore is prepared with minimal oil, so it remains quite low in total fat and calories. It's also rich in fiber, which makes it great for weight management, heart health, and especially blood sugar control. If you like, round out this dish with some tofu or chicken to get a bit of lean protein, and serve over a bed of brown rice for some more fiber, as well.

Preparation time: *40 minutes*

Cooking time: *20 minutes*

Yield: *4 servings*

2 ounces dehydrated wild mushrooms	2 cups baby bok choy, sliced in half
¼ cup boiling water	1 red bell pepper, seeded and julienned
1 tablespoon light soy sauce	½ carrot, thinly sliced on the diagonal
2 cloves garlic, minced	1 cup broccoli florets
1½ teaspoons grated fresh gingerroot	1 cup snow peas, trimmed
2 tablespoons canola oil	

1 Place the mushrooms in a heatproof bowl and cover them with the boiling water. Allow them to reconstitute for 30 minutes. Remove the mushrooms from the water. Chop them and reserve. Strain the liquid through a coffee filter to remove the grit. Combine the mushroom liquid, soy sauce, garlic, and gingerroot. Set aside.

2 Heat the oil in a wok or nonstick skillet. Stir-fry the mushrooms, bok choy, red pepper, carrots, and broccoli for 3 minutes. Add the soy sauce mixture and snow peas. Reduce the heat and continue cooking until the veggies are crisp tender and the sauce thickens.

Per serving: *Kcalories 137 (From Fat 66); Fat 7g (Saturated 1g); Cholesterol 0mg; Sodium 176mg; Carbohydrate 17g (Dietary Fiber 4g); Protein 4g.*

Moderation is the key when enjoying any fried foods. Many diabetics are encouraged to stay away from fried food entirely. In general, it's good advice because so many foods are heavily battered with starchy concoctions that no one needs to eat. But on occasion, you can enjoy fried foods that are lightly *dredged,* or lightly coated, in flour, as in the Vegetable Fritto Misto.

🍅 *Vegetable Fritto Misto*

This dish from Cetrella in Half Moon Bay, California (see Appendix A), calls for significant amounts of milk and white flour, but not to worry. Because they're used only to coat the vegetables, neither provides a significant amount of calories or carbohydrates. The flour and milk help create a thick, crispy coating on the veggies when they're sautéed. Though canola oil is a wonderful source of monounsaturated, heart-healthy fat, it's still very dense in calories, so be thrifty here! When the veggies are finished, drain them well on paper towels to get rid of some of the excess oil. You may also want to pair these veggies with a light entrée, such as fish or chicken, both low-calorie, lean sources of protein.

Preparation time: *30 minutes*

Cooking time: *35 minutes*

Yield: *4 servings*

4 tablespoons canola oil	*2 cups lowfat milk*
½ cup artichoke hearts	*2 cups flour*
½ head cauliflower, chopped into florets	*Salt and pepper*
10 pitted green olives	*Lemon wedges (optional)*
1 large portobello mushroom, large dice	

1 Heat the oil in a deep skillet until it starts smoking. While you're waiting for the oil to heat, place the artichoke hearts, cauliflower, olives, and mushrooms in the milk in a shallow bowl and soak. Place the soaked veggies in a resealable plastic bag with the flour. Shake to coat the veggies with flour. Put the floured vegetables into a strainer and shake off the excess flour.

2 Carefully place the vegetables in batches into the hot oil. Fry for 3 to 5 minutes, or until golden brown.

3 Remove the vegetables from the oil onto paper towels and season lightly with salt and pepper. Place them in a bowl and serve with a wedge or two of lemon, if desired.

Tip: *To ensure that your food absorbs the least amount of oil possible, make sure the oil is very hot before you begin frying it. This step ensures that your food gets a quick, crispy outer coating without getting saturated in oil.*

Per serving: *Kcalories 192 (From Fat 90); Fat 10g (Saturated 1g); Cholesterol 1mg; Sodium 480mg; Carbohydrate 22g (Dietary Fiber 3g); Protein 5g.*

Expanding Your Meal Options with Vegetarian Entrees

When you hear the word "vegetarian," you might think bland tofu or piles of raw vegetables. But vegetarian cuisine is undergoing a true renaissance, as new vegan and vegetarian restaurants open in cities large and small. More people are choosing to eat vegetarian meals as part of their regular diets. Vegetarian meals can be part of a healthy diabetic diet.

○ Vietnamese Style Stuffed Grape Leaves

These stuffed grape leaves, created by Millenium in San Francisco, are served on lettuce leaves with Asian aromatics like Thai basil, cilantro, and mint. The sweet and spicy plum miso dipping sauce is very versatile. You can use it to dress salads, or Asian influenced pasta dishes, or as a dip for crudités.

Preparation time: *17 minutes*

Cooking time: *15 minutes*

Yield: *6 servings*

2 cups thinly sliced fresh shiitake mushrooms

2 teaspoons minced ginger

2 cloves garlic, minced

1 tablespoon Chinese fermented black soy-beans, minced

⅓ cup vegetable stock

1½ cups crumbled firm tofu

1½ cups cooked brown rice

4 tablespoons cilantro leaves

1 tablespoon Tamari or salt to taste

Black pepper to taste

6 wooden skewers, soaked in water

18 brined large grape leaves, rinsed and dried

1 tablespoon sesame seeds

18 Romaine or butter lettuce leaves

1 bunch cilantro

1 bunch mint

1 bunch Thai basil

1 Heat a nonstick sauté pan over medium heat, add the shiitakes, ginger, garlic, black beans, and vegetable stock. Cook the mushrooms until soft and most of the stock evaporates. Add the tofu, rice, and cilantro. Cook the mixture, stirring until heated through. Season mixture with Tamari (or salt if using) and black pepper. Set aside.

2 Place a grape leaf on a flat work surface. Place 1 heaping tablespoon of filling in the center of the leaf, then fold up the leaf like a spring roll or burrito. Repeat with 2 more rolls and then skewer 3 together. Repeat with remaining grape leaves and skewers.

3 Place the skewers on a sheet pan and lightly brush with plum sauce (see the next recipe). Sprinkle with sesame seeds. Broil for 2 minutes until heated through and the sauce caramelizes on top.

4 Serve 1 skewer per person with 3 lettuce leaves, and a sprig of cilantro, basil, and mint with 3 tablespoons of the sauce in a small bowl or on the plate.

Sweet and Spicy Plum — Miso Sauce

2 ripe red-fleshed plums, seed removed, diced	*2 tablespoons agave nectar*
1 clove garlic peeled	*1 tablespoon rice vinegar*
1 tablespoon minced ginger	*4 tablespoons white or chickpea miso*
1 Thai chile	*½ cup water*

Place all ingredients in a blender and blend until smooth. Adjust the sweetener and vinegar to taste.

Per serving: *Kcalories 252 (Calories from Fat 64); Fat 5g (Saturated 7g); Cholesterol 0mg; Sodium 851mg; Carbohydrate 37g (Dietary Fiber 5g); Protein 14g.*

🍎 Asparagus Pizza with Fontina and Truffle Oil

This pizza dough is made with three different flours — white, whole wheat and rye. Tante Marie's Cooking School in San Francisco developed this plan.

Preparation time: *minutes*

Cooking time: *minutes*

Yield: *6 servings*

1 package dry active yeast	*2 tablespoons olive oil*
½ cup warm water (110 to 115 degrees)	*1 pound fresh asparagus*
1 to 2 cups white flour	*Cornmeal as needed*
1 cup whole wheat flour	*1 cup fontina, or Monterey Jack cheese, grated*
3 tablespoons rye flour	*¼ cup good quality Parmesan, grated*
1 teaspoon salt, divided	*½ tablespoon white truffle oil*
⅔ cup warm water	

1 To make the dough, dissolve the yeast in the ½ cup water in a small warmed bowl. Stir in ½ cup white flour, cover, and let rest for 10 to 15 minutes until bubbles form on the surface.

2 Meanwhile, in a larger bowl, mix ½ cup of white flour, whole-wheat flour, and rye flour, and 1½ teaspoons salt. Make a well in the center and add the yeast mixture and the remaining warm water and olive oil. Mix well and knead until the dough is smooth, adding more flour if necessary. Place the dough in a lightly oiled bowl and turn over in order to coat the top of the dough. Cover and put in a warm place for at least 1½ hours.

3 Bring a medium size pan of water to a boil over high heat, and cut the asparagus into ¼ inch slices, discarding the tough stems. Blanch and shock the asparagus. For details on how to blanch and shock vegetables, take a look at the section, "Blanching vegetables for optimum taste and nutrition," earlier in this chapter. Set the asparagus aside until ready to use.

4 Place a large baking stone on the bottom shelf of an oven. Preheat the oven to 500 degrees 30 minutes before baking.

5 Punch down the dough and place on a lightly floured wooden board or counter. Cut into 6 equal pieces. Cover the dough you are not working with a bowl or a dry towel. With your hands, shape one of the pieces of dough into a round disc. Then roll it flatter with a rolling pin. Place this on a *pizza peel* (a large paddle with a long handle used to transfer a raw pizza to the oven) covered with 1 tablespoon cornmeal, and stretch into a thin round with your fingers. Make sure the pizza dough can slide, and isn't stuck to the pizza peel. Cover the dough with the fontina cheese, then the asparagus, then the Parmesan. Repeat with remaining pieces of dough.

6 Place pizza in the oven and bake for 15 to 20 minutes until it is lightly browned on the bottom. Remove from the oven and sprinkle with the truffle oil and serve.

Tip: *The pizza dough will remain usable at least all day if kept cool, and more if refrigerated after the first rising. If you do refrigerate the dough, allow at least one hour for it to come to room temperature.*

Per serving: *Kcalories 265 (Calories from Fat 116); Fat 13g (Saturated 5g); Cholesterol 24mg; Sodium 600mg; Carbohydrate 28g (Dietary Fiber 4g); Protein 12g.*

⊙ *Asparagus Bread Pudding Layered with Fontina*

Bread pudding may not seem to be a diabetic friendly meal, but this recipe from Tante Marie's Cooking School in San Francisco is made with whole-grain bread and loaded with tasty asparagus.

Preparation time: *45 minutes*

Cooking time: *60 minutes*

Yield: *4 servings*

Non-stick cooking spray

6 to 8 thick slices whole-grain bread, dry

1 ½ to 2 cups nonfat milk

2 pounds asparagus

2 eggs

1 teaspoon salt

2 teaspoons freshly ground black pepper

2 tablespoons freshly grated Parmesan cheese

½ cup Fontina cheese, Swiss cheese or other white cheese, shredded

1 Preheat oven to 350 degrees. Spray a 2-quart soufflé dish with non-stick cooking spray; set aside.

2 Place the bread in a single layer in a shallow dish. Pour 1 ½ cups milk over the bread. Let the bread soak until the bread has absorbed the milk and becomes soft, about 30 minutes. Press the bread slices to extract the milk. Measure the milk; you should be able to squeeze ½ cup milk from the bread. If not, make up the difference with the additional ½ cup milk as needed. Set the milk and bread aside.

3 Meanwhile, trim the asparagus, removing the woody ends. Cut the remaining stalks on the diagonal into thin slivers each about 2 inches long and ⅜ of an inch thick. Blanch slivered asparagus until barely tender. Shock the blanched asparagus immediately. Drain and set aside.

4 In a bowl, beat together the eggs, salt, pepper, and the ½ cup milk from the bread soaking until well blended. Layer ⅓ of the bread in the prepared dish. Set 6 or 8 asparagus slivers aside and top the bread layer with half of the remaining asparagus. Spread ⅓ of each of the cheeses over the asparagus.

5 Repeat the layers, using half of the remaining bread, all of the remaining asparagus, and half of the remaining cheese. Arrange the remaining bread on top, spread the remaining cheese over it, and garnish with the reserved asparagus slivers. Pour the milk-egg mixture over the layers.

6 Bake in the preheated oven until the top is golden brown and a knife inserted in the middle of the pudding comes out clean, about 45 minutes.

Per serving: *Kcalories 260 (Calories from Fat 86); Fat 10g (Saturated 4g); Cholesterol 126mg; Sodium 1,018mg; Carbohydrate 29g (Dietary Fiber 5g); Protein 18g.*

☞ Baby Artichokes, Gigante Beans, and Summer Vegetable Cartoccio with Creamy Polenta

Cartoccio, or baking the vegetables in packets of parchment or foil, captures all the aromatics of the herbs and makes for an elegant presentation. Millennium in San Francisco shows you how easy it is to create this elegant meal at home.

Preparation time: *45 minutes*

Cooking time: *30 minutes*

Yield: *6 servings*

1 quart of water

1 head of garlic, cloves peeled or 18 medium to large garlic cloves

Juice from ½ lemon

6 baby to mid-size artichokes

6 pieces of bakers parchment or foil cut into 8-10 inch squares

1½ cup of cooked gigante beans, or canellini beans

12 oyster mushrooms

3 ripe Roma or other tomato, quartered

2 summer squash, diced

Other vegetables of choice

½ bunch basil, leaves picked

6 small sprigs of rosemary

1 lemon sliced into 6 slices

1 tablespoon capers

Salt, pepper, and chile flakes to taste

1 cup vegetable stock or white wine

1 Preheat the oven to 400 degrees.

2 Blanch the garlic cloves in 1 quart of water for 1 minute; then drain and set aside. Add the lemon juice to the boiling water. Clean the artichokes, and cut them in half. Blanch until the heart of the artichoke is just soft. Drain and reserve.

3 Place 1 piece of parchment (or foil if using) on a flat surface. Place 2 artichoke halves in the center, followed by 3 cloves of garlic, ¼ cup of the beans, 2 oyster mushrooms, 2 pieces of tomato, some of the summer squash, plus any other vegetable you are using. Top with basil leaves, rosemary sprig, a slice of lemon, a few capers, salt, pepper, and chile flakes if using. Pour 2 tablespoons of the stock or wine over the ingredients. Fold the parchment over the filling, and crimp the edges until sealed. Place sealed packet on a baking pan. Repeat with remaining parchment and ingredients.

4 Bake for 15 minutes. Place the baked cartoccio in a large shallow bowl with a portion of the Creamy Polenta (see the next recipe) and present to your guests.

Creamy Polenta

1½ cups polenta

6 cups vegetables stock or water

1 tablespoon nutritional yeast

Salt and pepper to taste

1 Heat the stock or water in a sauce pan to boiling. Whisk in the polenta, turn down the heat to a simmer and continue whisking for 2 minutes. Cook the polenta, whisking often for 20 minutes or until the polenta pulls away from the side of the pan and the grains are soft.

2 Whisk in the nutritional yeast and adjust salt and pepper to taste. Remove from heat and reserve. Set aside. When reheating, add more water to thin if needed.

Per serving: Kcalories 446 (Calories from Fat 26); Fat 0g (Saturated 0); Cholesterol 0mg; Sodium 1,000mg; Carbohydrate 93g (Dietary Fiber 24g); Protein 28g.

Chapter 12

Boning Up on Fish Cookery

Seafood is a great protein source, especially for diabetics. It has lower saturated fat, cholesterol, and carbohydrates than any other protein source. Much of it has a mild flavor that takes on the flavor of its accompanying ingredients and preparation methods, so you can have an almost endless variety of flavors and dishes. It cooks up quickly, so it can be ready when you are.

In this chapter, we convince you (in case you need it) that seafood is an excellent food choice to include in a diabetic diet. We give you plenty of recipes and fun new ways to prepare all kinds of fish dishes. And finally, we give you tips for preparing shellfish.

Identifying Good Reasons to Serve Seafood

Like meat and poultry, seafood supplies high-quality protein, balancing the fats and carbohydrates in the meal and providing calories that have little effect on blood glucose. But the benefits of eating fish extend beyond this:

> ✔ The oceans are a rich reservoir of minerals, and all creatures that live in the sea are in part made of these minerals. When you eat fish, you are likely also to be consuming iodine, selenium, phosphorus, potassium, iron, and calcium.

✔ Eating seafood regularly may help improve kidney function in patients with severe diabetes.

✔ Seafood is a good source of B vitamins, especially niacin, and also contains fat-soluble vitamin A. In addition, fatty fish are one of the few food sources of vitamin D.

✔ The most important nutrient in fish may well be the omega-3 fatty acids. These polyunsaturated fatty acids are especially high in the fat and oils of fish that live in cold water. (Because these oils stay liquid at room temperature, they may help insulate the fish against the cold.) The omega-3 fatty acids appear to lower the undesirable form of cholesterol, LDL cholesterol, and to raise the desirable form, HDL cholesterol. These fats also have an anti-inflammatory effect. The fish with the highest percentage of these healthy oils are salmon, sardines, tuna, and mackerel.

Healthy Americans are encouraged to eat two seafood servings per week on a regular basis.

Preparing Fish in Healthy Ways

You don't need to deep-fry your catch of the day or order deep-fried fish when you eat out in order to get fish that tastes good. Not only is this type of fish loaded with fat, but the type of fat is usually unhealthy. When fats heat to high temperatures, such as in deep-frying, toxic by-products are formed. It is far better to eat seafood prepared by methods such as baking, pan roasting, or grilling — all delicious and healthy ways of cooking fish. The following sections cover a variety of methods you can use to cook fish the healthy way.

Baking your way to fish bliss

Baking is one of the first techniques most people learn when they're learning to cook. In fact, many people don't "learn" to bake; they simply seem to know how to bake. Technically speaking, *baking* means to cook something by surrounding it with dry heat. In most cases, you bake in an oven, a closed environment where you control the temperature.

Baking doesn't mean boring. Try out this flavorful baked cod to see how baking can be both easy and delicious.

Horseradish-Crusted Cod with Lentils

This recipe, from Derek Dickerson, owner of Derek's Bistro in Pasadena, California (see Appendix A), shows that you can develop a great-tasting meal for a person with diabetes. The cod is a lean source of protein and prepared simply by baking, a great lowfat cooking technique. The fillets are topped with a touch of horseradish, which lends a ton of flavor but very little added fat and calories. The lentils are full of fiber and complex carbohydrate, making them a perfect choice. They are combined with crème fraîche, a heavy cream with a nutty flavor. This ingredient is included in such a modest amount, however, that it contributes very little fat and calories. The lentils, however, are left creamy and decadent.

Preparation time: *20 minutes*

Cooking time: *30 minutes*

Yield: *4 servings*

1 pound Puy lentils (or substitute the lentils of your choice)

2 sprigs fresh parsley

4 tablespoons crème fraîche (or substitute 3 tablespoons heavy cream and 1 tablespoon sour cream)

¼ cup chopped fresh parsley

Salt and pepper

4 teaspoons horseradish sauce

4 cod fillets, 6 ounces each

4 tablespoons panko bread crumbs (substitute crushed cornflakes if you can't find these Japanese bread crumbs in the Asian section of your market)

1 teaspoon olive oil

1 Preheat the oven to 375 degrees. Place the lentils in a large saucepan with enough cold water to cover them, plus an extra couple of inches. Add the whole sprigs of the parsley and bring to a boil. Simmer for 25 minutes, or until tender. Discard the parsley sprigs. Drain the lentils and toss with the crème fraîche and chopped parsley. Season to taste. Set aside and keep warm.

2 Spread the horseradish sauce over each fish fillet and then press in the bread crumbs to coat. Grease a nonstick baking sheet with the olive oil. Place the fish fillets on the baking sheet and bake for 14 to 17 minutes, until the fish is just cooked and the bread crumbs are golden.

3 Place one-fourth of the lentils on each of four plates. Top each with one piece of baked fish.

Per serving: *Kcalories 590 (From Fat 77); Fat 9g (Saturated 4g); Cholesterol 81mg; Sodium 281mg; Carbohydrate 73g (Dietary Fiber 26g); Protein 58g.*

Poaching to perfection

Poaching is a method of cooking that gently cooks the food in a small amount of liquid, just below the boiling point. In the case of seafood, this liquid is often highly flavored with herbs, wine, stock, and other seasonings. Give poaching a shot with this terrific salmon recipe.

Poached King Salmon with Steamed Asparagus and Tapenade Salsa

This recipe comes to your kitchen from that of Chef Didier Labbe of the Clementine restaurant in San Francisco (see Appendix A). The salmon is poached, which is the lightest method of cooking, requiring only water. Adding wine and other herbs to the cooking liquid, however, is a great way to infuse good flavor into poached poultry or fish, as this recipe calls for. This dish is a wonderful source of omega-3 fatty acids as well as other beneficial heart-healthy fats.

Combined with asparagus, the vitamin A content of this dish is off the chart, so eat up for eye health! Asparagus also lends a significant source of fiber, some good protein, and a bunch of folate. For women of childbearing age, folate is essential for the prevention of birth defects and has even healthier outcomes in diabetic patients as well. For everyone else, adequate folate intakes can also lower something called homocysteine, high levels of which are linked to heart disease.

By the way, if you don't have the time or energy to prepare your own fish stock, you can find the prepared version at many grocery stores and specialty food stores. Just remember, homemade always tastes better and is better for you, too!

Preparation time: *45 minutes*

Cooking time: *15 minutes*

Yield: *4 servings*

Fish Stock (see the following recipe)

½ pound green asparagus

½ pound white asparagus (if not available, use an additional ½ pound green asparagus)

4 salmon fillets, 6 ounces each

Tapenade Salsa (see the accompanying recipe)

1 Prepare the fish stock.

2 While the stock is cooking, prepare the asparagus. Add the asparagus to lightly salted, boiling water and cook until tender. Immediately remove the asparagus from the boiling water and shock it in a cold-water bath. (Check out Chapter 11 for tips on blanching and shocking vegetables.)

3 Bring prepared fish stock to a gentle simmer over medium heat. Add the salmon fillets to the simmering fish stock and cook for 5 minutes. Remove from broth and keep warm.

4 Prepare the tapenade salsa (see the accompanying recipe).

5 Just before serving, reheat the asparagus in the simmering fish stock, approximately 5 minutes.

6 Serve each salmon fillet with the asparagus tips and top with the Tapenade Salsa.

Fish Stock

1 pound fish bones

2 cups water, divided

1 small onion, diced

½ pound leeks, sliced and well rinsed

1 pinch ground cloves

¼ cup dry white wine

Juice of 1 lemon

1 In a large sauté pan, add the fish bones to 1 cup of cold water and bring to a simmer.

2 Add the onion, leeks, clove, and white wine and return to a simmer; then add the remaining 1 cup water and the lemon juice. Continue to cook the bones for an additional 30 minutes.

3 Strain the broth through a fine mesh strainer. Reserve the broth; discard the bones and other solids.

> *Tip: You can purchase fish bones at fish markets or at specialty food stores that sell fresh fish. Alternatively, you can find a fish stock base, like Redi-Base, on the Web at* www.redibase.com/about.htm#redibase. *It's a concentrate version of stock.*

Tapenade Salsa

2 ounces anchovies

1 cup pitted black olives

2 cloves garlic

1 cup olive oil

2 tablespoons balsamic vinegar

1 In a food processor, combine the anchovies, olives, and garlic until the mixture becomes a paste, about 45 seconds.

2 In a separate bowl, combine the olive oil and vinegar.

3 Combine the two mixtures and stir.

> *Per serving: Kcalories 838 (From Fat 639); Fat 71g (Saturated 10g); Cholesterol 109mg; Sodium 1,226mg; Carbohydrate 7g (Dietary Fiber 1g); Protein 43g.*

Pan roasting seafood sensations

In the strictest culinary terms, *pan roasting* is a two-step process that first sears and seals a thicker piece of meat or chicken in a pan on the stovetop and then finishes that piece in the oven, in the same pan you started in. So when we're talking about seafood, the term *pan roasting* is probably not exactly accurate. Because seafood cooks so fast, there's usually not a need to finish it in the oven. But you can make a terrific sauce in the same pan you seared your fish in.

Whatever you call it, pan-roasted food is downright good, as these next three recipes prove. Use a quality sauté pan that heats evenly. And make sure to heat it up well before you place your fish in to ensure an even, quick crust.

Tilapia Franchaise

If you're new to the world of seafood, tilapia is a good place to start. It's a mild-flavored white fish that really takes on the flavors of the food it's cooked with. This dish is simple to make, but very impressive for guests, because you cook the whole thing in a single pan. Sear the fish and then create the rich sauce — all without changing pans or washing a single dish. What could be simpler?

Preparation time: *10 minutes*

Cooking time: *15 minutes*

Yield: *2 servings*

Nonstick cooking spray	*½ cup whole-wheat flour*
2 pieces (6 ounces each) tilapia (or other flat white fish)	*¼ cup white cooking wine*
	1 tablespoon lemon juice
1 egg	*½ cup low-salt chicken broth*

1 Coat a medium skillet with the cooking spray and place over medium heat.

2 Rinse and dry the tilapia. In a small bowl, lightly beat the egg. Place the flour in a flat plate. Lightly coat both sides of the fish with the flour, coat the fish with the egg, and place directly in the hot skillet.

3 When the fish is golden brown on the first side (approximately 4 minutes), flip it over to brown the other side.

4 When the fish is golden brown (roughly after 2 to 3 minutes), reduce the heat to low. Add the wine and let it reduce to half the amount. Add the lemon juice and broth and let the liquid reduce as it cooks the fish.

5 When the liquid has reduced to approximately one quarter and appears to have slightly thickened, remove from the heat and serve.

Tip: *Serve with fresh vegetables, salad, whole-wheat couscous, or brown rice for some extra fiber.*

Per serving: Kcalories 291(From Fat 45); Fat 5g (Saturated 2g); Cholesterol 190mg; Sodium 156mg; Carbohydrate 23g (Dietary Fiber 4g); Protein 40g.

Pan-Roasted Salmon Fillet with Lemon-Dill Butter Sauce

Lewis Rossman, from Cetrella in Half Moon Bay, California (see Appendix A), offers an excellent pan-roasted recipe. The sauce is fantastic, the butter adds the right creaminess, the lemon juice provides the perfect acidity, and the pungent dill ties them together. Look for baby leeks because they're more tender and subtle flavored for a great addition to the salad. And be sure to check out the instructions for the right way to wash and slice leeks in Chapter 8.

Preparation time: *25 minutes*

Cooking time: *15 minutes*

Yield: *2 servings*

½ cucumber

1 bunch arugula

6 baby leeks, trimmed, cleaned, and blanched (or substitute 1 large leek, sliced; check out Chapter 8 for details on cleaning and slicing leeks)

Salt and pepper

3 tablespoons olive oil, divided

2 salmon fillets (6 ounces each), 1 inch thick

1 tablespoon Meyer lemon juice

3 tablespoons butter

3 sprigs dill, chopped

1 Prepare the cucumber salad first. Chop the cucumber into half moons and place in a bowl with the arugula and the baby leeks. Season with salt and pepper to taste and 1 tablespoon of the olive oil.

2 To cook the fish, heat a sauté pan with the remaining 2 tablespoons olive oil. Season the fish with salt and pepper and, when the pan is hot, add the fillets. Cook for 3½ minutes on each side (medium-rare to medium). Place the salad in the center of the plate and put the fish on top.

3 To make the sauce, wipe clean the same sauté pan and add the lemon juice. Allow the juice to reduce by half and add the butter. Swirl the butter vigorously into the lemon juice and season with salt and pepper to taste and the chopped dill. Pour over the fish.

Per serving: Kcalories 589 (From Fat 396); Fat 23g (Saturated 14g); Cholesterol 143mg; Sodium 431mg; Carbohydrate 10g (Dietary Fiber 2g); Protein 39g.

A *fumet* (pronounced foo-MAY) is a heavily concentrated stock. In the case of the next recipe, it's a stock made from shrimp shells. You can make a fumet by boiling fish heads, bones, shellfish shells, or whole fish with wine, aromatic herbs, and vegetables and then reducing it to concentrate the flavor.

Use a fumet to season sauces and soups or to braise or poach fish or vegetables. Its subtle flavor imparts the delicate essence of seafood with a slight acidity (thanks to the wine), but it doesn't overpower the main event.

If you'd rather not make your own fumet, look for fish stock or fish stock glace or base (an even more concentrated product that must be reconstituted with water before using) at your local fish or gourmet market.

Pan-Roasted Cod with Shrimp and Mirliton Squash

Here is a wonderful contribution from Chef Kevin Rathbun, of Rathbun's in Atlanta, Georgia (see Appendix A). If you're keeping in mind blood sugar control and heart health, fish is always a great choice — and this recipe makes use of two. The cod and shrimp come together well with the squash ragout.

Mirliton squash, also known as chayote squash, is similar to other squash varieties, and it makes for a wonderful addition to soups, stews, and casseroles. Look for a small, avocado-sized squash with a firm pale green skin. It has a white mild-flavored flesh that takes on the subtle flavors of the shrimp fumet very well. Its peak season runs from December to March, so if you can't find it, zucchini works well too. This dish is rich in lean protein, low in carbs and saturated fat, and full of vitamins A and C.

Preparation time: *1 hour*

Cooking time: *40 minutes*

Yield: *4 servings*

Fumet:

Shrimp shells, from twenty 26/30 shrimp (from shrimp in ragout or purchased at a local fish market; see the note at the end of the recipe)

1 shallot, chopped

1 bay leaf

1 thyme sprig

½ cup Chardonnay

Ragout:

20 white shrimp, 26/30s, peeled and deveined

2 cups ¼-inch cubes of peeled chayote squash (also called mirliton), blanched (see Chapter 11 for blanching instructions)

1 cup peeled, cubed tomato

½ cup Shrimp Fumet

2 tablespoons butter

2 teaspoons fresh lemon juice

1 teaspoon kosher salt

2 tablespoons parsley (whole leaves)

Cod:

4 cod fillets (6 ounces each)

Salt and pepper

2 teaspoons flour

2 tablespoons olive oil

1 Preheat the oven to 350 degrees. Place the shrimp shells, shallot, bay leaf, thyme, chardonnay, and enough water to cover the ingredients in a small saucepot. Slowly bring to a boil and simmer for 15 to 20 minutes to extract some flavor from the shells. After the flavor has been extracted, strain the liquid. Discard the shells and other solids and reserve the liquid.

2 Make the ragout: In a medium saucepan, place the shrimp, squash, tomato, fumet, butter, lemon juice, salt, and parsley. Simmer until the shrimp is done, approximately 5 to 7 minutes, and hold until ready to serve. Adjust seasoning as needed.

3 Lightly season the cod fillets with salt and pepper to taste and dust one side with flour.

4 Heat the olive oil in a sauté pan and place the cod fillets flour side down in the oil. Sauté to a golden brown, approximately 4 minutes, and then turn and transfer to the oven for 4 to 6 minutes.

5 When the cod is finished baking in the oven, place each fillet in a bowl and pour the ragout on top.

Note: *Shrimp fall into various size categories, and 26/30 means you get 26 to 30 shrimp in each pound. For more information, see Chapter 7.*

Per serving: Kcalories 292 (From Fat 126); Fat 14g (Saturated 5g); Cholesterol 134mg; Sodium 776mg; Carbohydrate 7g (Dietary Fiber 2g); Protein 34g.

Getting your grill on

Grilling is similar to broiling, but the heat comes from a different direction. In grilling, the heat source is under the food. In broiling, the heat source is above the food.

Tuna is an excellent fish for grilling. Its meat is firm, not flaky like white fish. It stands up nicely to spices and flavorings. And because it's usually served extremely rare, it takes very little time to cook. Try grilled tuna in the following recipe.

In recent years, there has been a growing concern regarding the methyl mercury content of some fish. Water pollution may increase the level of this metal to toxic amounts in certain areas. The U.S. Food and Drug Administration (FDA) cautions pregnant and nursing women, as well as women of childbearing age, to limit consumption of swordfish, shark, king mackerel, and tile fish to less than 7 ounces per week. These fish are shown to have the greatest mercury levels compared with other fish species. Ahi tuna is generally considered to be safe. However, if you're concerned about the mercury content of fish, visit the FDA Web site, www.fda.gov, to find out more.

Grilled Ahi Tuna with Asian Slaw

If you're in the mood for something that's light yet delicious and satisfying, this dish from food writer Heather Dismore is perfect. It's full of protein yet low in total calories and fat. The slaw provides a good source of vegetables, and the dressing helps to round out the dish with few added calories.

Fresh tuna is best when prepared very rare in the middle — nearly raw. For this reason, be sure to purchase sushi-grade tuna at the fish market. It's safer, less likely to be contaminated, and therefore less likely to cause foodborne illness. Pregnant and nursing women should always avoid all raw fish, including rare tuna. Otherwise, be sure to meet the American Heart Association's recommendation to consume 2 servings of fish per week.

Preparation time: *30 minutes, plus 2 hours for marinating*

Cooking time: *6 to 10 minutes*

Yield: *4 servings*

4 ahi tuna steaks, about 2 pounds (be sure they're sushi grade)

Marinade:

¼ cup light soy sauce

¼ cup mirin (sweet rice wine)

1 tablespoon toasted sesame oil

2 tablespoons rice wine vinegar

2 tablespoons minced fresh gingerroot

2½ tablespoons minced green onions

3 tablespoons minced garlic

Dressing:

⅔ cup rice wine vinegar

½ tablespoon Splenda (or to taste)

1 teaspoon honey

1 teaspoon light soy sauce

3 tablespoons chopped cilantro

1 teaspoon finely grated gingerroot

1 tablespoon toasted sesame seeds

Slaw:

1 small head napa cabbage, shredded

½ cup shredded carrot

¼ cup chopped green onion

¼ cup julienned red pepper

¼ cup julienned yellow pepper

½ cup julienned daikon radish

1 Make the marinade by combining the soy sauce, mirin, sesame oil, vinegar, ginger, green onions, and garlic in a resealable plastic bag. Place the ahi steaks in the bag. Gently coat the steaks in the marinade. Place in the refrigerator for 2 hours, turning occasionally.

2 About a half hour before the ahi has finished marinating, prepare the slaw: First mix the dressing ingredients (vinegar, Splenda, honey, soy sauce, cilantro, gingerroot, and sesame seeds) in a large bowl. In another large bowl, mix the slaw ingredients (cabbage, carrots, onion, red and yellow peppers, and radish). Toss the cabbage mixture with most of the dressing. Reserve a small amount of dressing for later.

3 Let stand for 20 minutes at room temperature. If you'd prefer to refrigerate the slaw, extend standing time to 1 hour (and start preparing it about 40 minutes after you start marinating the tuna). Preheat the grill.

4 Grill the ahi tuna 2 to 3 minutes per side. (Broil about 5 inches from the heating element, if you prefer.) The outside should be gray brown; however, the inside will remain red. Be sure not to overcook the steaks, as they will quickly dry out and lose flavor.

5 Slice the tuna thinly and serve with the slaw. Drizzle the reserved dressing on top.

Per serving of ahi tuna: Kcalories 258(From Fat 27); Fat 3g (Saturated 1g); Cholesterol 99mg; Sodium 232mg; Carbohydrate 2g (Dietary Fiber 0g); Protein 51g.

Per serving of slaw and dressing: Kcalories 57 (from Fat 12); Fat 1 g (Saturated 0 g); Cholesterol 0 mg; Sodium 73mg; Carbohydrate 10g (Dietary Fiber 3g); Protein 3g.

B.B.Q. Cedar-Planked Salmon

Chef Vitaly Paley of Paley's Place in Portland, Oregon (see Appendix A), has created a sumptuous feast of salmon with this cedar barbecue. You can prepare it in the oven or on an outdoor grill. As the planks roast on the fire, the salmon retains the aromas and begins to employ the earthy cedar flavor of the wooden planks. *Note:* You can find cedar planks at a lumber store — specifically look for untreated cedar shingles — or in kitchen supply stores or gourmet shops that sell lots of knickknacks.

Wild salmon is preferred — it contains more beneficial omega-3 fatty acids and far less saturated fat than its farmed counterpart. Salmon is a gift of nature and a gift to your health as well. Enjoy this fatty fish and reap its medicinal benefits.

Special tool: *1 cedar plank, 1 to 2 inches larger than salmon fillet all the way around, soaked in water for at least 2 hours*

Preparation time: *30 minutes, plus optional marinating time of 1 to 2 hours*

Cooking time: *20 minutes*

Yield: *6 servings*

½ tablespoon salt	5 tablespoons olive oil, divided
½ cup brown sugar	6 garlic cloves, finely chopped
Zest from 1 orange	½ cup chiffonade basil (roll the basil together tightly and then thinly slice width-wise to form long, stringy strips)
1 salmon fillet (2 pounds), pin bone removed (ask the person at the seafood counter to do this step for you)	1 large onion, peeled and thinly sliced

1 Preheat the oven to 450 degrees.

2 Mix up the dry marinade. In a small bowl mix the salt, brown sugar, and orange zest and spread it generously on both sides of the salmon fillet. (You can marinate the fish 1 to 2 hours in advance, if you prefer. Refrigerate the fish while it's marinating if you marinate it in advance.)

3 Brush one side of the cedar plank with 3 tablespoons of the olive oil and place it in the oven for 15 to 20 minutes.

4 Spread the garlic on the olive-oil-coated side of the plank and then place the salmon fillet on top. Sprinkle the salmon fillet with the basil. Cover the fish generously with the sliced onions and then drizzle it with the remaining 2 tablespoons olive oil.

5 Place the planked fish in the preheated oven. Cook the salmon for approximately 10 to 15 minutes, or until the fish is medium-rare and a probe thermometer reads 120 degrees. The cooking time will vary with the thickness of your fish. Allow approximately 10 minutes per inch of thickness.

If you prefer to cook the salmon on a grill, follow these instructions: Preheat the grill to medium-high heat. Place the oiled plank directly on the grill. Let the plank smoke a bit before adding the fish. If the plank catches on fire, spritz it with water. Close the grill and cook the salmon for approximately 10 to 15 minutes, or until the fish is medium-rare and a probe thermometer reads 120 degrees. The cooking time will vary with the thickness of your fish. Allow approximately 10 minutes per inch of thickness.

Per serving: Kcalories 373 (From Fat 153); Fat 17g (Saturated 2g); Cholesterol 86mg; Sodium 700mg; Carbohydrate 21g (Dietary Fiber 1g); Protein 33g.

Broiling your seafood bounty

You may find that many recipes call for broiling. Basically, you broil food by cooking it using a heat source from above, usually called (you guessed it) a broiler. Typically, food is heated for relatively short periods of time at a high heat, which usually creates a crispy coating. In most cases, broiling is a lowfat cooking technique requiring little additional fat *and* allowing the natural fats present in the food to drip away. All in all, a pretty healthy combination!

Broiled Salmon with Herb Sauce and Cucumbers

As if there weren't already a bunch of reasons to include salmon in your diet, here's one more. Salmon is a wonderful source of selenium, which happens to be another disease-fighting antioxidant. Add that to the long list of this seafood's many health benefits!

This salmon recipe, coming to us from Barbetta Restaurant in New York (see Appendix A), is broiled and paired with a sauce flavored with a variety of herbs. Although most creamy sauces are usually quite high in fat and calories, this one remains extremely light. The recipe takes advantage of lowfat yogurt instead of its full-fat counterpart. You can make simple substitutions like this with most dairy products, thus sacrificing a lot of fat and calories with barely noticeable change in taste.

Preparation time: *20 minutes*

Cooking time: *10 minutes*

Yield: *4 servings*

¼ cup finely chopped fresh chives

2½ tablespoons extra-virgin olive oil, divided

1 cup finely chopped fresh parsley, divided

½ cup finely chopped fresh cilantro

10 ounces plain lowfat yogurt

Juice of 1 lemon

1 medium cucumber, unpeeled, thinly sliced

4 fresh salmon fillets; 6 ounces each

Salt and pepper

1 Place an oven-safe grill pan (or broiler pan) in the oven. Preheat the broiler (on low setting if possible).

2 Place the chives in a blender with 1 tablespoon of the oil. Blend for approximately 1 minute, until well combined. Place the chives mixture in a small bowl. Add half of the chopped parsley and all of the cilantro, the yogurt, and lemon juice. Set aside.

3 Mix the cucumber slices with remaining chopped parsley.

4 Prepare 4 dinner plates by spreading the herb sauce in each one. Arrange the cucumber slices over the sauce. Put aside.

5 Brush the salmon fillets with 1 tablespoon of the olive oil. Sprinkle with salt and pepper to taste.

6 Remove the grill pan from the oven. Brush it with the remaining olive oil. Place the salmon fillets in the heated, oiled pan.

7 Place the grill pan under the broiler, about 5 inches from the heating element.

8 Cook for 5 to 7 minutes, until the top of the salmon acquires a golden to light brown color. Flip the fish to the other side. Allow the fillets to remain in the oven an additional 2 to 3 minutes.

9 Place one salmon fillet in the center of each dinner plate, over the cucumber slices and sauce.

Per serving: Kcalories 351 (From Fat 145); Fat 16g (Saturated 3g); Cholesterol 101mg; Sodium 334mg; Carbohydrate 9g (Dietary Fiber 1g); Protein 42g.

Surveying Superior Shellfish

The term *shellfish* includes seafood such as shrimp, lobster, oysters, clams, mussels, and scallops, which all have a shell instead of fins and gills. It also includes some seafood that have a not-so-obvious shell, like octopus and squid.

Shellfish are sold by their size and weight. For tips on how to pick the right shellfish for your recipe, check out Chapter 7.

The texture of these tasty tidbits ranges from exceptionally tender, in the case of lobster and some shrimp, to a bit chewy, in the case of octopus. It's probably not a surprise that the tenderness of these delicate creatures depends, in part, on how well you cook them.

Avoid overcooking shellfish. Doing so causes the texture to become rubbery and unpleasant.

Rock Shrimp Ceviche

With this ceviche (pronounced se-VEECH or se-vee-CHEE) dish from Lewis Rossman at Cetrella Bistro and Café in Half Moon Bay, California (see Appendix A), you and your company are in for a treat. It's even simple to prepare. Rock shrimp is a sweet shrimp with an almost lobsterlike flavor and texture. It's an extremely succulent shrimp that cooks quickly, so it's a natural choice for this no-heat cooking method. Born out of the necessity of using acid to retard food spoilage, ceviche is prepared through a delicious and healthy cooking technique. In a nutshell, raw seafood, usually whitefish or shrimp, is placed in an acid, most often lime juice, which in essence "cooks" the fish. Leave it to marinate for an hour, and it's ready to serve. Ceviche makes for a great first course, especially in the hot summer months, as it is quite light and refreshing and contains almost no fat. Enjoy!

Preparation time: *10 minutes, plus marinating time of 1 hour*

Yield: *4 servings*

1 pound rock shrimp, roughly chopped	*½ cup fresh lime juice (about 4 limes)*
1 mango, small dice	*1 pinch chili flakes*
1 shallot, finely chopped	*Salt and pepper*
½ cup chopped fresh cilantro	

Place the rock shrimp in a bowl and mix together with the mango, shallot, cilantro, lime juice, and chili flakes. Season with salt and pepper to taste and place in the refrigerator for 1 hour. The ceviche looks particularly attractive served in a martini glass.

Note: *Use only very fresh (or freshly frozen and then very recently thawed) seafood in ceviche because it never reaches temperatures high enough to kill strong bacteria.*

Per serving: *Kcalories 131 (From Fat 10); Fat 1g (Saturated 0g); Cholesterol 168mg; Sodium 340mg; Carbohydrate 13g (Dietary Fiber 1g); Protein 19g.*

Seared Diver Scallops with Bacon and Shallot Reduction

If you're looking to show off some cooking skills, this scallop dish from Chef Kyle Ketchum at Lark in Detroit, Michigan (see Appendix A), is sure to impress. Just a small amount of bacon as a condiment helps to achieve some big flavor — even without breaking the day's saturated fat and cholesterol limit. Scallops are great sources of protein while remaining low in total and saturated fat, so they're a healthier alternative to red meats. Serve this dish atop a bed of whole-wheat couscous to complete the meal.

Diver scallops are sea scallops that are harvested by, well, divers. They can be a bit more expensive than standard sea scallops since they're harvested by people rather than by boats dragging chains along the ocean floor, but typically they're less gritty and have a better texture. Plus, they're more environmentally friendly because divers generally take only the larger mature scallops, leaving the smaller younger scallops to grow for future scallop eaters.

U10 refers to the size of the scallops used in this recipe and means that one pound of these scallops contains less than 10 (or Under 10) scallops per pound.

Preparation time: *30 minutes*

Cooking time: *30 minutes*

Yield: *2 servings*

4 slices slab bacon, cut into ½-inch strips

1 shallot, peeled and thinly sliced

½ cup low-sodium chicken stock

2 tablespoons butter

1 tablespoon chopped fresh chives

Salt and pepper

6 U10 diver scallops (you can substitute 1 pound of sea scallops)

2 tablespoons olive oil

12 asparagus stalks (approximately ¼ pound), cleaned, trimmed, and blanched (see Chapter 11 for blanching instructions)

¼ cup Balsamic Syrup (see the following recipe)

1 Add the bacon to a small sauté pan and cook for 2 minutes. Add the shallots and continue cooking for an additional 3 minutes. Add the chicken stock and butter and bring to a simmer until the stock has reduced by half and the onions are tender, approximately 20 minutes. Add the chives and season to taste with salt and pepper. Set aside.

2 Preheat a medium sauté pan over high heat. Season the scallops evenly on both sides with salt and pepper. Add the oil to the hot pan and sauté the scallops approximately 2 minutes per side. Remove the scallops from the pan and place 3 scallops in the center of each plate. Reheat the asparagus in the skillet you used to cook the scallops. Put the bacon and shallot reduction (from Step 1) around the scallops. Arrange the asparagus around the scallops. Drizzle the Balsamic Syrup over the scallops and asparagus.

Per serving: Kcalories 652 (From Fat 306); Fat 34g (Saturated 11g); Cholesterol 154mg; Sodium 1,090mg; Carbohydrate 29g (Dietary Fiber 2g); Protein 52g.

Balsamic Syrup

1 cup balsamic vinegar   *1½ teaspoons Splenda*

Combine the balsamic vinegar and Splenda in a medium saucepan. Cook over medium-high heat until the sauce thickens and reduces to ¼ cup, approximately 30 minutes.

Per serving (2 tablespoons): *Kcalories 80 (From Fat 2); Fat 0g (Saturated 0g); Cholesterol 0mg; Sodium 31mg; Carbohydrate 19g (Dietary Fiber 0g); Protein 0g.*

Chapter 13

Flocking to Poultry

*W*hen you first received your diagnosis of diabetes, you may have assumed that your culinary life would include nothing more than broiled chicken breasts and steamed vegetables. Hopefully, if you've read any of this book at this point, you realize this assumption couldn't be farther from reality.

In this chapter, we show you how to safely use poultry in your diet. We give you tips to keep the most popular piece of chicken — the breast — tasty, moist, and downright exciting. And finally, we give you some great ways to include turkey in your regimen.

Including Poultry in Your Diet

Nutritionists define a portion as 3.5 ounces. What this serving size looks like on your dinner plate, with chicken for instance, is typically either a half chicken breast or a chicken drumstick and thigh. To reduce the fat content, eat the meat but don't eat the skin.

Maintaining good sanitary practices in your kitchen is important when you're working with poultry, no matter how much poultry you're cooking. Keep the following hints in mind to minimize bacterial contamination from poultry:

✔ Rinse any poultry pieces and pat them dry before using them. This step helps remove bacteria that are often present in poultry.

✔ Don't place raw poultry near, over, or in any foods that won't be cooked before they're eaten. Proper cooking kills most bacteria found in poultry, but never let the liquid in raw poultry drip onto salads, sauces, condiments, and the like.

✔ Keep a separate color cutting board only used for raw poultry. You can significantly reduce the chances that you cut lettuce on the same board you sliced chicken on if they're different colors.

✔ Clean your knife after cutting raw poultry. Wash it thoroughly in hot, soapy water.

✔ Thoroughly sanitize any surfaces that come into contact with any raw poultry or its juices. Use an antibacterial cleaner that's specifically made for this purpose.

✔ Always cook poultry to the appropriate food-safe temperature, as listed in Table 13-1.

Table 13-1	Safe Cooking Temperatures for Poultry
Product	*Temperature*
Ground turkey, chicken	165
Poultry breasts	170
Chicken, whole	180
Duck and goose	180
Poultry thighs, wings	180
Turkey, whole	180

Making the Best of Chicken Breasts

The breast is the leanest of all the chicken's parts, with the lowest total and saturated fat content, thus making it the healthiest choice for your heart.

Chicken Breasts with Lemon and Garlic

This dish, by Christopher Lee from the Eccolo restaurant in Berkeley, California (see Appendix A), takes full advantage of a chicken breast's white, lean meat. Just remember to remove the skin after the chicken has cooked.

Preparation time: *20 minutes*

Cooking time: *25 minutes*

Yield: *6 servings*

6 chicken breasts, 6 ounces each, bone in, with skin

Salt

2 tablespoons extra-virgin olive oil, divided

30 garlic cloves

4 tablespoons butter

Juice of 2 lemons, divided

1 cup dry white wine

3 cups chicken stock or water

A few thyme sprigs

Zest of 1 lemon, divided

1 A few hours before cooking, season the chicken breasts with salt. Refrigerate the chicken and bring to room temperature when ready to use.

2 In a small sauté pan, heat 1 tablespoon of the olive oil and add the garlic. Cook it over medium-low heat, allowing it to brown but not burn. Shake the pan occasionally or stir the garlic with a spoon to keep it from burning. Add a little water if the garlic starts to brown too much. Cook the garlic until it is soft, about 15 to 20 minutes.

3 Once the garlic is soft, in a large Dutch oven over medium heat, heat the remaining olive oil and 2 tablespoons of butter and slowly brown the chicken, skin side down, until the skin is golden and crisp. Turn the breasts over and reduce the heat to medium-low.

4 Once you flip the breasts, add the garlic and olive oil sauce to the chicken pan. Add half the lemon juice, the white wine, the chicken stock, the thyme, and half the lemon zest. Bring the sauce to a simmer and cover. Continue cooking for approximately 5 to 7 minutes, or until the breasts are cooked through and tender, but not dried out. Check the chicken and sauce occasionally, stirring as needed. If the pan begins to dry, add a little water to maintain about a half inch of liquid in the pan.

5 When the chicken is cooked and its juices run clear, remove it from the pan to a warm serving platter. Keep warm. Increase the heat in the skillet until the sauce begins to boil, and then shut off the heat and add the remaining 2 tablespoons butter. Adjust the seasonings with salt, pepper, and the remaining lemon juice, if desired. Pour the sauce over the chicken.

6 Garnish with the remaining lemon zest. Remove the chicken skin before eating.

Per serving: *Kcalories 288 (From Fat 153); Fat 17g (Saturated 7g); Cholesterol 91mg; Sodium 660mg; Carbohydrate 7g (Dietary Fiber 1g); Protein 26g.*

Chicken Scampi

When we say you can enjoy good food that is good for you, this dish is an example of exactly what we mean. Food writer Heather Dismore created this dish that's delicious and lowfat. The total fat and saturated fat content are low simply because you're using skinless chicken breast — the leanest part of the chicken. The recipe calls for some butter, but just enough to enrich the flavor without significantly raising the fat content. The chicken is full of wonderful flavor from fresh herbs, lemon juice, wine, and a sprinkle of Parmesan cheese. The longer you can marinate the chicken, the more flavor it will have when done.

Preparation time: *6 to 7 hours (mostly marinating time)*

Cooking time: *20 to 30 minutes*

Yield: *4 servings*

¼ teaspoon pepper

2 cloves garlic, minced, divided

¼ teaspoon salt

2 tablespoons roughly chopped fresh oregano

¼ cup roughly chopped fresh parsley

3 tablespoons lemon juice

¼ cup white wine, divided

5 skinless, boneless chicken breast halves, 4 ounces each, cut into 1-inch strips

1 tablespoon olive oil

¼ cup chicken stock

1 tablespoon butter

½ cup Roma tomatoes, diced

Salt and pepper to taste

3 tablespoons grated Parmesan cheese

1 Combine the pepper, half the garlic, the salt, oregano, parsley, lemon juice, and half of the wine in a resealable plastic bag. Add the chicken. Mix gently to coat the chicken with the marinade. Marinate in the refrigerator for several hours (overnight is best).

2 When ready to cook the chicken, preheat the broiler, on low if your range has this setting. Remove the chicken from the marinade (save the remaining marinade) and place in a shallow pan. Broil 8 inches from the heat, turning once, until the chicken is no longer pink inside (about 15 minutes).

3 While the chicken is broiling, heat the olive oil in a sauté pan. Sauté the remaining garlic, until fragrant, but not browned. Add the remaining white wine to the sauté pan and scrape to remove any bits on the pan. Add the remaining marinade and chicken stock. Bring to a boil. Reduce the sauce by half. Stir in the butter and tomatoes. Season with salt and pepper, as needed. Pour the sauce over the chicken. Top with the Parmesan cheese.

Per serving: Kcalories 241 (From Fat 100); Fat 11g (Saturated 4g); Cholesterol 89mg; Sodium 496mg; Carbohydrate 3g (Dietary Fiber 1g); Protein 31g.

A *paillard* (pronounced *pie*-yarhd) is a fancy French word that basically means a cutlet, or a slice of meat that's been pounded to a thin, even thickness (or thinness depending on your viewpoint). Some people call it a medallion (when they're small) or scaloppine. This process has two benefits.

✔ The meat cooks evenly, because there are no thicker or thinner sections.

✔ The meat cooks fairly quickly because it's thin.

Try this handy technique for yourself by taking a look at Figure 13-1 and following the next recipe.

Figure 13-1: Pound chicken into paillards with a rolling pin or mallet.

Chicken Cutlets Pounded to an Even Thickness

Place cutlets between two pieces of plastic wrap.

whack! And pound with a mallet or the bottom of a heavy pan.

Paillard of Chicken Breast with Fennel and Parmigiano

Laura Maioglio, owner of Barbetta Restaurant in New York City (see Appendix A), has provided this wonderful dish, to be enjoyed any time of the year. However, it's perfect for the summer months, because it's a light dish with fresh ingredients, and can be cooked on the barbecue, as well. The fennel and Parmigiano cheese offer two very opposing flavors but come together with the chive and sun-dried tomato vinaigrette. The ingredients create deep layers of flavor, requiring very little added salt.

Notice that the skin has been removed prior to cooking the chicken. By searing the breasts in a hot pan, the juices become locked within the chicken's crisp coat, keeping the breast from drying out.

Preparation time: *30 minutes*

Cooking time: *30 minutes*

Yield: *4 servings*

1 bunch fresh chives	*1¼ pounds cherry tomatoes*
5 tablespoons extra-virgin olive oil, divided	*Salt and pepper*
Pinch of salt	*4 full boneless skinless chicken breasts, 6 ounces each, pounded flat*
1 bulb fennel	*3 ounces sun-dried tomatoes in olive oil, puréed*
4 cups baby arugula	
4 ounces Parmigiano, sliced paper thin	*2 lemons, halved*

1 Chop the chives. In a blender, blend the chives with 3 tablespoons of olive oil. Add the pinch of salt.

2 Slice the fennel into paper-thin slices.

3 Arrange four dinner plates with baby arugula on one side and fennel slices layered with Parmigiano slices over arugula. Halve the cherry tomatoes and place on either side of the salad.

4 Lightly sprinkle salt and pepper on both sides of the chicken breasts.

5 Warm the remaining 2 tablespoons of olive oil in a large saucepan. When the pan is very hot, place the 4 chicken breasts in the pan. Cook the breasts until they've acquired a golden color. Flip the breasts over and do the same to the other side. The breasts shouldn't cook more than 2 to 3 minutes on each side. Don't let the breasts become dry.

6 Place 1 chicken breast paillard on each plate next to the salad. Season with salt and pepper. With a spoon or squirt bottle, dribble the chive sauce and the tomatoes over and around the chicken breast paillards to create a colorful design.

7 Dress the salad plate with a drizzle of olive oil and a lemon half.

Tip: Fennel is a terrific herb you may not be familiar with. The thick bulb (sometimes called the "head") has a thick, cabbagelike texture and the rich flavor and aroma of licorice. (You can see what fennel looks like in Chapter 9.) Save the stringy tops, which resemble dill weed, for a fun and unusual garnish.

Per serving (with 2 tablespoons chive and sun-dried tomato vinaigrette): Kcalories 589 (From Fat 300); Fat 33g (Saturated 9g); Cholesterol 116mg; Sodium 904mg; Carbohydrate 24g (Dietary Fiber 7g); Protein 51g.

Marinating chicken for hours or even overnight is a great way to maximize flavor and add moisture to chicken breasts. Make up your own marinades based on what you're in the mood for. Here are some ideas to get you started.

✔ Balsamic vinegar, olive oil, and oregano

✔ Light soy sauce, lime juice, minced garlic, and minced ginger

✔ Lowfat salad dressing, like Italian or Greek vinaigrette

Include an acid of some sort in your marinade to help break down some connective tissue in the meat, making it more tender and helping it to absorb the marinade flavor more completely. Good acid choices include citrus juice and vinegar. The marinade in the following recipe features lemon juice.

Roast Free-Range Chicken Breast Stuffed with Porcini Mushrooms, Caramelized Leeks, and Pancetta

This dish is fantastic (courtesy of the Baricelli Inn in Cleveland — see Appendix A) and surprisingly simple. Although you want to keep the skin on while cooking the chicken, be sure to remove it after you sit down to eat. The skin is full of artery-clogging saturated fat. You won't even need the skin when you taste the pancetta. Pancetta is essentially Italian bacon, although it has a higher fat content and slightly saltier flavor than traditional bacon. For this reason, use it in moderation, as more of a condiment, than a main ingredient in dishes. Just a small amount can impart a delicious smoky flavor.

To create the delightful sauce, you need to rehydrate dried mushrooms. Rehydrating is easy, but remember: Always strain the liquid used to rehydrate mushrooms before adding it to any recipe. Gently pour it through a coffee filter to remove any dirt or grit.

Preparation time: *30 minutes*

Cooking time: *50 minutes*

Yield: *4 servings*

½ cup dried porcini mushrooms

2 cups warm water, divided

3 sun-dried tomatoes

4 ounces lean pancetta (approximately 8 thin slices), diced

2 tablespoons butter

1 medium leek, tough greens removed, rinsed well, diced small

4 chicken breasts, skin on, boned and tenders removed, about 6 ounces each

Salt and pepper

1 teaspoon finely chopped fresh thyme

4 cups watercress, washed

1 tablespoon extra-virgin olive oil

1 tablespoon balsamic vinegar

2 cups low-sodium chicken stock

1 Place the oven rack in the lower area of the oven. Preheat the oven to 400 degrees. Set aside a large roasting pan.

2 Place the porcini mushrooms in 1 cup of warm water. Let rest for 15 minutes. Repeat the process in a separate cup of water with the sun-dried tomatoes. Strain the porcini from the water and reserve the water. Cut the mushrooms into fine juliennes. Strain the sun-dried tomatoes from the water and discard the water. Cut the tomatoes into fine juliennes.

3 Sauté the pancetta in a pan until fat is rendered out, but not browned, 3 to 4 minutes.

4 Heat the butter in a small sauté pan over medium heat. When hot, add the leeks and cook until lightly browned, about 4½ minutes. Add the mushrooms, tomatoes, and pancetta to the sauté pan.

5 To assemble the chicken breasts, pull the skin back and season both sides with salt and pepper. Sprinkle with thyme on both sides. Spread about ½ cup of the mushroom mixture over each chicken breast. Cover with skin. Place in the reserved roasting pan. Top the chicken breasts with any additional stuffing mixture that is remaining.

6 Place in the oven and roast until browned, approximately 25 to 30 minutes. Transfer the chicken to a warm platter.

7 Toss the watercress with the olive oil and vinegar.

8 Deglaze the pan. Combine the porcini mushroom water and chicken stock in the pan used for the chicken. Simmer until reduced to ⅓ cup, about 6 to 8 minutes.

9 Serve the chicken breasts over the watercress and pour the sauce on top.

Per serving: Kcalories 527 (From Fat 266); Fat 30g (Saturated 10g); Cholesterol 145mg; Sodium 846mg; Carbohydrate 15g (Dietary Fiber 4g); Protein 50g.

Talking Turkey to Liven Up Your Meals

A standard 3½-ounce serving of white meat turkey, without the skin, has only a gram of saturated fat, which is even less than the same size serving of a chicken breast. Turkey is also a good source of B vitamins and many minerals, including iron, potassium, selenium, and zinc, especially in the dark meat.

If you buy a whole turkey, you tend to get more meat for your money by buying a larger bird. With a small bird, in the 12- to 15-pound range, much of what you get is bones, so you may be disappointed with the meager meat that results from all your hard work. If you have more leftovers than you can (or want to) eat in a couple of days, freeze the extra with a touch of chicken broth to help keep it moist.

"Rotisserie"-Roasted Turkey Breast

Rotisserie chicken is available in just about every grocery store in the country. It's a great convenience food, and a relatively healthy one as well. But if you're watching your salt intake, you may not be able to enjoy this tasty food regularly. Heather Dismore created this low-sodium version of the perennial favorite with turkey. Roast the turkey up out of its own fat (either on a rack or on foil balls) for a true "rotisserie" experience at home.

Preparation time: *20 minutes*

Cooking time: *2 hours and 15 minutes*

Yield: *Varies based on weight of turkey, 6-ounce serving size*

1 tablespoon olive oil	*4 tablespoons lemon pepper*
1 turkey breast, 6 to 7 pounds, with skin	*1 tablespoon ground sage*

1 Preheat the oven to 400 degrees. Rub the olive oil into the turkey breast. Place the turkey breast in a roasting pan with a rack. (If you don't have a rack, roll up 6 balls of foil and then place under the turkey in the roasting pan to elevate the turkey breast.) To get a rotisserie-like final product, you need to make sure the turkey doesn't sit in any fat as it cooks. Set aside.

2 In a small bowl, combine the lemon pepper and ground sage. Sprinkle the combined seasonings evenly over oiled turkey breast. Place the roasting pan in the oven. Cook for 45 minutes at 400 degrees. Then reduce the oven temperature to 300 degrees to finish cooking, approximately 1½ hours, depending on the size of your bird. Cook the turkey until it reaches an internal temperature of 165 degrees with a meat thermometer.

Tip: *Use this easy dry rub on any poultry you like. It's great with chicken, Cornish game hens, capons, and game birds.*

Per serving (with skin): *Kcalories 329 (From Fat 122); Fat 14g (Saturated 4g); Cholesterol 125mg; Sodium 589mg; Carbohydrate 1g (Dietary Fiber 0g); Protein 48g.*

Classic: Turkey Loaf with Portobello Sauce

Meatloaf is a homey food that became chic in recent years. You'll find it served in trendy gourmet restaurants, a witty addition to elaborate menus. This recipe is a dressed-up version that calls for ground turkey and is topped with fancy portobello mushrooms, those meaty giants you can find in the produce section of most supermarkets. Have this meatloaf for dinner and then in a sandwich the next day for lunch.

Preparation time: *25 minutes*

Cooking time: *60 minutes*

Yield: *4 servings*

The meatloaf:

Nonstick cooking spray

1 medium onion, minced

1 stalk celery, minced

1 pound lean ground turkey

¼ cup chopped parsley

¼ cup fine bread crumbs

¼ cup skim milk

1 egg white, lightly beaten

1 clove garlic, minced

1 teaspoon dried thyme leaves

¼ teaspoon nutmeg

¼ teaspoon pepper

The sauce:

2 teaspoons unsalted margarine (see the tip at the end of the recipe)

1 large portobello mushroom, cleaned and cut into small pieces (about 1 cup)

1 cup low-sodium chicken broth

⅛ teaspoon ground nutmeg

⅛ teaspoon pepper

⅛ teaspoon salt

1 Preheat the oven to 350 degrees.

2 For the meatloaf, coat a large skillet with cooking spray and place over medium heat until hot. Add the onion and celery. Sauté, stirring often, until translucent, about 5 minutes.

3 Meanwhile, in a large bowl, combine the turkey, parsley, bread crumbs, milk, egg white, garlic, thyme, nutmeg, and pepper. Add the onion and celery and mix well.

4 Form into a loaf and place in a well-coated loaf pan. Bake 50 minutes or until the internal temperature is 165 degrees.

5 For the sauce, melt the margarine in a saucepan placed over medium heat. Add the mushrooms. Sauté, stirring, until tender.

6 Remove from the heat. Add the chicken broth, nutmeg, pepper, and salt. Return to heat. Cook until fragrant and slightly thickened, 5 minutes.

7 When the meatloaf is cooked, unmold, slice, and place portions on warmed dinner plates.

8 Ladle mushroom sauce over sliced turkey loaf.

Tip: *Look for brands of margarine that aren't made with hydrogenated oils, which contain trans fatty acids.*

Tip: *Ground turkey is a great substitute for ground beef. Choose ground turkey without skin, for the greatest savings in the saturated fat department. Use ground turkey anywhere you'd use beef, such as pasta sauce, burgers, or casseroles.*

Per serving: Kcalories 203 (From Fat 32); Fat 4g (Saturated 1g); Cholesterol 76mg; Sodium 243mg; Carbohydrate 11g (Dietary Fiber 2g); Protein 31g.

Chapter 14

Creating Balanced Meals with Meats

*P*rotein is an ideal food for people with diabetes because it contains only minimal carbohydrate and, consequently, it doesn't raise blood glucose levels significantly under normal circumstances. Every time you eat, you need to be sure to include some protein to balance the fat and carbohydrate in your diet. Meals that contain protein, as well as fat and starch, help stabilize blood glucose and can give you a more consistent supply of energy.

Your body uses protein to build and repair tissues. Meat is an excellent source of protein for this purpose because it contains all nine *essential* amino acids, those that must be obtained through diet. Meat is also a source of B vitamins and many minerals needed for good health. In particular, it is an excellent source of vitamin B12, essential for normal functioning of the nervous system, and iron for transporting oxygen to the cells.

In this chapter, we show you three great techniques for cooking meats to fit in with a diabetic diet: searing, braising, and roasting. We give you great recipes for each technique and other tips along the way.

Always cook meats to a safe temperature for appropriate degree of doneness. See Table 14-1 to find out what temperature to cook the meat of your choice.

Table 14-1	Safe Cooking Temperatures for Meats
Product	*Temperature (in degrees)*
Ground veal, beef, lamb, pork	160
Beef, medium rare	145
Beef, medium	160
Beef, well done	170
Veal, medium rare	145
Veal, medium	160
Veal, well done	170
Lamb, medium rare	145
Lamb, medium	160
Lamb, well done	170
Pork, medium rare	145
Pork, medium	160
Pork, well done	170
Ham, fresh (raw)	160
Ham, precooked (to reheat)	140

Searing Meats for Culinary Success

A cooking technique called searing is particularly helpful for keeping meat as lowfat and delicious as possible. *Searing* subjects meat to extremely high heat on the stovetop for a short period of time. Usually you sear one side and then the other. The technique produces a beautifully caramelized skin on the meat and essentially seals in its juices. This process helps to retain the moisture content of the meat and therefore much of the flavor.

Veal tenderloin is a healthy option compared with many other cuts of meat that can be quite high in saturated fat and cholesterol. Because it's naturally low in fat, cook veal quickly at high temperatures to keep as many of the natural juices as possible. Searing veal is a great choice.

Veal Tenderloin with Chanterelle Mushrooms in a Muscat Veal Reduction Sauce

A *medallion* is a small, coin-shaped piece of meat. Medallions are very thin, so once you sear them, you don't need to finish them in the oven. With just a short searing time, you'll create perfectly tender slices of veal. Serve this terrific recipe, from Baricelli Inn in Cleveland (see Appendix A), with cavatelli pasta and the Haricot Vert from Chapter 11, also contributed by the Baricelli Inn.

Preparation time: *15 minutes*

Cooking time: *15 minutes*

Yield: *4 servings*

1 tablespoon cracked black pepper (plus more to taste)

4 veal tenderloin medallions, approximately 6 ounces each (silver skin removed), pounded thin (check out Chapter 13 for details on pounding meat into cutlets)

½ cup flour

2 tablespoons extra-virgin olive oil

4 ounces wild mushrooms (chanterelle if available)

2 ounces Muscat wine

Salt to taste

6 ounces veal reduction sauce (reduced veal stock, also known as demi-glace)

1 Press ½ teaspoon black pepper into each veal medallion and dredge in the flour.

2 Heat a medium sauté pan over high heat. Add olive oil; sear the medallions on both sides (about 4 minutes on each side). Remove the medallions and set aside.

3 To the same sauté pan, add the mushrooms, Muscat, salt, remaining 1 teaspoon pepper, and veal stock and cook for 2 minutes over high heat. Adjust salt and pepper to taste. Pour the mixture over the veal slices.

Tip: *If you can't find veal reduction sauce in your grocery store, check online or at Williams-Sonoma.*

Per serving: *Kcalories 424 (From Fat 217); Fat 24g (Saturated 8g); Cholesterol 111mg; Sodium 471mg; Carbohydrate 18g (Dietary Fiber 1g); Protein 32g.*

If you sear a thicker piece of meat like a chop or even a roast, quickly sear the outside and then *finish* the meat in the oven. Searing seals in the natural juices, and roasting finishes the cooking process to desired perfection. Check out Table 14-1, earlier in this chapter, for tips on choosing the right temperature for your taste and your cut of meat.

Pan-Roasted Veal Chops with Corn and Gouda Ragout

Chef Kevin Rathbun of Rathbun's in Atlanta (see Appendix A) offers another dish bursting with flavor that won't break the day's calorie bank. The original recipe contains a bit more salt than we can recommend, so we made some minor modifications. But don't worry. You won't miss a thing — the dish remains full of other herbs and ingredients that offer intense flavors and great taste.

A *ragout* (pronounced ra-goo) is a thick, flavorful stewlike concoction that usually features meat and sometimes features vegetables. In this recipe, pan-roasted corn is paired with creamy Gouda cheese. It's great with the delicate veal medallions.

Preparation time: *1 hour and 15 minutes*

Cooking time: *45 minutes*

Yield: *4 servings*

Steak seasoning:

1 teaspoon kosher salt

1 tablespoon cracked black pepper

1 tablespoon minced garlic

1 tablespoon chopped fresh sage

Corn ragout:

2 cups yellow corn kernels, fresh or frozen

½ tablespoon minced garlic

1 cup milk

1 tablespoon chopped scallions

½ teaspoon pepper

Salt and pepper

¼ cup grated Gouda cheese

Veal chops:

4 veal chops, 7 ounces each

2 tablespoons steak seasoning (see Step 1)

2 tablespoons olive oil

1 To prepare the steak seasoning, preheat the oven to 250 degrees. Place the salt, pepper, garlic, and sage into a food processor and process 15 seconds. Transfer to an oven-safe dish and place in the oven for 30 minutes. After the garlic dries out, transfer back to the food processor and process 15 seconds. Set the seasoning aside. Increase the oven temperature to 400 degrees.

2 To make the ragout: Heat a cast-iron skillet over high heat, at least 5 to 6 minutes. Add the corn and continue to cook until it becomes charred, approximately 8 to 10 minutes. Add the garlic, milk, scallions, and pepper. Cook for 2 minutes. Salt and pepper to taste. Reserve.

3 Heat a large ovenproof sauté pan over high heat. Season the veal chops with the pre-pared steak seasoning. Add the olive oil to the heated skillet. Sear the chops in the olive oil until golden brown on both sides, approximately 4 minutes per side. Transfer to the 400-degree oven and roast until desired doneness. Check out Table 14-1 to find the right temperature for you and test your chops with a meat thermometer.

4 When ready to serve, place the corn ragout on plates and sprinkle the Gouda cheese over the corn. Place the veal chops on top of the corn and serve.

Per serving: Kcalories 351 (From Fat 162); Fat 18g (Saturated 5g); Cholesterol 104mg; Sodium 764mg; Carbohydrate 19g (Dietary Fiber 3g); Protein 30g.

Understanding the Basics of Braising

Braising is a terrific cooking method for meats, vegetables, and anything else you want to make tender and tasty. Basically, *braising* involves cooking a cut of meat in a small amount of liquid. The meat gently cooks and steams, or *braises,* at the same time. Braising is particularly effective for less expensive cuts of meat, because you cook it slowly and break down the tougher muscle over time.

Braising is also a great cooking method because it requires very little use of added fats, such as butter and oil. You can braise foods either in the oven or in a pot on the stove. Try it out with the following great recipe.

Beer-Braised Pork and Crisp-Herb Cabbage with Apple-Tarragon Dipping Sauce

Chef Tom Wolfe, from Peristyle in New Orleans (see Appendix A), has developed this diabetic-friendly dish (shown in the color section). Pork comes from a pig, so it must be high in fat, right? Well actually, that's only half true. In recent years, pork has gained attention as "the other white meat." As it turns out, the fat content of pork depends on the cut of the meat. The rump and rib roast, for example, are much higher in fat and cholesterol than the pork tenderloin, boneless sirloin chops, or boneless loin roasts. In this dish, try to use a lean cut of pork, such as the tenderloin, which is a naturally tender cut of meat and will remain moist from the slow-cook method of braising.

Preparation time: *1 hour and 45 minutes*

Cooking time: *1 hour*

Yield: *6 servings*

¼ teaspoon kosher salt	1 tablespoon melted butter
¼ tablespoon black pepper	2¼ cups amber beer
4 tablespoons low-sodium soy sauce	2½ tablespoons canola oil
2 tablespoons minced shallots	1 pound pork tenderloin sliced into 12 1-inch medallions
1 tablespoon chopped garlic	
1 tablespoon Dijon mustard	1 red pepper, julienned

1 Combine the kosher salt, pepper, soy sauce, shallots, garlic, mustard, butter, and beer. Marinate the pork in this mixture in a resealable plastic bag in the refrigerator for 30 to 60 minutes prior to cooking.

2 Heat the oil in a medium-hot large sauté pan. Add the pork medallions, reserving the marinade, and cook until golden brown, about 3 to 4 minutes on each side.

3 Reduce the heat to medium-low and add the reserved marinade and the red pepper. Simmer on low, uncovered, for 25 to 30 minutes. Sauce should be reduced by one-half.

4 To serve, place the cabbage (see the next recipe) on a warm plate. Place 2 pork medallions next to the mound of cabbage. Pour the dipping sauce (see the accompanying recipe) into a ramekin and place it next to the pork and cabbage.

Crisp-Herb Cabbage

1 head cabbage, thinly shredded

1 medium red onion, julienned

½ tablespoon chopped garlic (about 2 cloves)

½ cup chopped parsley

¼ cup chopped fresh basil

1½ teaspoons chopped fresh thyme

½ cup rice vinegar (seasoned)

¼ cup white vinegar

1 tablespoon kosher salt

½ tablespoon crushed red pepper flakes

2 packets Splenda

½ teaspoon allspice

½ teaspoon ground coriander

Juice from 2 lemons

1 Combine the cabbage, onion, garlic, parsley, basil, and thyme in a large mixing bowl.

2 Combine the rice vinegar and white vinegar in a small bowl. Add to the cabbage mixture.

3 Add the salt, red pepper flakes, Splenda, allspice, coriander, and lemon juice to the bowl and mix ingredients well.

4 Let stand at room temperature 45 minutes while getting the other ingredients together.

Apple-Tarragon Dipping Sauce

1 cup water

½ cup rice vinegar

Juice of 1 lemon

2 peeled and diced Granny Smith apples

1 teaspoon chopped garlic

1 bay leaf

¼ teaspoon ground cinnamon

¼ teaspoon ground allspice

½ teaspoon crushed red pepper flakes

1 tablespoon chopped tarragon

Combine all the dipping sauce ingredients in a medium saucepan and bring to a boil. Simmer 20 to 25 minutes, until the apples are tender. Remove the bay leaf. Purée in a food processor until smooth, approximately 3 to 4 minutes.

Per serving (pork, cabbage, and dipping sauce): Kcalories 284 (From Fat 103); Fat 12g (Saturated 3g); Cholesterol 47mg; Sodium 1,946mg; Carbohydrate 29g (Dietary Fiber 6g); Protein 19g.

Recommending Roasting

Roasting is a simple technique that requires little effort. Season meat with herbs and spices and cook it in the oven until it reaches a desired degree of doneness. You just need to ensure that the meat doesn't dry out, a possibility with this dry-heat method of cooking. Here are some suggestions:

- ✔ Slow-roast meat at a low temperature, 350 degrees and below.

- ✔ Wrap meat in foil for most of the cooking time and remove only for the last half hour of cooking — to allow the meat to brown.

- ✔ Cook roasts with the bone still attached, when possible, because the meat cooks faster and has more flavor that way.

Try roasting lamb with the next recipe. Leave the bones on the chops for quicker cooking and a beautiful presentation.

Roasted Lamb Sirloin with Herbes de Provence, Spinach, and Onion Ragout with Lamb Au Jus

Herbes de Provence is simply a mix of herbs commonly used in southern French cooking. They happen to go wonderfully well with this lamb dish, by Chef Didier Labbe from the Clementine restaurant in San Francisco (see Appendix A). Lamb is typically one of those meats with more fat, so do your best to choose a leaner cut, like the sirloin. Choose cuts with the least amount of white marbling, (or fat) within the meat and, as with all meat dishes, remember to trim excess fat whenever possible!

The ragout contributes a wonderful flavor to the lamb and spinach, and the only ingredient is onion! Be creative with your blender — you can make many wonderful, flavorful sauces and spreads by using just a single fruit or vegetable.

Preparation time: *45 minutes*

Cooking time: *1 hour*

Yield: *4 servings*

4 lamb sirloin chops, 6 ounces each	2 cups water
2 tablespoons Dijon mustard	1 bunch spinach
¼ cup herbes de Provence	½ cup port wine
Salt and pepper	1 tablespoon chopped garlic
2 tablespoons olive oil, divided	2 tablespoons butter
3 white onions, sliced	

1 Preheat the oven to 400 degrees.

2 Place the lamb sirloin chops in a roasting pan. Spread the Dijon mustard evenly over the lamb chops. Sprinkle on herbes de Provence and lightly salt and pepper. Drizzle lightly with 1 tablespoon of the olive oil and roast 15 minutes. Reduce the heat to 325 degrees and continue roasting until the chops are medium rare (light pink inside), or when a meat thermometer inserted in the center of a chop reaches 145 degrees.

3 While the chops are cooking, combine the onions and water in a large sauté pan or 3-quart saucepan. Cover and simmer until the onions become soft. Remove the onions from the pan and process them in a food processor until they're smooth.

4 In the same sauté pan, heat the remaining olive oil. Add the spinach. Cover and cook the spinach for about 3 to 4 minutes. Fold the onion purée into the spinach, season it lightly with salt and pepper, and set it aside, but keep warm.

5 Remove the chops from the roasting pan to another dish and cover them with foil to keep them warm.

6 Place the baking pan on the stove. On low heat, deglaze the pan by adding the port wine, garlic, and butter. Reduce the mixture by one-fourth.

7 To serve, place the spinach mixture in the middle of each plate. Place one lamb chop on top of the spinach and pour the port wine sauce over it.

Per serving: Kcalories 281 (From Fat 124); Fat 14g (Saturated 6g); Cholesterol 84mg; Sodium 460mg; Carbohydrate 15g (Dietary Fiber 6g); Protein 26g.

Chapter 15

Having a Little Bite with Snacks

In This Chapter

▶ Looking at handy snack options

▶ Using dips and sauces in snacks

▶ Munching on mini-meals

How many times have you heard, "It's all about portion control"? Well, in this case, the conventional wisdom is true. If your blood glucose levels benefit from a steady stream of food, portion control and snacking are your new best friends. Consider a snack before or after a workout to give you an energy boost. Plan on having a light bite between lunch and dinner. Just keep track of it all and make sure your eating plan is well rounded.

Any food that's part of your healthy daily regimen can be a good snack choice, especially in the right portion sizes. Here's a list of good snack choices for diabetics:

✔ A piece of string cheese and 4 whole-wheat crackers

✔ 8 dried apricot halves

✔ ¾ cup oatmeal (not the sugary just-add-water variety)

✔ Handful of roasted soy nuts

✔ 6 smoked almonds

✔ ½ cup tuna, light mayo, and dill pickle relish

✔ 6 ounces vegetable juice

✔ ½ cup cottage cheese

Watch out for snacks from vending machines and prepackaged foods like pudding cups, instant flavored oatmeal, and toaster pastries. Although they can be convenient, they can also be loaded with sugar, salt, and fat. Read your labels carefully before making your food choices. For more on reading food nutrition labels as a diabetic, check out Chapter 5.

In this chapter, we show you how to stock up on handy snacks, supplement snacks with dips and sauces, and whip up light and easy mini-meals.

Keeping Healthy Snacks at the Ready

Many people grab whatever they can find for a quick snack because they're incredibly hungry. It's easy to reach for a bag of chips, a candy bar, or a soda if they're handy. Instead of keeping these convenient, high-fat, high-sodium, high-sugar foods handy, stock your fridge, freezer, and pantry with healthy snacks that can satisfy you and keep you eating on your plan. For example, you can make snack-size servings of cut-up fresh veggies, ready and waiting in the fridge.

For a special beverage treat, keep some sugar-free drink mix single-serving tubes handy. Just add their contents to your water bottle for an instant treat.

Mixing it up with whole grains

Stock your pantry today with healthy whole-grain snacks like GORP. Here we include whole grains, nuts, and dried fruit for a good all-around snack choice. Feel free to substitute your favorite fruits and nuts as you experiment with this tasty treat.

Tante Marie's Muesli

You might be familiar with the commercially prepared boxed version of this healthy treat. The retail version is often packed with extra refined sugar that is not part of a diabetic diet. Tante Marie's Cooking School in San Francisco (www.tantemarie.com) shows you how you can make your own that tastes better and is much more diabetic-friendly.

If you prefer your oats toasted, place the rolled oats on a baking sheet in an oven preheated to 350 degrees for about 15 minutes, stirring from time to time. You can substitute rolled wheat and/or rye flakes for oats. Muesli can be served softened with yogurt and served with fresh fruit as they do in Switzerland, or served with milk.

Preparation time: *10 minutes*

Yield: *6 servings*

3 cups rolled oats (regular, not instant)

½ cup bran

½ cup wheat germ

1 cup raisins

1 cup chopped dried apples

½ cup toasted hazelnuts and/or almonds (no salt added)

2 tablespooons brown sugar (not packed)

1 Place all the ingredients in a large bowl, and mix well.

2 Store in an airtight container in your pantry for up to one week.

Per serving: Kcalories 387 (Calories from Fat 87); Fat 10g (Saturated 1g); Cholesterol 0mg; Sodium 23 mg; Carbohydrate 69g (Dietary Fiber 12g); Protein 12g.

Why should you choose whole-grain snacks?

If you can have 6 saltines or 4 whole-wheat crackers and you're really hungry, which should you choose? At first glance, the answer may seem obvious. Choose the saltines because you get 6 (compared to the 4 whole wheat crackers). But believe it or not, 4 whole-wheat crackers will keep you fuller, longer. The whole grain is the key. Your body works harder and longer to digest the whole-wheat crackers.

With saltine crackers, the flour manufacturer has done much of the work for you by refining the flour, removing most of the fiber and nutrients. By making your body work for its nutrition, you help it work more efficiently, in turn helping you to stabilize your blood glucose levels. For more about adding grains to your diet, check out Chapter 10.

Filling your freezer with treats

Some people just can't seem to stay away from the snacks after dinner, especially the sweet ones. Maybe you just want something simple like a bowl of ice cream or a more elegant chocolate mousse or cheesecake. Instead, consider stocking your freezer with the following healthy, quick-grab snacks.

- ✔ **Flavored ice cubes:** Fill ice cube trays with your favorite sugar-free drinks, like any flavor of Crystal Light. Freeze until frozen and then transfer the individual ice cubes to a resealable plastic bag. Add a few lemonade ice cubes to your next glass of strawberry kiwi beverage. Experiment with flavors you like.

- ✔ **Grapes:** Clean the grapes and remove them from their stems. Place individual grapes on a clean baking sheet in the freezer. When the grapes are frozen, transfer them to a resealable plastic bag. Grab a few when your sweet tooth attacks.

- ✔ **Sugar-free frozen pops:** Many manufacturers are making freezer pops from 100 percent juice or sweetening them with sugar substitutes.

- ✔ **Yogurt tubes:** Squeezable yogurt tubes can make a terrific quick snack. Toss a few in the freezer for an extra creamy frozen treat.

This type of yogurt can have added sugar, so read your labels carefully to make sure you know what you're eating, and confirm that it fits with your eating goals.

Choosing kid-friendly snacks

Many children are afflicted by diabetes. Often, their parents and other caregivers need to learn about the disease from scratch. Check out Chapter 22 for more tips on helping kids cope with diabetes. Also, check out *Diabetes For Dummies,* 2nd edition, written by Alan Rubin, MD, and published by Wiley, for more great kid-friendly tips.

Here's a list of snacks designed with diabetic kids in mind. Teach kids how to snack well early in life, and they'll be better equipped to deal with diabetes as they grow.

- Snack-sized bag of light microwave popcorn

- Whole-wheat pretzels with mustard

- Cup of lowfat yogurt

- Sugar-free gelatin cup

- Lunchmeat rollup

- An apple with a small dollop of peanut butter

- Celery sticks dipped in lowfat ranch dressing

- Turkey hot dog

- ½ cup cottage cheese

- 1 ounce part-skim string cheese

- ¼ cup roasted peanuts

Adding Dips and Sauces to Snacks

Condiments are typically used to flavor or complement other foods. But some condiments are so delicious and craveable that you may want to eat them all by themselves. *Condiment* may be a bit of an understatement for the tasty recipes in this section. They can both be terrific spreads for sandwiches or lettuce wraps. Use them as sauces to top grilled chicken or firm fish.

Dips are a creative way to get in lots of vegetables. Unfortunately, most dips tend to be very high in calories and fat. What is considered a light snack can quickly turn into a full meal's worth of calories and fat. So skip the fat and keep the flavor with this excellent vegetable dip. (Check out Chapter 7 for more dips to try.)

Roasted Veggie Dip

This dip from Heather Dismore is an excellent appetizer, food topper, condiment, or omelet filling — you name it, it can work. The roasting of the vegetables brings out their natural sugars, and the spices give it a kick. Snack on this no-fat dip with whole-wheat crackers or check out our list of approved dippers in Chapter 7.

Preparation time: *20 minutes*

Cooking time: *35 minutes*

Yield: *6 servings*

½ eggplant, peeled, thick sliced	Nonstick cooking spray
1 zucchini, thick sliced	½ teaspoon cayenne pepper
1 yellow squash, thick sliced	1 teaspoon seasoning salt
½ red onion, thick sliced	1 teaspoon chili powder
4 cloves garlic, roughly chopped	Salt and pepper

1 Preheat the oven to 400 degrees. Spray the eggplant, zucchini, squash, onion, and garlic with the cooking spray, coating well.

2 In a small bowl, combine the cayenne pepper, seasoning salt, and chili powder. Add one-fourth of the seasoning to the vegetables. Toss well to combine. Add another one-fourth of the seasoning and toss well. Repeat until the vegetables are evenly coated and all the seasoning is added. Adding the seasonings in stages helps combine the seasonings evenly.

3 Spray a baking pan with the cooking spray. Add the vegetables in a single layer. Cook vegetables in the oven, until browned, stirring occasionally, roughly 35 minutes.

4 Place the roasted veggies in the bowl of a food processor. Process to desired consistency. Season with salt and pepper as necessary.

Per serving: *Kcalories 32 (From Fat 3); Fat 0g (Saturated 0g); Cholesterol 0mg; Sodium 257mg; Carbohydrate 7g (Dietary Fiber 3g); Protein 2g.*

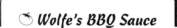

⏱ Wolfe's BBQ Sauce

Chef Tom Wolfe, from Peristyle in New Orleans (see Appendix A), has let you in on the secret of his famous barbecue sauce — and it is good! You might have perused the nutrition labels of some of your favorite sauces before and noticed just how high the sugar content can really be. A great substitution that Chef Tom made here was to use sugar-free syrup instead of the usual version, which, you may have guessed, is entirely sugar. This is a good reminder to make substitutions like this whenever you can. Save your blood sugars without sacrificing your favorite foods. This sauce (in the color section) is approved for dipping grilled chicken and veggies, slathering on a hunk of firm fish, or topping a pita for an impromptu barbecue chicken pizza. But definitely try it with the Barbecue Chicken Potato Hash in Chapter 13.

Preparation time: *10 minutes*

Cooking time: *15 minutes*

Yield: *8 servings*

1½ cups ketchup	*1 teaspoon chili powder*
1 cup light pancake syrup	*1 teaspoon onion powder*
1½ tablespoons low-sodium soy sauce	*1 teaspoon fresh chopped garlic*
1½ tablespoons Worcestershire sauce	*1 teaspoon pepper*
¾ tablespoon sesame oil	*½ teaspoon salt*
1 teaspoon minced ginger	

Place all ingredients in a nonmetallic saucepan on low. Warm the sauce for 10 minutes, stirring occasionally. For thicker sauce, continue to cook for 2 to 3 more minutes. Remove from the heat and cool.

Per serving: *Kcalories 131 (From Fat 29); Fat 3g (Saturated 1g); Cholesterol 0mg; Sodium 872mg; Carbohydrate 26g (Dietary Fiber 1g); Protein 1g.*

Preparing Mini-Meals

Eating small portions of well-balanced meals can be a great way to fit a nutritious and filling snack into your day. Maybe you ate a light brunch and are waiting for a late dinner. Maybe you had a really early breakfast and can't fit a full lunch in until late in the day. Or maybe you just find it easier to maintain even blood sugar levels by eating five or six small meals each day. Whatever the reason, mini-meals can help you eat right.

Choosing chicken

For diabetics, chicken is a great basis for a mini-meal because it provides protein that is slowly changed to sugar in your body. Try the following two recipes to enjoy a taste of chicken.

Greek-Style Chicken Wraps

These wraps are quick and easy. They might remind you of a Greek gyro sandwich, but they're lower in fat because we use boneless skinless chicken breast in our version. Experiment with different herbs, like basil, and cheeses, like feta, to find the flavor combinations you like. Also, keep this chicken ready and in the freezer for emergency snacking. It's great to toss with salad greens, chop into a quick casserole, or make these wraps in minutes.

Preparation time: *20 minutes*

Cooking time: *25 minutes*

Yield: *2 servings*

Nonstick cooking spray

2 boneless, skinless chicken breasts, 4 ounces each, pounded thin

1 tablespoon lemon juice

1 teaspoon oregano, crushed and dried

2 thin slices Vidalia onion

2 whole-wheat tortillas, 10-inch variety

¼ cup lowfat plain yogurt

¼ cup peeled, seeded, and chopped cucumber

¼ cup crumbled feta cheese

1 teaspoon chopped fresh mint

1 Preheat the oven to 350 degrees. Coat an 8 x 8 inch baking dish with nonstick cooking spray. Brush the chicken breast on both sides with lemon juice and oregano. Place the chicken breast and onion in the baking dish. Bake for approximately 25 minutes.

2 When the chicken is done, transfer to a cutting board and cut into ½-inch strips.

3 Spread out the tortillas on a flat surface. Spread equal parts of yogurt on top of the tortillas. Top with equal parts chicken, onion, cucumber, cheese, and mint.

4 Roll up the wraps and serve warm.

Per serving: *Kcalories 372 (From Fat 97); Fat 11g (Saturated 4g); Cholesterol 81mg; Sodium 767mg; Carbohydrate 36g (Dietary Fiber 7g); Protein 33g.*

Quick Chicken Tostadas

Mexican food is often considered to be pretty high in fat and cholesterol, but it doesn't have to be. In fact, common ingredients in Mexican cooking, such as beans, chicken, olives, and tomatoes, are very healthy. Not so good, on the other hand, are fried tortillas, extra cheese, and high-fat sour cream. If you have a craving for nachos or quesadillas, traditionally very high in calories and saturated fat, try these light tostadas instead, courtesy of Heather Dismore. They're full of flavor and incorporate traditional Mexican ingredients but have half the calories and fat. When preparing tacos or other Mexican-style dishes at home, be sparing with the toppings (cheese, sour cream, and guacamole), which contribute the most significant amount of calories and fat.

Preparation time: *20 minutes*

Cooking time: *10 minutes*

Yield: *6 servings*

6 whole-wheat flour tortillas	*Salt and pepper*
Nonstick cooking spray	*1 cup shredded cheddar cheese*
¾ pound cooked chicken (see the tip at the end of the recipe)	*1 tablespoon minced cilantro or green onions (optional)*
¾ cup salsa	*2 tablespoons minced black olives (optional)*
¼ teaspoon cayenne pepper	*6 tablespoons lowfat sour cream (optional)*
¼ teaspoon chili powder	*3 tablespoons prepared guacamole (optional)*
1 cup diced red pepper	

1 Preheat the oven to 400 degrees. Spray each tortilla lightly with cooking spray. Place prepared tortillas on a baking sheet and place in the oven. Toast the tortillas until crisp, approximately 2 to 3 minutes. Remove from the oven and set aside. Reduce the oven temperature to 375 degrees.

2 Mix the chicken, salsa, cayenne pepper, chili powder, red pepper, and salt and pepper to taste together in a mixing bowl. Top each tostada with one-sixth of the chicken mixture.

3 For each tostada, top the chicken mixture with one-sixth of the cheddar cheese. Return the tostadas to the oven. Cook until the chicken is heated through and the cheese is melted, approximately 5 to 7 minutes.

4 If desired, top each tostada with ½ teaspoon cilantro or green onions, 1 tablespoon sour cream, and 1 teaspoon black olives.

Tip: For this recipe, you can purchase roasted chicken breast, or you can cook the chicken breast yourself by poaching it, which means cooking it in water just below the boiling point until it is cooked through (no longer pink inside).

Per serving: Kcalories 316 (From Fat 121); Fat 13g (Saturated 5g); Cholesterol 68mg; Sodium 668mg; Carbohydrate 31g (Dietary Fiber 2g); Protein 29g.

Selecting seafood

Seafood, tuna in particular, is a great item for a diabetic to choose as a mini-meal because, like chicken, it's mostly protein and does not raise your sugar rapidly. The following dish is easy to reduce to a snack size portion: Eat only one skewer full of tasty goodness, and you cut the kilocalories (and the other nutritional analysis) in half. Enjoy!

Tuna Dijon Brochettes

Tuna isn't just for salad anymore. Fresh tuna has a beautiful ruby red color, a firm texture, and a meaty flavor. It goes well with spicy sauces and spices, like Dijon mustard. With sweet pineapple and mild veggies, you get a full flavor experience.

Special tools: *2 metal skewers, 8 inches long*

Preparation time: *25 minutes*

Cooking time: *6 to 8 minutes*

Yield: *1 serving*

8 ounces tuna, fresh, cut into 6 equal chunks

1 tablespoon Dijon mustard

4 mushrooms

4 squares red pepper, 1 inch each

4 slices zucchini, ¼-inch thick

4 chunks fresh, peeled pineapple, 1 inch each

4 medium cherry tomatoes

Salt and pepper

Nonstick cooking spray

1 Preheat the broiler. In a bowl, coat the tuna chunks with the mustard.

2 Skewer the tuna, mushrooms, peppers, zucchini, pineapple, and cherry tomatoes, alternating each item twice, beginning and ending with a tuna chunk.

3 Sprinkle each skewer with salt and pepper to taste. Coat a baking sheet with the cooking spray and place the skewers on the baking sheet. Broil for 6 to 8 minutes.

Per serving: Kcalories 351 (From Fat 40); Fat 4g (Saturated 1g); Cholesterol 98mg; Sodium 762mg; Carbohydrate 23g (Dietary Fiber 5g); Protein 56g.

Stocking your snack drawer at work

Getting through the workday and avoiding food pitfalls can be challenging for anyone, particularly so for the diabetic. The best defense against the shared snacks of coffeecakes, muffins, bagels, and doughnuts near the coffee station is a good offense. Keep a healthy snack drawer at work for snacking emergencies, and you're sure to save yourself some calories and blood sugar spikes and dips. And remember: A well-stocked snack drawer can be a lifesaver on early days when you don't have time to eat breakfast before heading for work.

Here are some ideas for a diabetic's snack drawer:

✔ Light popcorn in snack-sized microwaveable bags

✔ Individual servings of nuts

✔ Lowfat and low-sodium canned soups

✔ Fat-free, sugar-free gelatin and pudding

✔ Low-sugar protein bars

✔ Canned nutritional supplement drinks, like Glucerna or Ensure

✔ Individual servings of sugar-free drink mixes

✔ Individual cans of low-sodium vegetable juice

✔ No-sugar-added juice boxes or bottles

When possible, choose individual serving sizes. They're proportioned to take the brainwork out of grabbing a quick snack when you're starved. Plus, keeping track of how much you eat is much easier when the nutritional information is on each snack.

Picking pasta

Indulge in your cravings for Italian food with this version of the traditional potato pasta, gnocchi. Potatoes, or pasta for that matter, may be tough to work into your eating plan, but if you love Italian food, you don't have to give it up completely. In addition to this great flour-free option, check out zucchini and cucumber linguine with clams found in Chapter 11. You get all the Italian flavor without any traditional pasta and the costly carbs.

⟲ *Spinach-Ricotta Gnocchi*

Here's a great twist on the traditional gnocchi, or potato pasta. Chef Christopher Fernandez at Poggio in Sausalito, California (see Appendix A), has creatively substituted the white flour base to this usually high-carbohydrate food for ricotta cheese, a signifi- cant source of protein. In doing so, the gnocchi will have far less of an effect on your blood sugars and allow you to once again eat what you might have once considered sinful! Enjoy this with your favorite red Italian pasta sauce.

Special tools: *Cheesecloth, pastry bag*

Preparation time: *1 hour*

Cooking time: *4 to 5 minutes*

Yield: *4 servings*

½ pound part-skim ricotta cheese	*Pinch ground nutmeg*
1 gallon water	*Salt to taste*
¼ pound fresh spinach	*2 tablespoons potato starch*
1 cup grated Parmesan cheese	*1 tablespoon dehydrated potato flakes*
1 egg, beaten	*2 tablespoons plus 2 cups flour*

1 Place the ricotta in a strainer lined with cheesecloth and let sit overnight in the refriger- ator to remove excess liquid.

2 Bring the 1 gallon of water to a boil, add the spinach, and boil for 30 seconds. Strain the spinach and place the spinach on a baking sheet lined with parchment paper. Place the spinach in the refrigerator to cool. Once cooled, squeeze out all the excess water from the spinach. Chop the spinach as fine as you can on a cutting board. This may take some time, but the finer the better.

3 To make the gnocchi, place the chopped spinach, ricotta, Parmesan cheese, egg, nutmeg, and a pinch of salt into a large mixing bowl. Mix until the spinach has been evenly distributed, and add the potato starch, dehydrated potato, and 2 tablespoons of the flour to bind the mixture. Bring a small pot of water to a boil and drop a spoon-sized piece of gnocchi to test the consistency and flavor. If the gnocchi is too wet and falls apart, add another egg and some flour. The key to this gnocchi is to add the minimum amount of binder so that the gnocchi are as light as possible.

4 Place a 6-quart pot on the stove with plenty of salted water to boil the gnocchi. Bring the water to a boil and turn down until you're ready to cook the gnocchi.

5 Place the remaining 2 cups of flour in a long baking pan. Shake the flour evenly around in the pan. Place the gnocchi mixture into a pastry bag with a large straight tip about ½ inch in diameter. Pipe the gnocchi mixture in a long line directly into the flour, as if you were making a long snakelike piece. You can make a couple of lines like this in the flour.

6 With a knife, cut the snakelike pieces into 1-inch pieces. With your hands, gently cover the gnocchi lightly with flour, shake off any excess flour, and place directly into boiling salt water. Cook the gnocchi for at least 5 minutes or until they float for 2 minutes. Remove from the water.

Tip: You can serve these immediately or hold them for later use. If you plan to hold the gnocchi, place the cooked gnocchi onto a lightly oiled sheet pan and place in the refrigerator. Once cooled, you can place the gnocchi in an airtight container until ready to use. You can reheat the gnocchi in boiling water for 4 to 5 minutes.

Per serving: Kcalories 282 (From Fat 109); Fat 12g (Saturated 7g); Cholesterol 86mg; Sodium 628mg; Carbohydrate 24g (Dietary Fiber 1g); Protein 19g.

Chapter 16

Smart Ways to Include Dessert in a Diabetic Diet

Sugar is not a dirty word, even for a diabetic. But it's no secret that the amount of sugar consumed by Americans today is out of control. Manufacturers sneak it into all kinds of products, including prepackaged rice pilaf mix, ketchup, and, of course, baked goods, under the names *high-fructose corn syrup* and *malt syrup*. Even though diabetes is a disease that involves impaired metabolism of carbohydrates, you can still enjoy desserts that contain starches and sugar. You just need to select your ingredients wisely and eat reasonably modest portions. But don't waste time feeling guilty because you can't stay away from sweets. Sweet is one of the basic tastes, just like sour and salty, and craving sweet foods is normal.

Of course, people crave sweets such as cookies, jelly doughnuts, pies, and candy made with refined white flour and white sugar, which provide little nutrition. Enriched white flour has had a significant portion of the nutrients in the original whole grain removed, and white sugar contains no vitamins or minerals at all.

In this chapter, we show you how to create appealing desserts that feature nutritious ingredients. We help you satisfy your cravings for sweet foods, including chocolate. We introduce a healthful sweetener, agave nectar, to flavor desserts the right way. And we give you a host of different presentations to impress your guests.

Finding a New Take on Fruit

Diabetic desserts have long consisted of sugar-free gelatin and fruit. There's certainly nothing wrong with that, but if you're bored with the standard take on fruit, we have several recipes that help you improve upon that old standard, fruit, and give it an update you'd be proud to serve to anyone.

⌕ Spiced Infusion with Tropical Fruits

Tobi Sovak, pastry chef at Derek's Bistro in Los Angeles (see Appendix A), gives you a way to enjoy a treat without all the sugar that comes with most sweets! Be aware that this dish still contains carbs, and like everything else, enjoying it in moderation is key.

Preparation time: *5 minutes*

Cooking time: *30 minutes, mostly steeping time*

Yield: *2 servings*

¼ cup Splenda for Baking	Zest of 1 lemon
2½ cups water	1 cinnamon stick
8 star anise	15 whole black peppercorns
2 vanilla beans	1 teaspoon coriander seed
2 tablespoons gingerroot	1½ cups fresh tropical fruits, such as mango, pineapple, star fruit, or passion fruit

1 Combine all the ingredients, except the fruit, in a large saucepan and bring to a boil. Turn off the heat, cover, and allow to steep ½ hour. Strain spices and herbs and allow to cool completely.

2 Serve on top of the fruit.

Per serving (sauce with 4 ounces fruit): *Kcalories 199 (From Fat 6); Fat 1g (Saturated 0g); Cholesterol 0mg; Sodium 18mg; Carbohydrate 50g (Dietary Fiber 7g); Protein 2g.*

Creating luscious fruit desserts with different flavorings

Even if you don't have time to prepare a full-blown fruit recipe, you can still concoct wonderful desserts and mouthwatering nibbles simply by using luscious fruit and adding a special ingredient or two. You can use all sorts of herbs, spices, and nuts to enhance the flavor of fruit. Some examples include:

✔ Peel a banana, freeze it, and then purée it in a food processor, along with almond or peanut butter, and you'll have a fruit version of ice cream.

✔ Purée ripe melon with lowfat vanilla yogurt, a dash of nutmeg and cinnamon, and a squirt of lemon for a refreshing fruit soup.

✔ Combine brown sugar substitute and lowfat vanilla yogurt. Layer the yogurt with fresh fruit to create a parfait.

✔ Grill pineapple slices and then lightly coat with lemon juice, a dash of honey, and cinnamon.

✔ Create fruit kabobs from your fresh favorites and marinate them in lemon juice, nutmeg, and crushed mint.

One of the easiest ways to spice up a fruit dessert is by adding, well, spices. Try sprinkling fresh fruit with traditional Indian spices like green cardamom or with a Latin-inspired combination of cayenne pepper and cinnamon. Get started with the spiced fruit in the next recipe.

Ginger and lemon brighten the sweet flavors of the cantaloupe and papaya in the following recipe. Choose cantaloupes that are heavy for their size and have a lightly sweet melon fragrance. A cantaloupe should be firm but give slightly when pressed. Avoid melons with mushy spots or discolorations.

The papaya is a large pear-shaped tropical fruit. It contains a bed of large peppery seeds in the center of the fruit. If you're looking for a ripe papaya to use immediately or refrigerate, choose richly colored papayas, with splotches of bright yellow, green, and some orange. Green papayas will ripen in a few days if left at room temperature and placed in a brown paper bag.

✆ Cantaloupe-Papaya Salad with Ginger Simple Syrup

Chef Kyle Ketchum of The Lark in West Bloomfield, Michigan (see Appendix A), offers this fruity dessert sure to please the taste buds. It's a simple recipe, using simple syrup. Simple syrup is made from sugar and water; here, however, we substitute Splenda — the non-sugar sweetener — for the same amount of sugar. Enjoy the natural fruit flavors of these antioxidant-packed fruits with a little something extra drizzled lightly on top.

Preparation time: *20 minutes*

Cooking time: *10 minutes*

Yield: *6 servings*

Syrup:	Fruit salad:
¼ cup (18 packets) Splenda	1 cantaloupe
½ cup water	2 papayas
2 inches fresh gingerroot, peeled	4 mint sprigs
1 tablespoon lemon zest	

1 Bring the Splenda and water to a boil in a small saucepan over moderate heat. Add the ginger and reduce the heat, allowing the liquid to simmer.

2 Stir until the Splenda dissolves and the ginger infuses the syrup, about 2 minutes. Remove the pan from heat and take out the ginger. Allow the syrup to cool at room temperature. Add the lemon zest.

3 Scoop out the meat of the fruits with a melon baller and then toss it with the simple syrup and mint when you're ready to serve it.

Per serving: Kcalories 78 (From Fat 1); Fat 0g (Saturated 0g); Cholesterol 0mg; Sodium 20mg; Carbohydrate 19g (Dietary Fiber 3g); Protein 1g.

☼ *Pears Baked in Red Wine alla Piemontese*

This recipe, courtesy of Barbetta in New York City (see Appendix A), is a classic way of preparing pears in Piemonte, Italy's northwesternmost region. The pears should be baked until the skins turn brown and crinkly — *strafugna* as they would say in the Piemontese dialect. Here, we substitute Splenda for sugar, which causes the pears to lack the almost candied taste of the traditional preparation. Splenda, however, is a natural-tasting artificial sweetener, so you'll still be satisfied with the pear's flavor. Keep in mind, however, that since fruit and wine have natural sugars, we can't completely discount the carbohydrate content of this dish, which (per serving) is equivalent to almost 3 starch servings. Consider enjoying this delightful dessert after a meal low in starch and only on occasion.

Preparation time: *15 minutes*

Cooking time: *1½ hours, plus cooling time*

Yield: *4 servings*

10 ounces dry red wine	*Juice of 2 lemons*
7 cloves	*1 cup Splenda*
1 cinnamon stick	*4 large Bosc pears, unpeeled*

1 Preheat the oven to 300 degrees.

2 Pour the wine into a 9-inch-square baking pan. Add the cloves, cinnamon, lemon juice, and Splenda and stir until the Splenda dissolves. Add the pears to the pan. Place them in the oven and bake for 1½ hours, brushing the pears with wine from the pan every 10 minutes.

3 Remove the pears from the oven. Allow them to cool at room temperature and serve.

Per serving: *Kcalories 160 (From Fat 8); Fat 1g (Saturated 0g); Cholesterol 0mg; Sodium 0mg; Carbohydrate 40g (Dietary Fiber 5g); Protein 1g.*

Juicing Your Way to Tasty and Healthy Treats

Fruit juice lacks the fiber of whole fruit, so all the natural sugars can really affect your blood sugar without all the fiber to slow it down. But with a little diligence, you can use fruit juice to flavor your desserts and still maintain your blood sugar levels.

Cranberry-Raspberry Granita

This refreshing treat, courtesy of Heather Dismore (and shown in the color section), makes for a sweet dessert — except it doesn't have any added sugar. Raspberries and cranberries are some of the best sources of antioxidants, and you don't even have to wait for summer to take advantage of these nutritional powerhouses. Most berries are available in frozen food sections of supermarkets and have all the great nutrition of their fresh versions.

Preparation time: *6 hours and 30 minutes, mostly unattended*

Yield: *6 servings*

2 cups 100% juice cranberry-raspberry juice blend

1 ½ cups raspberries (fresh or previously frozen, thawed, and drained)

½ cup Splenda sugar substitute

1 In a blender, combine the juice and raspberries. Mix well. Pour the mixture through a fine-mesh sieve placed over a mixing bowl. Press the mixture gently through the sieve, as necessary, to extract as much juice as possible. Discard the mixture in the sieve or reserve for another use.

2 Add the Splenda to the strained juice mixture and stir to mix well. Cover and freeze. Stir thoroughly with a fork about every 30 minutes, for 6 hours or so, or until the granita is frozen in a crumbly, grainy texture.

Per serving: Kcalories 71 (From Fat 2); Fat 0g (Saturated 0g); Cholesterol 0mg; Sodium 2mg; Carbohydrate 18g (Dietary Fiber 0g); Protein 0g.

Citrus fruits in particular make great juice choices for adding to desserts. Their strong flavors mean a little can go a long way. And many are tart rather than sweet, so they naturally have few sugars. For the scoop on how to juice your own citrus, check out Chapter 7.

Taking Advantage of Agave Nectar

Agave nectar is a delicious natural sweetener with a flavor similar to honey. It's derived from the same plant that gives us tequila. Compared to other sweeteners, it has a low glycemic index. It provides sweetness without the sugar rush (and subsequent crash) of refined sugars. Used in moderation, it can be part of a healthy diabetic diet.

Additionally, agave nectar, sometimes called agave syrup, is full of other health benefits, including improving bacterial balance in the gut. When mixed with salt, it's a beneficial treatment for wound care. Inulin, one of the components of agave, may help lower cholesterol, reduce the risk of some cancers, and improve the absorption of nutrients, like isoflavones, calcium, and magnesium.

Brown Rice Pudding

Sublime (www.sublimerestaurant.com) located in Ft. Lauderdale, Florida, brings you this twist on a traditional dessert favorite. Brown rice, because it retains its bran, has more fiber than white rice and takes longer to cook, so definitely allow extra time during the initial cooking phase.

Preparation time: *10 minutes*

Cooking time: *1 hour 45 minutes*

Yield: *6 servings*

1 ¼ cups brown rice	*½ cup raisins*
3 cups soymilk	*2 teaspoons agave nectar*
½ cup golden raisins	

1 Cook rice according to package directions, stirring often.

2 Combine the cooked rice with the soymilk, raisins, and agave nectar. Cover and cook the mixture over low heat for 1 hour, until most of the soymilk has evaporated and the rice is creamy.

Per serving: Kcalories 288 (Calories from Fat 32); Fat 3g (Saturated 1g); Cholesterol 0mg; Sodium 26mg; Carbohydrate 58g (Dietary Fiber 6g); Protein 8g.

Crispy Oatmeal Cookies

Vegetate in Washington, D.C. developed these cookies, sweetened only with agave nectar. They are surprisingly high in fiber and protein, especially compared to traditional cookies. These cookies can definitely help curb a sugar craving, without spiking your blood sugar.

Preparation time: *15 minutes*

Cooking time: *24 minutes*

Yield: *12 servings, 2 cookies per serving (2 dozen cookies total)*

½ cup grape seed oil	½ teaspoon baking soda
½ cup agave nectar	2 teaspoons cinnamon
¼ cup soy milk	½ cup white flour
1 teaspoon vanilla extract	½ cup whole-wheat flour
3 cups old-fashioned rolled oats	

1 Preheat oven to 350 degrees.

2 Mix grape seed oil, agave nectar, soy milk and vanilla. Add oats, baking soda, cinnamon, and flours to the liquid mixture. Mix until well combined.

3 Using a small spoon, drop dough on nonstick cookie sheet and flatten with wet fingers or spatula, roughly 2 inches apart.

4 Bake 12 minutes or until golden brown and crispy.

5 Removed baked cookies from cookie sheet and place on a cooling rack. Allow to cool completely. Store cooled cookies in an airtight container.

Per serving (2 cookies): Kcalories 236 (Calories from Fat 95); Fat 11g (Saturated 1g); Cholesterol 0mg; Sodium 54mg; Carbohydrate 32g (Dietary Fiber 4g); Protein 5g.

Choosing Chocolate for Dessert

What would life be without chocolate? Fortunately, you won't have to speculate or even discover the situation for yourself. Mix up your own tasty chocolate concoctions by substituting your favorite no-calorie sweetener for the regular sugar.

And whenever possible, choose the highest-quality cocoa powder you can afford. The flavor is much better, and since you're only having a small portion anyway, you definitely want the best-tasting bite you can get!

Mixing up some meringues

Meringue, essentially egg whites flavored and whipped to foamy peaks, is an extremely versatile food. You can create little clouds to hold fresh fruit, top a fruit pie, or even use it to cover a pound cake and ice cream (to create baked Alaska). Meringue is naturally lowfat and takes on the flavor of any extracts, like almond, mint, or chocolate, so experiment and enjoy!

⬬ *Chocolate Meringue Bits with Strawberries and Cream*

These little meringues, courtesy of Heather Dismore, are a surefire way to satisfy your chocolate cravings without all the calories and fat. We flavor them with cocoa powder and Splenda to give fantastic flavor. And the texture of these "lite bites" is outstanding. Top with fresh strawberries for a dash of fiber and vitamin C.

Preparation time: 30 minutes, plus standing time of 8 hours or overnight

Cooking time: 1 hour and 30 minutes

Yield: 40 1½-inch meringues

4 egg whites	*⅓ cup cocoa powder*
¼ teaspoon cream of tartar	*1 cup reduced-fat tub-style whipped topping*
1 teaspoon vanilla extract	*40 strawberries*
⅔ cup Splenda	

1 Preheat the oven to 225 degrees. Line 2 baking sheets with parchment paper.

2 Beat the egg whites, cream of tartar, and vanilla at high speed with an electric mixer until frothy. Add the Splenda, 1 tablespoon at a time, beating until stiff peaks form, roughly 5 to 7 minutes. Gently fold in the cocoa powder until completely incorporated.

3 Spoon heaping tablespoons of the mixture onto the baking sheets. Bake for 1 hour and 30 minutes; turn the oven off. Let the meringues stand in the closed oven for 8 hours or overnight. Store in an airtight container.

4 Just before serving, top each meringue with 1 scant teaspoon of whipped topping and a strawberry.

Per serving: Kcalories 13 (From Fat 3); Fat 0g (Saturated 0g); Cholesterol 0mg; Sodium 6mg; Carbohydrate 2g (Dietary Fiber 1g); Protein 1g.

Enjoying a coffee break

Coffee is one of the most available beverages in society these days. You can't even take a stroll through your local grocery store or mall without being assaulted by the aromas of your local coffee roaster. And fortunately, most of them offer delicious decaffeinated versions of these aromatic beverages. Steam up a little nonfat milk to go with it, and you're ready to relax for a few minutes.

For a decadent but diabetic-friendly coffee break, make your own decaf, nonfat coffee drink (sweetened with sugar-free sweeteners, of course) and pair it with our delicious, crunchy biscotti.

Chocolate-Almond Biscotti

Biscotti are a great treat, and now you can enjoy them homemade, and without all the calories and sugar. This rendition of the Italian "biscuit" (courtesy of Heather Dismore) is easy to make and takes no time. It's also half the calories and carbohydrates of the usual crusty cookie. See these treats in the color section.

Preparation time: *1 hour*

Cooking time: *45 minutes*

Yield: *20 servings*

Nonstick cooking spray	*⅛ teaspoon salt*
½ cup almonds, toasted and roughly chopped	*½ cup Splenda for Baking*
½ cup all-purpose flour	*1 egg*
⅓ cup whole-wheat flour	*1 egg white*
¼ cup unsweetened cocoa powder	*1 teaspoon vanilla extract*
2 teaspoons instant coffee crystals	*1 teaspoon almond extract*
½ teaspoon baking soda	

1 Preheat the oven to 350 degrees. Line a large baking sheet with aluminum foil. Spray the foil with nonstick cooking spray.

2 In a food processor, combine ¼ cup of the almonds and the all-purpose flour, whole-wheat flour, cocoa powder, coffee crystals, baking soda, and salt. Process until the nuts are finely ground, approximately 2 minutes. Transfer the mixture to a large mixing bowl.

3 In the food processor, combine the Splenda, egg, egg white, vanilla extract, and almond extract. Mix until the mixture is slightly thickened, roughly 2 minutes. Add the egg mixture to the flour mixture in the mixing bowl. Stir in the remaining ¼ cup almonds.

4 Use half the batter to form a log (approximately 5 to 7 inches long) on one-half of the foil-lined baking sheet. Repeat with the remaining dough on other half of the baking sheet. Bake until firm, approximately 15 minutes. Cool approximately 10 minutes. Reduce the oven temperature to 300 degrees.

5 Place the logs on a cutting board. Using a serrated bread knife, cut each log into approximately 10 ½-inch diagonal slices. Return the slices to the baking sheets. Bake until the cut sides feel dry to the touch, approximately 20 minutes. Cool completely and store in an airtight container.

Per serving (1 biscotti): *Kcalories 60 (From Fat 15); Fat 2g (Saturated 0g); Cholesterol 11mg; Sodium 30mg; Carbohydrate 10g (Dietary Fiber 1g); Protein 2g.*

Part III
Eating Away from Home

The 5th Wave
By Rich Tennant

"Give me 2 carbohydrate exchanges, 1 protein exchange, and if I have any room left, I'll take a 1/2 fat exchange."

In this part . . .

The chapters in this part tell you how to eat well and stay healthy wherever you are. You can always visit a fast-food franchise, but a lot of that food isn't good for you. So in these chapters, I help you to pick and choose well. That way, you can select a meal even when your only choice is the one fast-food restaurant off the next exit on the freeway.

Chapter 17

Making Eating Out a Nourishing Experience

*P*eople eat many of their meals in restaurants these days, so integrating restaurant eating into a nutritional plan is essential for a person with diabetes. The restaurant business is booming, and creative chefs have the same celebrity status as famous sports stars. And they deserve it. They use fresh ingredients to produce some of the most delicious and unique tastes imaginable. Unfortunately, nutrition isn't always uppermost in their minds. Our experience with the many chefs in this book proves that interest in good nutrition is increasing, but you're still on your own most of the time when selecting healthy foods. This chapter helps you ensure that your restaurant eating fits well into your nutritional plan.

Your situation may be much like the plight of the customer who called the waiter over and said, "Waiter, taste this soup." The waiter replied, "Is there something wrong with it?" "Never mind," said the customer, "just taste the soup." "But it smells and looks okay," said the waiter. "That's all right, just taste the soup," replied the customer. "But sir, there's no spoon," said the waiter. "Aha," said the customer. Or you may be like the diner who complains to the waiter, "Waiter, I can't find any steak in this steak pie." The waiter replies, "Well, there's no horse in the horseradish either." And if you find a fly in your soup, thank the waiter for the extra protein but ask him to serve it separately. The point is that you are ultimately responsible to ensure that you know what is in the food you order and make healthy choices.

Preparing for Restaurant Dining

If you live in (or are visiting) one of the cities that contains a restaurant we reference in this book (see Appendix A), the task of finding a restaurant that is appropriate for a person with diabetes is much easier for you. The chefs who have contributed to this book are health-conscious. They make an effort to keep the fat and the sugar low. But they have to respond to what they perceive to be their customer's needs. They think that one of the main "needs" is for a lot of food, so your portions will almost always be larger than necessary.

You have to evaluate the food you order by questioning your waitperson carefully. Even if the balance of energy sources is right, you will probably receive too much food and should take some home or leave some on your plate.

Because this book is limited to certain cities and restaurants, you may often find yourself having to choose a restaurant where you don't know the ingredients in the food or whether the menu items are healthy or not. How do you go about choosing a restaurant in this situation? Here are a few suggestions:

✔ No particular kind of food is better or worse than any other, with the exception of fast food (we discuss this issue in Chapter 18). You may think that vegetarian food is better than animal sources, but a dish of pasta in a creamy sauce is no better than a piece of fatty steak. Often, restaurants have several menu items that fit into your nutrition plan.

✔ Consider choosing a restaurant that you can walk to and from. The exercise you get will offset the extra calories you may consume.

✔ Many restaurants now publish their menus on the Internet. Before deciding to visit a particular restaurant, go to the establishment's Web site and make sure that it serves food you can eat.

✔ Don't go to the restaurant if the catch of the day is fish sticks.

✔ Call ahead and find out whether you can substitute items on the menu. Nonfranchise and non-fast-food restaurants are much more likely to let you substitute menu items. Fast-food restaurants are able to serve large numbers of people at lower prices by making the food entirely uniform. On the other hand, as Chapter 18 explains, this uniformity makes it easier to know the exact ingredients and methods of preparation. You need to ask only a few questions to know whether a restaurant will be accommodating. Ask whether the staff will

• Substitute skim milk for whole milk.

• Reduce the amount of butter and sugar in a dish.

- Serve gravies, salad dressings, and sauces on the side.

- Bake, broil, and poach instead of frying or sautéing.

✔ An older restaurant has the advantage of having experienced and well-trained waitstaff who know what the kitchen staff are willing to do for you, based on what has been done before.

✔ Find out whether the restaurant already has special meals or entrees for people with chronic diseases such as heart disease. They're much more likely to be health conscious in their cooking.

✔ When you choose a restaurant, consider what you've already eaten that day. For example, if you've already eaten your daily limit of carbohydrate, then the choice of a restaurant where pasta or rice is the major ingredient may not be a good one. People often choose a restaurant days in advance, so if you know ahead where you'll be dining, you can plan to modify your eating accordingly earlier in the day, especially if the restaurant specializes in foods you should eat in small quantities.

✔ Drink water or have a vegetable snack before you go to the restaurant so that hunger won't drive you to make bad choices.

✔ If you know that the restaurant serves huge portions of everything, don't go there unless you plan to share your meal or take part of your meal home.

Mrs. Wilson, who has type 2 diabetes, decided to go to a well-known delicatessen before she attended a musical play. She knew that they served huge portions, but she also knew that she could order a mini-version of many of the items. At the restaurant, she ordered a mini-Reuben sandwich, expecting to get half or less of the usual entree. What arrived was the entire Reuben sandwich without the usual potato salad and coleslaw. She couldn't take half of it home because she was going directly to the show. She knew that she'd feel bad leaving part of such a delicious sandwich, so she ended up eating most of it. Her blood glucose level later that night reflected the huge excess in calories that she had consumed.

You can see from the information in this section that you can do plenty, even before you reach the restaurant, to prepare for dining out. Your preparation may make the whole experience much more satisfying and less frustrating.

Beginning the Dining Experience

As you sit down to enjoy your meal, you can take many steps to make the experience of eating out the pleasure that it ought to be. A few simple considerations at this point allow you to enjoy the meal free of the concern that you are wrecking your nutritional program. Among the steps that you can take are the following:

- ✔ If you arrive early, avoid sitting in the bar with cocktails before you move to your table to eat your meal.

- ✔ Ask the hostess to seat you promptly so you don't have to wait and get too hungry or even hypoglycemic.

- ✔ Ask your waiter not to bring bread or to take it off the table if it is there already. That goes for chips and crackers as well.

- ✔ Ask for raw vegetables without a dip, what the restaurant menus call *crudités,* so you can munch on something before you order.

- ✔ Check your blood glucose before you order so you'll know how much carbohydrate is appropriate at that time.

- ✔ Wait to administer your short-acting insulin until you can be sure of the food delivery time.

Mr. Phillips, a 63-year-old man with type 2 diabetes, was trying to understand, with the help of his dietitian, why his blood glucose had risen to 386 mg/dl after a meal at a local Mexican restaurant. "I knew the portions were large, so I ordered a bean tortilla, and I didn't even eat the whole thing. I left half of it on my plate. I ate very little of the rice as well." The dietitian asked him if he had arrived early at the restaurant. "Oh yes, I forgot. I had to wait in the bar, and I had a virgin margarita." "That," said the dietitian, "explains your high blood glucose. The margarita is all carbohydrate."

Ordering from the Menu

The regular menu and the specials of the day or season are arranged to encourage you to order a big meal. One of the more interesting things that we learned as a result of working with the chefs whose recipes are found in this book, especially the European chefs now cooking in the United States, is the expectation of large portions on the part of U.S. restaurant-goers, compared to Europeans. The chefs were amazed at how much food they had to put on each plate to satisfy U.S. tastes. When you order meat, fish, or poultry, you often get at least twice as much as the recommended serving. Considering how frequently people eat out in the United States, it's no wonder the population is getting fatter.

Your strategy for ordering from the menu should include the following:

- ✔ Plan to leave some food or take home half your order, because the portions are always too large. You can also order a dish to share with another person.

- ✔ If you decide to have wine, order it by the glass. Diners almost always finish a bottle of wine, and unless eight of you share the bottle, you'll drink too much.

✔ Consider using an appetizer as your entree.

✔ Feel free to get a complete description, including portion size, of an appetizer or entree from the waitperson so that you aren't surprised when the food arrives. Pay particular attention to how the food is cooked — in fat or butter, for example.

✔ Consider a meal of soup and salad. This combination can be delicious, filling, low in calories, and low in carbohydrates.

✔ Order clear soups rather than cream soups.

✔ Ask for salad dressings and sauces on the side if possible. This way, you are in control of the amount you consume.

✔ You're probably wise to choose fish more often than meat, both to avoid fat and to take advantage of the cholesterol-lowering properties of fish. Remember, however, that fried fish can be as fat-laden as a steak.

✔ Let your server know that you need to eat soon. If your food will be delayed because the kitchen is slow or busy, insist that vegetable snacks be brought to the table.

The description of an entree usually offers clues that tell you whether it's a good choice for you. These words, in particular, indicate that the preparation keeps fat to a minimum:

✔ Baked

✔ Blackened

✔ Broiled

✔ Cooked in its own juice

✔ Grilled

✔ Poached

On the other hand, the following words point to a less desirable high-fat entree:

✔ Battered

✔ Buttered or in butter sauce

✔ Creamed or in cream sauce

✔ Deep-fried

✔ Escalloped

✔ Fried

✔ Golden brown

✔ In a plum sauce

- ✔ In cheese sauce
- ✔ Sautéed
- ✔ Sweet-and-sour
- ✔ With peanuts or cashews

Does it really matter if you order one kind of sauce versus another? Here are the calorie counts per tablespoon for various salad dressings. Remember that the energy in food is properly expressed in kilocalories, not calories, which are a thousand times smaller:

- ✔ **Blue cheese:** 82 kilocalories
- ✔ **Creamy Italian dressing:** 52 kilocalories
- ✔ **Lowfat French dressing:** 22 kilocalories
- ✔ **Red-wine vinegar:** 2 kilocalories

Planning at Each Meal and in Specific Kinds of Restaurants

You can make good choices at every meal, whether it's breakfast, lunch, or dinner. Every kind of food offers you the opportunity to select a lowfat, low-salt alternative. You just need to think about it and be aware of the possibilities. Helping you choose healthy meals is the purpose of this section.

When you go to any one of the ethnic restaurants discussed here, take a look at the waiters and waitresses. Are they overweight or obese? Usually they're not, yet they eat the food you're about to eat on a regular basis. This means you can order food in this restaurant and know that you have plenty of good healthy choices. (Check out Chapter 4 for an introduction to ethnic foods and how to prepare them yourself.)

Breakfast

The good choices at breakfast are fresh foods, which usually contain plenty of fiber. Fresh fruit and juice are good ways to start the meal, followed by hot cereals such as oatmeal or Wheatena, or high-fiber cold cereals such as shredded wheat or bran cereals. Always add skim milk or 1 percent fat milk instead of whole milk. Enjoy egg whites but not yolks, or make an omelet with two whites for every yolk.

Less desirable choices are foods such as quiche, bacon, fried or hash brown potatoes, croissants, pastries, and doughnuts. And be careful of the high calorie coffees. According to Starbuck's own Web site, a Strawberries and Crème Frappuccino Blended Crème-Whip has 570 kilocalories, including 130 kilocalories of fat.

Appetizers, salads, and soups

Raw and plain food beats those cooked and covered with butter or sour cream, and that rule applies to appetizers, salads, and soups, too. Raw carrots and celery can be enjoyed at any time and to almost any extent. Clear soups are always healthier. Salsa has become a popular accompaniment for crackers and chips instead of a high-fat dip. A delicious green salad is nutritious and filling.

By contrast, olives, nachos, and avocados have lots of fat. Nuts, chips, and cheese before dinner add lots of calories. Fried onion appetizers are currently very popular, and they're often dripping with fat. Watch out for the sour cream dips and the mayonnaise dips, since they, too, are full of fat.

Vegetarian food

As the population gets increasingly obese, there has been a trend to go to vegetarian restaurants. What is called vegetarian varies from no dairy products at all, which is referred to as vegans (people who use no animal products of any kind) to eating eggs and/or dairy. Vegans diets can provide all the nutritional needs of a patient, but must be carefully planned to do so. Alternatively, vegans dieters can take supplements of calcium, iodine, vitamin B12, and vitamin D.

Lacto-vegetarians eat dairy but not eggs while lacto-ovo-vegetarians eat eggs and milk. Semi-vegetarians eat some fish and poultry as well.

Wherever you fit in the continuum of vegetarians, you should know that your choice is a good one. In general, vegetarians are lighter in weight than non-vegetarians. If you have diabetes, it is easier to control, and if you are at risk for diabetes, you are less likely to get it if you eat vegetarian. Vegetarian eating is also associated with less cancer, strokes, and heart attacks.

You still have to make good choices in the vegetarian restaurant. Stay away from the creamy, buttery foods and enjoy the lighter dishes made with grains like quinoa. Use beans and lentils to get your protein without the accompanying fat of meat.

Seafood

Most fish are relatively low in fat and can be a healthy choice. But even the best fish can compromise your nutrition plan when they're fried. Fish that stand out in the lowfat category are cod, bass, halibut, swordfish, and tuna in water. Most of the shellfish varieties are also lowfat. Stay away from herring, tuna in oil, and fried anything.

Chinese food

You can eat some great Chinese food and not have to worry about upsetting your diet plan. Any of the soups on the menu will be delicious and fill you up. Stick to vegetable dishes with small amounts of meat in them. Avoid fried dishes, whether they're meats, tofu, or rice and noodles. Steamed dishes are a much better choice. Potstickers, an appetizer often found on the menu, and sweet-and-sour pork will really throw off your calorie count and your fat intake. Stay away from the almond cookies that often follow Chinese meals.

French food

While the old style of preparing French food promotes a lot of cream and gravy, a new style, called the new cuisine, emphasizes the freshest ingredients, usually cooked in their own sauce. This style has revolutionized the French restaurants. Still, some French chefs cling to the old ways, and their food is not for you, unless you're prepared to share your meal.

Most desserts in French restaurants are high in carbohydrate. Limit yourself to a taste or, better yet, don't tempt yourself by ordering the cake or custard in the first place. See if the pastry chef has a fruit dish, like a poached pear, that is both delicious and good for you.

Indian food

Rice and pita bread are good carbohydrate choices, but avoid foods made with coconut milk because of its fat content. Meat, fish, and poultry cooked in the tandoori manner (baked in an oven) are fine, but Indian chefs like to fry many foods; keep those to a minimum. Curries are fine as long as they're not made with coconut milk. Avoid ghee, which is clarified butter. Fried appetizers like samosas and creamy dishes do not help your blood glucose. Chicken tikka and chapatti are fine — they're made with delicious spices (for taste) but little fat.

Italian food

Stick to tomato-based sauces and avoid the creamy, buttery, cheesy sauces. Minestrone soup is a hearty vegetable soup that is low in fat. Pasta in general is fine as long as the sauce isn't fatty. The problem with the pasta, however, is that the quantity is almost always too great. Share it or take half home. Sausage, because of all the added fats, is a poor choice, whether served with pasta or placed on pizza. Pesto sauce can be made with little fat. If you love the taste of basil, as Dr. Rubin does, ask for a lowfat version of this classic sauce. Ask whether the kitchen staff will make garlic bread with roasted garlic alone, without the butter that often accompanies it. You'll be delighted with the delicious taste. Avoid Caesar salad and dishes made with a lot of cheese, such as cheese-filled ravioli.

Mexican food

Mexican food has become increasingly popular, but Mexican restaurants offer you many temptations to slip from your healthy eating plan. They often start with chips, nachos, and cheese. Tell your waiter to keep them off the table. Have salsa, not guacamole, as an appetizer. Stay away from anything refried; it means just what the word says. Avoid all dishes laden with cheese, as well as dishes heavy in sausage. Chicken with rice, grilled fish, and grilled chicken are excellent choices. Tortillas, burritos, and tostadas are delicious and good for you as long as you avoid the addition of a lot of cheese, sour cream, or guacamole. And keep in mind the importance of moderation. Mexican restaurants are known for large servings, so take some home.

Thai food

Other than the tendency to provide larger-than-needed portions, there is little that Thai restaurants do that is not good for the person with diabetes. The creative use of spices, emphasis on fish, and use of fresh vegetables make this cuisine a good choice for you. Just watch out for the spices.

Enjoying Your Food

If you've been conscientious in planning a delicious restaurant meal ahead of time, you deserve to really enjoy the food. But you need to continue thinking about healthy eating (and drinking) habits even as you sit down to the meal. All the great planning can come undone if you're careless at this point. Think about the following advice as you eat:

✔ If you have a glass of wine, consider the number of calories.

✔ Try using some behavior modification to prolong the meal and give your brain a chance to know that you've eaten: Eat slowly, chew each bite thoroughly, and put your fork down between each bite.

✔ Remember that the meal is a social occasion. Spend more time talking to your companions and less time concentrating on the food.

✔ Remove the skin if you're eating poultry, and allow the sauce to drip off the morsel of food on your fork if you're eating a dish cooked in a sauce.

✔ After you've carefully controlled the intake of food on your plate, don't add significant calories by tasting or finishing the food on your companion's plate.

Finishing with Dessert

For many people, the early parts of a meal are just a prelude to their favorite part, which is dessert. Most people have a sweet tooth, and dessert is often the way that they satisfy that need. The Italians don't call the part of the menu that features the desserts the *dulci* (which means "sweets") without reason. Dessert, in many restaurants, has become a showpiece. The pastry chef tries to show how sweet he or she can make the dessert while creating a culinary work of art. The term *decadent* is often used in describing the richness of these desserts.

Does this mean that you can't have any dessert at all? No. Making a wise choice simply requires a certain amount of awareness on your part. You need to ask yourself the question, "Is the taste of this dessert worth the potential damage it will do to my blood glucose and calorie intake?" If you can answer this question with a "yes," then have the dessert, but check your blood glucose and adjust your medications as needed after eating it. Then return to your nutritional plan without spending a lot of time regretting your lapse. You might even do a little extra exercise to counteract the calories.

On the other hand, if you want to answer the question with a "no," ask yourself these questions to help you avoid temptation:

✔ Do you really need or want the dessert?

✔ Will you remember it ten minutes later when you're at the theater?

✔ Could you share the dessert or just taste it?

✔ Is a fruit dessert available that you could enjoy instead?

To help you avoid that high-calorie dessert even further, think in terms of the number of minutes of active aerobic exercise you must do to account for the calories you consume in a dessert. If your exercise is walking, double these times. Here are some examples:

- ✔ Boston cream pie: 32 minutes
- ✔ Brownie: 32 minutes
- ✔ Apple pie: 34 minutes
- ✔ Hot fudge sundae: 38 minutes
- ✔ Cheesecake: 40 minutes
- ✔ Ice cream cone: 44 minutes
- ✔ Strawberry milkshake: 47 minutes

You may conclude that dessert is worth your time, but we'll leave that decision up to you.

Chapter 18

Fast Food on Your Itinerary

. . . .

In This Chapter

▶ Getting a feel for fast-food options

▶ Visiting the old South in Louisiana plantations

▶ Going through gold and silver country in Colorado

▶ Seeking Utah's beautiful natural attractions

▶ Travelling in Hemingway country, the Florida Keys

▶ Stepping in the footsteps of FDR and Eleanor, Maine to Campobello Island

. . . .

*W*ould you like to take a ride with Dr. Rubin and Cait? Here's your chance. You're invited to travel with them on the highways and byways of some of the most scenic areas of the country with the best destinations. You will stop along the way at some of the best-known fast-food restaurants. Luckily, you are with Cait, who knows the contents of all the foods in these restaurants, and Dr. Rubin, who is there to make sure that you enjoy yourself while staying on your eating program. If you want to get the details on these trips, you can refer to Frommer's very popular travel guides (published by Wiley). We give you just the bare essentials here.

We selected these specific restaurants because they're usually the most common examples of a particular class of fast-food restaurants. In no way do we mean to recommend them above others in their class.

In this chapter, we hit the high spots, the most commonly visited fast-food places. Keep in mind that one chapter isn't enough space to cover the hundreds of different fast-food franchises all over the country. In general, a burger in McDonald's looks like a burger at Burger King, but there are major variations.

Touring the Fast-Food Landscape

Is it even important to discuss fast-food restaurants? McDonald's claims that it serves 26 million customers every day in the United States. That's almost one in ten of all Americans. It has 13,700 restaurants, compared with 7,600 for Burger King; 5,900 for Wendy's; and 3,300 for Arby's. You bet they have a huge impact on eating in America.

People used to say that at fast-food restaurants you could get more nourishment from biting your lip than eating the food. This is definitely no longer the case. Because everyone is conscious of good nutrition these days, you can now find something healthful to eat in any fast-food restaurant.

Watch for a few key words that warn you not to order a particular item in these restaurants. If the food is called a double, big, jumbo, monster, or the ultimate, stay away from that selection. Also avoid any menu item with bacon or sausage.

The reason these establishments are called fast-food restaurants is that they have food preparation, ordering, and serving down to the least amount of time possible. Because we're in a hurry on our trips in this chapter and don't want to stop for a long time, there's nothing wrong with enjoying that convenience, but we want to make sure that the food is right for you.

Of course, some of these places aren't meant to rush into and out of. They are sit-down places, but the food is standardized and is prepared pretty fast, so the result is about the same. This chapter discusses those kinds of restaurants, too.

One advantage of franchise restaurants is that a hamburger in a Denny's in California is almost exactly the same as a hamburger in a Denny's in New Mexico or Oregon. You know exactly what you're getting, which makes the meal easier to fit into your diet. On the other hand, the quick serving and eating often doesn't allow your brain enough time to recognize that your body has eaten enough calories, and you may be tempted to order more food. Don't.

A study published in *The Lancet* in December 2004 that followed 3,000 people over 15 years showed that those who ate regularly at fast-food restaurants gained 10 pounds more than those who did not and were much more likely to develop diabetes. They did not have Cait and Dr. Rubin along to help them as you do. Cait has selected the restaurants in advance to save you the trouble of choosing them along the way.

In Chapter 2, I introduce you to trans fats, the absolutely worst kind of fat, because it not only raises bad cholesterol but lowers good cholesterol. These fats are also called hydrogenated or partially hydrogenated oils. Since 2006, food labels have had to list the amount of trans fats, and the better fast-food places are trying to eliminate them from their cooking. They're still present in large amounts, however, especially in foods like french-fried potatoes, batter-dipped fried onions, fried mozzarella sticks, and buffalo wings. The best way to avoid trans fats is to order food that is low in all fats. The fast-food restaurants that have *no* trans fats in their foods include:

- In-N-Out Burger
- Subway
- Taco Bell
- Pizza Hut
- Popeyes
- Little Caesars
- Papa Johns

The fast-food restaurants that are the worst offenders with the most items with trans fats are:

- Jack in the Box
- Burger King
- White Castle
- A & W
- Dairy Queen

On the trips I'm going to take in this chapter, I'm going to avoid the heavy offenders and emphasize the zero users.

No one should say that a person with diabetes can't go to a fast-food restaurant and remain on his or her nutritional plan. But these places do offer many seductive and unhealthy choices. You need to plan in advance what you're going to choose. You can't go wrong if you stick to the selections that we talk about in this chapter.

If you want to be sure of the nutritional *content* of various fast foods, refer to your favorite search engine on the Internet and enter the name of a specific franchise. All the details are there.

Driving From New Orleans to See Civil War Plantations

We start with a fairly short trip filled with old plantations that are open to the public. Plan this trip in the Spring or Fall because Summer is extremely hot here.

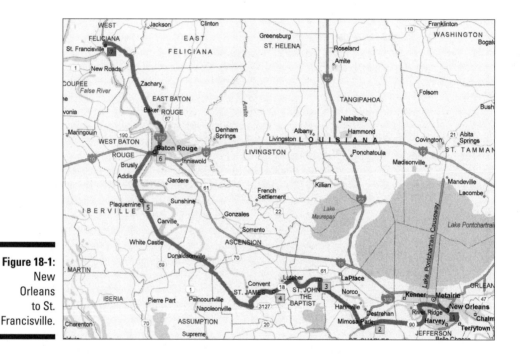

Figure 18-1:
New Orleans to St. Francisville.

After breakfast at our hotel, we leave New Orleans on I-10 going west and leave I-10 at exit 220 onto I-310. At exit 6 we find State Route 48, which takes us to the Destrehan Plantation. We spend an hour there and get back on I-310. Cait has picked out a Popeyes Restaurant a short distance away on US 90 in Boutte for lunch.

Popeyes is a popular chicken restaurant, where the chicken can be mild or spicy. Cait suggests that you have the mild chicken and recommends a wing, a leg, a thigh and a breast. It should be skinless and with no breading. That saves lots of calories. It adds up to only 200 kilocalories, most of which is 51 grams of protein with only 9½ grams of fat and no carbohydrate. If you have it breaded and with the skin, for example the thigh goes from 80 to 280 kilocalories, while the breast goes from 120 to 350 kilocalories. Cait has really saved you from a lot of excess calories.

You can add some carbohydrate with a piece of corn on the cob. It has 37 grams of carbohydrate and 190 kilocalories. Or have some Cajun Rice at 170 kilocalories and 22 grams of carbs. Try to drink water for your beverage. Cait recommends that you skip the dessert, a cinnamon apple turnover that has 34 grams of sugars.

We continue following the River Road, which runs on either side of the Mississippi to Garyville and the San Francisco Plantation House where we spend another couple of hours. Continuing west we get to the Laura Plantation and spend time there. We find a place to stay at Vacherie, a little farther along the River Road.

We are up early the next morning heading for Donaldsonville on State Route 3089 where Cait knows there is a McDonald's for breakfast. Cait suggests an Egg McMuffin, which has 300 kilocalories with 12g of fat, 260mg of cholesterol and 30g of carbohydrate. She tells us to skip the breakfasts with sausages and bacon and warns us against the Big Breakfasts and the Deluxe Breakfasts that have almost 1,000 kilocalories or more per serving. A small glass of orange juice is 12 ounces, so we share a glass and each get 70 kilocalories that way.

Cait has her usual black coffee, which helps to explain why she remains so slim (her good diet and all the exercise she does). She avoids the lattes and the cappuccinos that bring the calories up to almost 300.

Leaving McDonald's we head on State Route 1 farther west to Nottoway Plantation, visit there, and go on to Baton Rouge where we find the Magnolia Mound Plantation, and then end the trip at St. Francisville, where we find the beautiful Rosedown Plantation.

Finding Gold and Silver in Colorado

Take this trip in the summer and you can do it in a day, although it's better to take your time and give it two days. We all start out in Colorado Springs, Colorado heading north on U. S. 24, stopping at the Garden of the Gods, an amazing series of geological formations. We continue to the Florissant Fossil Beds National Monument, where plants, insects, and trees are preserved. Continuing on U. S. 24, we get to Hartsel, where we take State Route 9 north. Cait suggests we continue to Breckenridge. From Breckenridge we stay on 9 for 10 miles where it joins I-70, getting off in Dillon, where we will have lunch. It's a total of 120 miles from Colorado Springs.

She has picked out Arby's in Dillon. She wanted to try Ruby Tuesdays but the nutritional information is so sparse that she did not know what to recommend. Arby's has its problems as well. Many of its items have trans fats and are high in salt. She suggests we have the Chopped Turkey Club Salad. It is only 230 kilocalories, of which 95 come from 11g of fat. The sodium is a little high at 801mg. The Chopped Farmhouse Chicken-Grilled is an alternate choice with less sodium. Both dishes have 9g of carbohydrate. Cait tells us not to add Dijon Honey Mustard Dressing, which adds 180 kilocalories, almost all from fat. The Toasted Subs are loaded with salt and calories and are not a good choice, similar to the Market Fresh Sandwiches. For example, the Ultimate BLT Sandwich is 779 kilocalories with 45g of fat and 1,571mg of sodium.

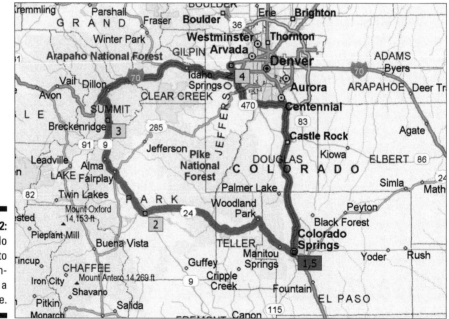

Figure 18-2: Colorado Springs to Breckenridge in a large circle.

Returning to I-70, we head to Georgetown, a center for the mining of both silver and gold. There is plenty to see in Georgetown about mining and we visit the Hamill House Museum.

After Georgetown, we continue back on I-70 heading east. It joins up with US 40 right into Golden, Colorado, where the Coors Brewing Company is located and can be visited. There are plenty of nice local restaurants in Golden, so we eat at one and stay in Golden for the night. The next day we will pick up US 6 and follow it through Denver to where it joins with I-25 and then go south for a visit to the Air Force Academy at exit 156B.

We head back to Colorado Springs on I-25. Cait wanted to stop at PF Chang's in Colorado Springs for lunch but the items contain so much salt and do not list trans fats, so she vetoes this idea. Instead she takes us off exit 150 to a nearby Taco Bell. She suggests any of the tacos, gorditas, or chalupas, but not the burritos, which are too salty. The recommended items generally have about 300 kilocalories, 600mg of sodium, 12 to 18g of fat, and 30g of carbohydrate. They are very tasty, and we enjoy our lunch before departing.

Visiting Utah's Major Attractions

We have decided to take a shorter trip of 82 miles from Salt Lake City, Utah to Mirror Lake. We head east on I-80 early in the morning towards Park City, getting off at exit 141 where Cait knows there is a Starbucks.

At Starbucks you can drink a lot of calories if you order a fancy coffee like a Double Chocolaty Chip Frappuccino Blended Crème-whip at 510 kilocalories. If you order a cup of today's blend, it's 5 kilocalories. Unfortunately, Starbucks does not give you nutritional information for their cakes and pastries, but half a bagel toasted will be just fine. A little jam on it won't hurt a bit, either. It sets you back just 100 kilocalories. Of course, if you add things like cream cheese, all bets are off.

Getting back in our car, we head to Park City. We have dinner and breakfast in our hotel. The next morning we get on the road early. We are headed to Wasatch-Cache National Forest on Route 248, then up to the Upper Provo River Falls on Route 150 to Washington Lake, a beautiful spot. We pass through Bald Mountain Pass and stop for more scenery at Mirror Lake. Then we retrace our route back to Salt Lake City, getting off I-80 at exit 126 where Cait has selected a Wendy's.

Wendy's offers many good choices for the traveler with diabetes. The Mandarin Chicken Salad has only 180 kilocalories, only 2g of fat, and 16g of carbohydrate. It's mostly protein (24g). The Chicken Caesar is about the same. Watch out for the chili — too much salt. Stay away from the shakes and the Frostys — too many calories. Avoid the Baconator with 830 kilocalories and 1,880g of sodium. If you must have meat, the ¼-lb Hamburger Patty is not a bad selection. But don't have any doubles or triples. And try not to add cheese to your hamburger. It quickly raises the calorie and salt count.

After lunch we visit Temple Square in Salt Lake City, the center of Mormonism.

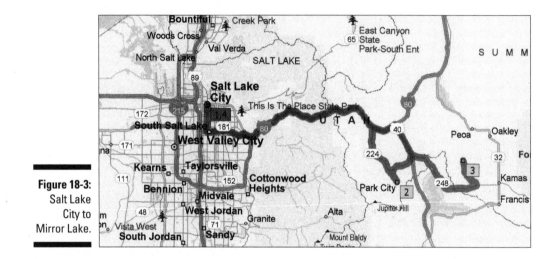

Figure 18-3:
Salt Lake
City to
Mirror Lake.

Enjoying Hemingway Country: The Florida Keys

We are back in the southeastern United States, taking a wonderful ride from Key Largo to Key West, where Hemingway made his home. There is water on either side of the road and plenty of beautiful beaches to stop at. The distance is 106 miles, but we will take three days, since we want to do plenty of swimming and other water sports. The entire trip is on US 1. We begin in Florida City and head south.

We stop in Key Largo for some snorkeling and then have lunch. Cait has already selected a Subway Restaurant right along US 1 in Key Largo. She has checked the nutritional information, which is pretty complete. Subway very nicely lists their food by grams of fat. In the 6-grams-of-fat or less column, there are plenty of sandwiches to choose from. The only problem is that they all have a fair amount of sodium.

Cait suggests we share a sandwich, and you suggest we buy two sandwiches and cut them in three pieces, then each have two of the pieces. Great idea! That reduces both the calories and the salt by ⅓. But we can't get the foot-long sandwiches, which just have too much salt, even if we share them. You like the 6-inch Sweet Onion Chicken Teriyaki, and Cait likes the 6-inch Veggie Delite. I like everything. Not bad at all and no trans fats. The total we each end up with is about 200 kilocalories with 33g of carbohydrate, 17g of protein, and 3g of fat.

We continue to Tavernier, where we stop at the Florida Keys Wild Bird Rehabilitation Center and then go on to Lignumvitae Key Botanical State Park, to which we take a boat. Finally we arrive in Long Key, where we are staying, and have dinner at the hotel.

The following morning we do some snorkeling and then head to Grassy Key in the city of Marathon, where we visit the Dolphin Research Center. We are all hungry for some breakfast, so Cait suggests the IHOP along US 1 in Marathon.

Cait suggests either a couple of buttermilk pancakes, a couple of harvest grain 'n nut pancakes, a couple of buckwheat pancakes, or a waffle. Each of these contains about 225 kilocalories with 6g of fat and 34g of carbohydrate. Of course, we have to have some pancake syrup but go very light on this. Still, it adds another 115 kilocalories from 29g of carbohydrate. Four ounces of orange juice adds an additional 15g of carbohydrate. I drink tea, but you and Cait have your morning coffee.

We continue to Bahia Honda Key and the Bahia Honda State Park for some hiking. We follow the road a few more miles to Big Pine Key, where we are staying, and have dinner and breakfast in our hotel.

Next morning we continue to Key West, where we visit the Hemingway Home and Museum and the Mel Fisher Maritime Museum, which houses a fascinating collection of artifacts from the sunken Spanish galleon, Atocha. Then it's off to Mallory Square to celebrate the sunset.

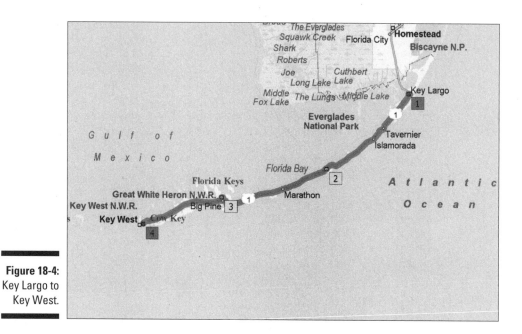

Figure 18-4:
Key Largo to
Key West.

Discovering Where FDR and Eleanor Hung Out: Maine

Franklin Delano Roosevelt, our 32nd president, loved to stay at Campobello Island in Maine. You, Cait, and I begin this trip on US 1 in West Gouldsboro, Maine about 1,800 miles from the same US 1 we just took to Key West. The distance is 100 miles, but there are lots of detours and plenty of things to do, so we will stay one night along the way.

We head out on US 1 to Columbia Falls, where we visit the Ruggles House, an old mansion with plenty of interesting architecture. North of Columbia Falls we take Route 187 to Jonesport and visit Great Wass Island for hiking, ocean views, and wildlife. Route 187 takes us back to US 1 and on to Machias.

We find the Dunkin' Donuts that Cait has discovered. Of course, we are going to bypass the 500 kilocalorie cookies, the 620 kilocalorie Coffee Cake Muffin, and the 300 to 500-plus kilocalorie donuts. What self-control! Instead we are each having one of the Oven Roasted Flatbread Sandwiches that does not contain cheese, like the Southwest Chicken, the Egg White Veggie, or the Egg White Turkey at around 300 kilocalories, 9g of fat, and 38g of carbohydrate. When we finish, Cait tells us we have followed the program so well that we can share any donut three ways. What a treat!

We stay overnight in Machias and leave on Route 191 for some driving along the coast, rejoining US 1 after a while. Not far away is Quoddy Head State Park, which happens to be the easternmost point in the country. After some viewing and hiking, we head back to Route 189 to Lubec. Lubec has no fast-food restaurants, according to Cait, so we splurge at Murphy's Village Restaurant, where the food is good, the service is good, and the people are friendly. Sorry, I won't tell you what we had there!

We cross the Franklin Roosevelt Memorial Bridge over to Campobello. We stop at the Visitor Center, and then we visit the Roosevelt Cottage. The so-called Cottage is 34 rooms and there is plenty of FDR history to be seen.

Figure 18-5:
Gouldsboro
to
Campobello
Island,
Maine.

Part IV
The Part of Tens

The 5th Wave   By Rich Tennant

"I'm having you fitted with a monitoring device that will help reduce blood glucose during meals by automatically signaling the brain to reduce food absorption. It's called a belt."

In this part . . .

In the chapters in this part, I provide ten steps to improve your eating habits and ten food substitutions that you can easily make within a recipe. You can explore ten strategies to normalize your blood glucose and ten ways to promote healthy eating in children.

Chapter 19

Ten (or So) Simple Steps to Change Your Eating Habits

. . . .

In This Chapter

▶ Keeping a food diary and discovering the reasons behind your behavior

▶ Making time and sitting down for all meals

▶ Using water and vegetables for many purposes

▶ Cooking with half the fat (and stripping it away)

▶ Flavoring with condiments, herbs, and spices instead of salt

▶ Sticking to the *b*'s — braising, broiling, boiling, and barbecuing

. . . .

*F*ollowing a nutritional plan sometimes seems so complicated. But really, if you follow the few simple rules outlined in this chapter, you can make the process much easier. This chapter provides you with ten (or so) simple things you can do today. None of them cost anything other than time. Doing them one at a time makes a big difference in your calorie and fat intake. Adding one after another makes the results huge. Your weight, blood pressure, and blood glucose all fall. Who could ask for anything more?

Maintaining a Food Diary

Try this little diversion: For the next two days, write down everything you eat and drink. Before you go to bed on the evening of the second day, take a separate piece of paper and try to reconstruct what you have eaten for the past two days without looking at your original list. Then compare the two lists. The differences in the lists will startle you. The point of this exercise is to show you that you're doing a lot of mindless eating. Trying to follow a nutritional plan from memory doesn't work.

A food diary not only shows you what you're eating all the time but also makes it easy to select items to reduce in portion size or eliminate altogether. When you go to your doctor, the fact that your diary lists birdseed for every meal helps confirm your statement that you eat like a bird.

You might even want to include something in your diary about how you're feeling and what you're doing. This information, besides turning your diary into a more personal statement, allows you to see the associations between your mood and your food. Keeping your exercise record in the diary makes it even more useful, reminding you of when you did (or did not) exercise.

Finally, your dietitian can easily plug your food intake into a computer program to analyze such valuable information as calorie breakdown, amount of salt, levels of saturated fat, and amount of cholesterol.

Figuring Out Why You Eat the Way You Do

You may recognize that you do a lot of your eating for emotional reasons. Try to remember how you ate in your family as you were growing up. What did eating mean to you and your family? Was it a way of connecting with others in the family, or was it used in some other way? Does eating trigger feelings that you want to have again and that make you feel happy or good in some other way? Or do you associate eating with negative emotions? Do you eat the way you do out of loneliness, boredom, depression, happiness, or anger; as a reward; or as a way to save time? You may come up with several reasons, but you need to understand them and begin to respond to those triggers with other actions besides eating.

After you begin to clarify the emotional aspect of your eating, you can look for ways to have the same emotions without the eating part of it. What are other things you can do to feel happy or connected? Do you eat out of boredom? What can you do to keep yourself from being bored?

This sounds like psychology, and it is. You may have to seek the help of a psychologist to find out exactly what eating means to you. Meanwhile, because that type of counseling is often a long process, try doing the other things recommended in this chapter to gain control of your eating.

All habits, including eating habits, come from repetition. Every time you do something the same way, it encourages you to do it the same way the next time. By breaking the chain, you can make healthful changes. Here are some things you can do right now until you figure out why you eat:

✔ Never eat and do something else at the same time, such as watch TV.

✔ Eat in only one place in your home, preferably at the table, your designated eating place.

✔ Eat on smaller plates.

✔ Never eat from the bag, the container, or the carton.

✔ Chew your food slowly and pick up all food with utensils, not fingers, after you've swallowed the previous bite.

✔ Always leave food on your plate to develop the habit of stopping eating when you're full.

✔ Keep food only in the kitchen and out of sight, not on counters.

✔ Avoid junk food that has no nutritional value but only calories.

✔ Eat three meals and even a couple of healthy snacks every day.

✔ Select a healthy alternative to eating, such as exercise, a creative hobby, or even conversations with your spouse.

✔ Choose non-food rewards, such as new clothes for your new shape.

Perform one of these actions at a time. When you've made that action a part of your behavior, try a second action. Build up to many changes. You'll be delighted with the results.

Eating Every Meal

When you miss meals, you become hungry. If you have type 1 diabetes, you can't safely miss meals, especially if you give yourself regular or lispro insulin. Instead of letting yourself become hungry, eat your meals at regular times so that you don't overcompensate at the next meal (or at a snack shortly after the meal you missed) when you're suffering from low blood glucose. Many people overtreat low blood glucose by eating too many sugar calories, resulting in high blood glucose later on.

You should not miss meals as a weight-loss method, particularly if you take a drug that lowers blood glucose into hypoglycemic levels. A pregnant woman with diabetes especially should not miss meals. She must make up for the fact that her baby extracts large amounts of glucose from her blood. Both mother and growing fetus are adversely affected if the mother's body must turn to stored fat for energy.

Eating smaller meals and having snacks in between is probably the best way to eat because doing so raises blood glucose the least, provides a constant source of energy, and allows control of the blood glucose using the least amount of external or internal insulin.

The fact is, following your complete nutritional plan in fewer than three meals is extremely difficult.

Sitting Down for Meals

Eating food with others is one of the pleasures of life. As an added advantage, it also slows the pace of your eating, which allows your brain to recognize when you're full so you stop eating at the appropriate time. By sitting down and eating more slowly, you slow the absorption of carbohydrates, thus slowing the rise in your blood glucose.

Another advantage of sitting down and eating with others is that they serve as a brake on how much you eat. When people eat alone, they tend to eat more. In the company of others, you're restrained by social controls. By eating while sitting at the table, you see only the food on the table. When you stand and eat, you can easily walk to the kitchen, where all the rest of the food is (if you're not there already).

You usually limit the food served at the table to what is on your plate, so you aren't exposed to excessive food. You can make sure that the only foods brought to the table are acceptable food choices, especially if they're prepared as attractively as possible. A lot of your eating is done because the food looks so good, so make the right foods the best-looking foods.

Drinking Water throughout the Day

Seventy percent of your body is water, and all your many organs and cells require water to function properly. Most people, especially older people, don't get enough water. Older people often have the additional disadvantage of losing their ability to sense when they're thirsty. The consequences may include weakness and fatigue, not to mention constipation.

Water can replace all the sodas and juice drinks that add unwanted calories to your day. You soon lose your taste for those drinks and discover that you don't need (or miss) the aftertaste of soda and juice that you took for granted. Those drinks also raise the blood glucose very rapidly and are often used to treat low blood glucose.

One of our patients admitted to drinking 10 to 12 cans of cola drinks daily. He had a high blood glucose that returned to normal when he broke his cola habit.

Make drinking water a part of your daily habits. Drink some when you brush your teeth. Drink more with meals and snacks. Many people don't want to drink much water close to bedtime because if they do, they'll have to get up during the night to go to the bathroom — all the more reason to make sure you get your daily water ration, which should be at least eight 8-ounce glasses, early in the day.

Consuming Vegetables throughout the Day

What makes you think that you can use broccoli only as a side dish with your dinner meat or fish? How can you possibly get in your daily three to five servings of vegetables if you think like this? What would happen if you drank vegetable juice for breakfast? Suppose you added vegetables to an omelet? How about a salad at lunch instead of that large sandwich containing way too much carbohydrate?

You can find so many different kinds of vegetables in the grocery, yet most people limit themselves to very few of them. Your whole meal can consist of vegetables with a small amount of protein thrown in just as a garnish. Try a vegetarian restaurant to see for yourself how delicious freshly prepared vegetables can be.

We're not talking about the starchy vegetables, such as beans, peas, and lentils that really belong in the starch list of exchanges, but rather the vegetables that contain much less carbohydrate. These vegetables include asparagus, bok choy, green beans, cabbage, carrots, cauliflower, chard, collards, onions, summer squash, turnips, and water chestnuts.

Use these vegetables in meals and for snacks. They fill you up but add very few calories. Some are just as good when frozen and defrosted (because they are flash frozen immediately after picking) as they are when fresh. Especially good snack vegetables include baby carrots, cucumbers, and pieces of sweet pepper.

Reducing Added Fat

If you use recipes that have been handed down in your family, they often contain much unnecessary added fat. The same can be said for recipes created by chefs who aren't conscious of the harmful effects of high fat intake. We carefully selected the recipes in this book to minimize added fat. You should try to do the same thing when you cook.

Cooking food doesn't generally require the extra fat. We can remember when a pancake recipe required a cup of vegetable oil, but we now know that you can make delicious pancakes without all that oil. Although vegetable oil is better for you than animal fats like lard and butter, it still has plenty of calories — in fact, as many as animal fats. A gram of fat contains 9 kilocalories, no matter the source.

Try reducing the suggested fat by 50 percent. See whether the taste suffers or if preparing the food is more difficult.

How much difference does reducing the fat make in terms of kilocalories? A cup of oil is 8 ounces, and each ounce is 28.35 grams. Because each gram has 9 kilocalories, a cup of oil contains about 2,000 kilocalories. You get rid of 1,000 kcalories by reducing the fat in half. If your recipe serves four people, each person is getting 250 kilocalories less fat. Is that a worthwhile reduction? You bet!

Chapter 20 is full of great substitutions.

Removing the Attached Fat

Many foods, such as sausage and luncheon meats, contain so much fat that lowering their fat content isn't possible. You should mostly avoid these foods. But other protein sources, such as chicken, steak, roast beef, and pork, have large amounts of visible fat attached to them, so you can remove this fat before you prepare the food. In the case of poultry, removing the skin removes most of the fat. Selecting white meat rather than dark further reduces the fat in poultry.

As fat cooks on a grill, it often flames, which causes the meat to burn. Removing the fat before you cook it makes the cooking process safer (because the burning fat won't spray around), and the resulting meat is much lower in calories.

Leaving Out the Salt

For reasons that are unclear to us, most Americans like a lot of salt in their food. Consequently, these people taste mostly salt and not much of the food. Try getting rid of the salt in your recipes. You can always add it later if you miss the flavor that salt adds. At first, you may think that the food tastes bland. Then you'll begin to discover the subtle tastes that were in the food all along but were overpowered by the salt.

Why do we emphasize cutting salt levels? We know that salt raises blood pressure. Recent studies, particularly the United Kingdom Prospective Diabetes Study, which was a major breakthrough published in 1998, have shown that you can slow or prevent diabetic complications by reducing blood pressure.

You can try the approach of slowly removing salt from the recipe. If it calls for a teaspoon of salt, add only ¾ teaspoon. You won't notice the difference. Next time, try ½ teaspoon. And so on. In the recipes in this book, we have tried to use less salt wherever possible, with the permission of the chefs who created the recipes. Most chefs have been very open to eliminating salt.

Adding Taste with Condiments, Herbs, and Spices

This section explores a case of getting something for almost nothing. If you like a lot of distinctive flavors in your food, try using various condiments, herbs, and spices to replace the flavors of fat and salt. Experimenting with these flavors can bring entirely new tastes to old favorite recipes. Surely, the new millennium is all about breaking free from old habits of eating, which may not be so good for you, and replacing them with new tastes.

Many of the chefs in this book — who are some of the most renowned chefs in the world — have achieved their fame by virtue of their willingness to go in new taste directions. They have combined foods that no one put together before and used spices not traditionally used in foods from their particular ethnic origin. The result has been an explosion of new tastes combined with better nutrition.

Foods that you associate with bland taste, such as some fish, come alive when you add the right herbs and spices. You may never have liked those foods before, but you will now. Not only do they taste different, but they smell wonderful and exotic. They have the additional advantage of being very good for you.

Examples of condiments that add great taste and few calories are salsa, hot sauce, mustard, and horseradish. Herbs that add flavor include rosemary, thyme, and basil. They are best added toward the end of cooking to preserve their flavor if fresh, or at the beginning of cooking to bring out their flavor if dried.

Cooking by the B's

The best methods of cooking all begin with a *b*, such as braising, broiling, boiling, and barbecuing. These methods of preparation don't add fat and often remove a lot of the fat within the food. Broiling a hamburger, for example, often eliminates as much fat from a moderate-fat hamburger as buying a reduced-fat hamburger to begin with. Frying, sautéing, and other methods that depend on butter or fat add exactly the things that you want to remove.

If you must use fat, use a cooking spray that reduces the amount of added fat.

Chapter 20

Ten Easy Vegetarian Substitutions

. . . .

In This Chapter

▶ Replacing meat

▶ Substituting for milk

▶ Enjoying cheese in another form

. . . .

*Y*ou will be surprised at how easy it is to eliminate meat and dairy and substitute with something just as delicious. Sometimes the food will taste different, so you have to try different vegetable products to see what works best. You may even find that the taste of the food when vegetable sources are used is better than when animal sources are used. It takes getting used to, but the advantages for your health are worth the effort.

Take a good look at the vegetarian recipes in this book. They show you that vegetarian cooking is just as complex and interesting as cooking with meat, fish, or poultry. If you try several of them, as Cait and Dr. Rubin did, you will find that they are just as delicious as the non-vegetarian recipes.

Using Several Foods for Animal Protein

There are a number of vegetarian foods that can take the place of meat, depending on what you feel like eating. Baked portobello mushrooms can taste amazingly close to a steak with the same texture and juiciness. Tofu can replace chicken in lots of dishes, especially stir-fried food.

Textured vegetable protein (TVP) is made from soy. It comes in small dry chunks that resemble dried vegetables. It cooks quickly, supplying vegetable protein without fat. You can use TVP to replace meat in soups and stews. It is available in large supermarkets and natural food stores.

Eggplant and mushrooms are other vegetables that replace meat with ease, especially in the southern United States. Eggplant can be stuffed, roasted, marinated, grilled, even fried (not recommended). Combine it with tomato and onions and you have ratatouille.

Spilling the Beans

You know that your muscles are made of protein, so naturally when you think of protein, you think of meat. The time has come to recognize that protein comes from many sources, however. Vegetables have proteins, too, and they don't have the fat that meats provide.

People have suggested that you can't eat only vegetable protein sources because they lack some of the building blocks required for muscle growth, and that you can find those building blocks only in animal protein. As always, an exception breaks that rule: the soybean. Soybeans contain all the different building blocks you need to build your own protein.

Even without soybeans, you can get all the building blocks you need by eating several different vegetable protein sources together, such as rice and beans or yogurt with chopped nuts.

The best nonmeat sources of protein are legumes like dried beans and peas. Other protein sources include nuts and seeds, but they contain quite a bit of fat, so the calorie count swells. The following vegetable protein sources provide the equivalent of an ounce of animal protein:

- ¼ cup of seeds (like sunflower seeds)
- ⅓ cup of nuts (like pecans and peanuts)
- ½ cup of cooked dry beans
- ½ cup of baked beans
- ½ cup of tofu

Avoiding Meat and Chicken Stock

Soup recipes need a stock usually, and most of them call for meat or chicken stock. Vegetable stock will fill the bill very well, though you will get a change in taste. You'll also probably get much less salt. But vegetable stock is not the only thing you can use. Garlic broth can be made to do the job. The ingredients for 8 cups of garlic broth are:

> ✔ 3 small heads of garlic, smashed and peeled
>
> ✔ 1 tablespoon of olive oil
>
> ✔ Coarse salt to taste
>
> ✔ Freshly ground pepper to taste
>
> ✔ 9 cups of water

You can also use water or wine with 1 to 2 tablespoons of soy sauce per cup of liquid. There is no need to use meat or chicken stock again.

Replacing Cheeses

If you want to go the vegan way and avoid dairy, there are lots of ways to replace the cheeses that you commonly use in recipes. Here are some suggestions:

> ✔ There are vegan cheeses available in supermarkets that taste just like cheddar cheese, mozzarella, and Monterey jack.
>
> ✔ Crumbled tofu can take the place of cottage cheese and ricotta cheese.
>
> ✔ Tofu cream cheese can replace regular cream cheese.

They can be used on pizzas, in sauces, and anything that requires melting cheese.

Avoiding Cow's Milk

This is an easy one. Soy milk is an excellent replacement for cow's milk. It is made by cleaning and soaking soy beans overnight, then puréeing them. The solids are strained out, and the liquid is boiled for ten minutes. You can buy soy milk right next to cow's milk in the market. Some of the benefits include:

> ✔ It has more protein and fiber than cow's milk.
>
> ✔ It has isoflavones, chemicals that are thought to prevent cancers, heart disease, and osteoporosis.
>
> ✔ It has about 2 percent fat but no cholesterol.
>
> ✔ Older women can use soy milk to reduce menopausal symptoms, especially hot flashes.

Soy milk does not have calcium like cow's milk so you will need to get your calcium elsewhere. Almonds, beans, and green leafy vegetables are good sources.

Choosing to Replace Milk Chocolate

Dark chocolate has flavonols, which are antioxidants that may be protective against cancer, but milk chocolate does not have the same benefits because the proteins in the milk bind the flavonols so they are unavailable. Chocolate also has caffeine. Since cocoa, the basis for chocolate, is naturally bitter, high fructose corn syrup and refined sugar as well as fats are added to sweeten it.

Carob is a naturally sweet, caffeine-free substitute. It comes from the fruit pods of carob trees found in the Middle East and the Mediterranean. The beans are dried, roasted, and ground to make carob powder. Carob powder is high in fiber, unlike chocolate. But don't think that carob is for dieting. When it is used to make candies and so forth, it can contain just as many calories as chocolate.

Avoiding Mayonnaise

A tablespoon of mayonnaise has 49 kilocalories, most of which is fat, though not necessarily the bad saturated fat. People tend to put a lot of mayonnaise on sandwiches, adding 49 kilocalories for each tablespoon, so it doesn't take long to add a lot of calories just from this condiment.

Instead of standard mayonnaise, try tofu mayonnaise:

- 1 clove garlic
- 8 ounces tofu, drained
- 2 tablespoons fresh lemon juice
- 1 tablespoon olive oil
- 1 teaspoon Dijon mustard
- Sea salt

Blend together for 25 seconds until smooth. Makes 1 cup.

Now you can enjoy the taste of mayonnaise with far fewer calories.

Banishing Eggs

There are plenty of substitutes for eggs. The substitutes don't have the fat found in the standard mayonnaise, but they can be used for baking. You can't use the substitutes, however, for replacing more than 2 eggs in a recipe. It won't work. Here are some substitutes you can use for 1 egg:

- 1½ teaspoons commercial powdered egg replacer
- 1 mashed small ripe banana
- ¼ cup blended soft tofu
- 1 cup unsweetened applesauce
- ¼ cup pureed prunes

You want to experiment a little and see how the substitute tastes compared with an egg. It may even be better in many recipes.

Avoiding Sour Cream

Sour cream is only mildly sour but it is full of fats. It contains 14 grams of butterfat in a 4-ounce serving. That's saturated fat (bad fat) we are talking about. If you are trying to stay vegetarian, you can't use yogurt, which would make a low fat substitute. But you can use tofu sour cream. Here's a fat free recipe that makes delicious tofu sour cream:

- 10.5-ounce package of light firm tofu
- 4 teaspoons lemon juice
- 2 teaspoons apple cider vinegar
- 1 teaspoon sweetener
- ½ teaspoon salt

Process in a blender until creamy and smooth. You'll get all the taste without the fat.

Enjoying Non-Dairy Ice Cream

Wouldn't you know, the food merchants have given us all kinds of choices for people who want ice cream without dairy. Some of the choices include:

- Gelato
- Sorbet
- Dairy-free ice cream sandwiches
- Fudge popsicles

The best are soy-based. There are also plenty of recipes to be found on the Internet for making your own. Just put "vegetarian ice cream" in the search box of your favorite Web browser. Or pick up a book called "The Vegan Scoop: 150 Recipes for Dairy-Free Ice Cream" by Wheeler del Torro.

Chapter 21

Ten Strategies to Normalize Your Blood Glucose

. . . .

In This Chapter

▶ Knowing your blood glucose level

▶ Exercising and taking medications to stay in control

▶ Reacting immediately to foot and dental problems

▶ Keeping a positive attitude while planning for unexpected situations

▶ Staying aware of new developments and using expert help

▶ Avoiding methods that don't work

. . . .

In *Diabetes For Dummies,* 2nd Edition, we describe the management of diabetes in detail. In this chapter, you find the highlights of that extensive discussion. Although this book is about eating, controlling your blood glucose requires much more from you. Everything we suggest is directed toward normalizing your blood glucose.

Doctors consider your blood glucose *normal* when it's less than 100 mg/dl (5.5 mmol/L) if you've eaten nothing for 8 to 12 hours. If you've eaten, your blood glucose is normal if it's less than 140 mg/dl (7.8 mmol/L) two hours after eating. If you never see a blood glucose level higher than 140, you're doing very well, indeed. See Chapter 1 for a full explanation of mg/dl (milligrams per deciliter) and mmol/L (millimoles per liter).

You can use many tricks to achieve this level of control. In this chapter, you find the best of the lot. All of our patients can remember receiving and using some advice that made a huge difference in their lives with diabetes. If you have a tip that you want to share, please send an e-mail to drrubin@ drrubin.com. We'll try to get it into the next edition of this book.

Knowing Your Blood Glucose

No excuse is adequate for you to not know your blood glucose at all times, although we've heard some pretty far-out excuses over the years — close to "The dog ate my glucose meter." The ability to measure blood glucose accurately and rapidly is the greatest advance in diabetes care since the discovery of insulin. Yet many people don't track their blood glucose.

Sure, sticking your finger hurts, but laser devices now make it painless, and even the needles are so fine that you barely feel them. How can you know what to do about your blood glucose if you don't know what it is in the first place?

The number of glucose meters you can choose is vast, and they're all good. Your insurance company may prefer one type of meter, or your doctor may have computer hardware and software for only one type. Other than those limitations, the choice is yours.

If you have very stable blood glucose levels, test once a day — some days in the morning before breakfast, other days in the evening before supper. Varying the time of day you test your blood glucose gives you and your doctor a clearer picture of your control under different circumstances. If your diabetes requires insulin or is unstable, you need to test at least before meals and at bedtime in order to select your insulin dose.

Painless devices for measuring blood glucose are right around the corner. The closeness of this great advance is a particularly good reason to keep aware of new developments (see "Becoming Aware of New Developments" later in this chapter about tracking advancements).

Using Exercise to Control Your Glucose

When people are asked how much exercise they do, about a third say that they do nothing at all. If you're a person with diabetes and consider yourself a part of that group that doesn't exercise, then you aren't taking advantage of a major tool — not just for controlling your blood glucose but also for improving your physical and mental state in general. When a large group of people who were expected to develop diabetes because both parents had diabetes participated in a regular exercise program in one recent study, 80 percent who stayed on the program didn't develop diabetes.

Don't think that exercise means hours of exhaustion followed by a period of recovery. We're talking about a brisk walk, lasting no more than 60 minutes, every day and not necessarily all at once. If you want to do more, that's fine, but just about anyone can do this much. People who can't walk for some reason can get their exercise by moving their arms. To lose weight as a result of exercise, you need to do 90 minutes a day, every day.

Exercise can provide several benefits to your overall health. Exercise does the following:

- Lowers the blood glucose by using it for energy
- Helps with weight loss
- Lowers bad cholesterol and triglyceride fats and raises good cholesterol
- Lowers blood pressure
- Reduces stress levels
- Reduces the need for drugs and insulin shots

When we see a new person with diabetes, we give him or her a bottle of pills. These pills aren't to be taken by mouth; they're to be spilled on the floor and picked up every day. It's our way of making sure that a new patient gets at least a little exercise every day.

Taking Your Medications

You have the advantage of having some of the best drugs for diabetes available to you, which wasn't true as recently as ten years ago. A few years ago, as specialists in diabetes, we struggled to keep our patients in good control to avoid complications of diabetes. Now, with the right combination of medications (and by using some of the other tools in this chapter), just about any patient can achieve excellent control. But no medication works if you don't take it.

The word *compliance* applies here. Compliance refers to the willingness of people to follow instructions — specifically, taking their medications. People tend to be very compliant at the beginning of treatment, but as they improve, compliance falls off. Diabetic control falls off along with it.

The fact is, as you get older, the forces that contribute to a worsening of your blood glucose tend to get stronger. You want to do all you can to reverse that tendency. Taking your medications is an essential part of your overall program.

If you're confused by all the medications you take, get yourself a medication box that holds each day's medications in separate compartments so you make sure the compartment for each day is empty by the next day. Any doctor who prescribes more than two medicines to you should be able to get one for you, and you can definitely get them in drugstores.

Seeking Immediate Help for Foot Problems

One error that leads to a lot of grief in diabetes is failure to seek immediate help for any foot problems. Your doctor may see you and examine your feet only once in two or three months. You need to look at your feet every day. At the first sign of any skin breakdown or other abnormality (such as discoloration), you must see your doctor. In diabetes, foot problems can go from minor to major in a very brief time. We don't pull punches in this area, because seeing your doctor is so important — major problems may mean amputation of toes or more. (See Chapter 1 for more information about foot problems as they relate to diabetes.)

You can reverse most foot problems, if you catch and treat them early. You may require a different shoe or need to keep weight off the foot for a time — minor inconveniences compared to an amputation.

Besides inspecting your feet daily, here are some other actions you can take:

- Testing bath water with your hands to check its temperature, because numb feet can't sense if the water is scalding hot
- Ensuring that nothing is inside your shoe before you put it on
- Wearing new shoes only a short time before checking for damage

Taking immediate action goes for any infection you develop as a diabetic. Infections raise the blood glucose while you're sick. Try to avoid taking steroids for anything if you possibly can. Steroids really make the glucose shoot up.

Brushing Off Dental Problems

Keeping your teeth in excellent condition is important, but especially if you have diabetes. "Excellent condition" means brushing them twice a day and using dental floss at the end of the day to reach where the toothbrush never goes. It also means visits to the dentist on a regular basis for cleaning and examination.

We have seen many people with diabetes have dental problems as a result of poor dental hygiene. As a side effect, controlling the blood glucose is much harder. After patients cure their teeth, they require much less medication.

People with diabetes don't have more cavities than non-diabetics, but they do have more gum disease if their glucose isn't under control. Gum disease results from the high glucose that bathes the mouth — a perfect medium for bacteria. Keeping your glucose under control helps you avoid losing teeth as a result of gum disease, as well as the further deterioration in glucose control.

Maintaining a Positive Attitude

Your mental approach to your diabetes plays a major role in determining your success in controlling the disease. Think of diabetes as a challenge — like high school math or asking out your first date. As you overcome challenges in one area of your life, the skills you master help you in other areas. Looking at something as a challenge allows you to use all your creativity.

When you approach something with pessimism and negativity, you tend to not see all the possible ways you can succeed. You may take the attitude that "It doesn't matter what I do." That attitude leads to failure to take medications, failure to eat properly, failure to exercise, and so forth.

Simply understanding the workings of your body, which comes with treating your diabetes, probably makes you healthier than the couch potato who understands little more than the most recent sitcom.

Some people do get depressed when they find out they have diabetes. If you're depressed and your depression isn't improving after several weeks, consider seeking professional help.

Planning for the Unexpected

Life is full of surprises — like when you were told you have diabetes. You probably weren't ready to hear that news. But you can make yourself ready to deal with surprises that may damage your glucose control.

Most of those surprises have to do with food. You may be offered the wrong kind of food, too much food, or too little food, or the timing of food doesn't correspond to the requirements of your medication. You need to have plans for all these situations before they occur.

You can always reduce your portions when the food is the wrong kind or excessive, and you can carry portable calories (like glucose tablets) when food is insufficient or delayed.

Other surprises have to do with your medication, like leaving it in your luggage — which is on its way to Europe while you're headed to Hawaii. Keep your important medications with you in your carry-on luggage, not in checked luggage. Again, your ability to think ahead can prevent you from ever being separated from your medication.

Not everything is going to go right all the time. However, you can minimize the damage by planning ahead.

Becoming Aware of New Developments

The pace of new discoveries in diabetes is so rapid that keeping on top of the field is difficult even for us, the experts. How much more difficult must it be for you? You don't have access to all the publications, the drug company representatives, and the medical journals that we see every day.

However, you can keep current in a number of ways. The following tips can help you stay up-to-date on all the advances:

- ✔ Begin by taking a course in diabetes from a certified diabetes educator. Such a course gives you a basis for a future understanding of advances in diabetes. The American Diabetes Association (www.diabetes.org) provides the names of certified diabetes educators.

- ✔ Get a copy of Dr. Rubin's book *Diabetes For Dummies,* 2nd Edition (Wiley), which explains every aspect of diabetes for the nonprofessional.

- ✔ Join a diabetes organization, particularly the American Diabetes Association. You'll start to receive the association's excellent publication, *Diabetes Forecast,* in the mail, which often contains the cutting edge of diabetes research as well as available treatments.

- ✔ Go to Dr. Rubin's Web site (www.drrubin.com) where you can find linkable addresses for the best and latest information about diabetes on the Net.

- ✔ Finally, don't hesitate to question your doctor or ask to see a diabetes specialist if your doctor's answers don't satisfy you.

The cure for diabetes may be in next week's newspaper. Give yourself every opportunity to find and understand it.

Utilizing the Experts

The available knowledge about diabetes is huge and growing rapidly. Fortunately, you can turn to multiple people for help. Take advantage of them all at one time or another, including the following people:

- ✔ Your primary physician, who takes care of diabetes and all your other medical concerns
- ✔ A diabetes specialist, who is aware of the latest and greatest in diabetes treatment
- ✔ An eye doctor, who must examine you at least once a year
- ✔ A foot doctor, to trim your toenails and treat foot problems
- ✔ A dietitian, to help you plan your nutritional program
- ✔ A diabetes educator, to teach you a basic understanding of this disease
- ✔ A pharmacist, who can help you understand your medications
- ✔ A mental health worker, if you run into adjustment problems

Take advantage of any or all of these people when you need them. Most insurance companies are enlightened enough to pay for them if you use them.

Avoiding What Doesn't Work

Not wasting your time and money on worthless treatments is important. When you consider the almost 20 million people with diabetes in the United States alone, they provide a huge potential market for people with "the latest wonder cure for diabetes." Before you waste your money, check out the claims of these crooks with your diabetes experts.

You can find plenty of treatments for diabetes on the Internet. One way you can be sure that the claims are based on science is to look for verification from the Health on the Net Foundation, which you can find at www.hon.ch/HomePage/Home-Page.html. Its stamp of approval means the site adheres to principles that every legitimate scientist agrees with.

Don't make any substantial changes in your diabetes management without first discussing them with your physician.

Chapter 22

Ten Ways to Encourage Children to Eat More Fruits and Vegetables

Children don't hate vegetables any more than they hate ice cream. It is what we teach them that determines their feelings about food. If we show them that we love vegetables and consider them delicious, that's how they will feel about vegetables. They love to follow our example.

Fruit is no problem. Try taking a bowl of sweet strawberries, blueberries, or raspberries away from a small child! It's not quite as dangerous as taking a bone from a dog, but close. Most children have a natural love for sweet. There is nothing like a sweet peach or nectarine to excite a child. Just try to get ripe fruit, not the too-early-picked, hard-as-a-rock, tart stuff that passes for fruit in many markets.

There are numerous things you can do to encourage your child to eat vegetables. In this chapter, I will provide just ten. I am sure you can come up with a few others.

One thing I don't encourage is this idea of concealing the vegetables from the child. The message you send is that vegetables are so unpleasant that you have to fool the child to get him to eat them, exactly the message that will lead to a life of avoiding vegetables.

Starting Early

Children learn their eating habits at a very young age, age 2 or even younger. From the time they can eat solid or even semi-solid food, they should be given choices of vegetables. I do not recommend using bottled vegetables, since they are often filled with salt and sugar, but rather making the vegetables into small portions yourself.

Give the child the vegetable to eat by itself, not with a choice of fatty things or sweet things that he will gravitate towards. Do not threaten that the "good stuff" comes only after the vegetables are eaten. Vegetables must be seen as part of the good stuff.

And, of course, set an example. Let him see you eating and enjoying the vegetables. The message will come through loud and clear.

Letting Children Pick

Children love to feel that they have power. Give them the power to pick the vegetables in the market that they and you will eat. Move around to the different colors, explaining that the reason for the different colors is that each color represents a different kind of food that they need in their body. Get a rainbow of vegetables.

Try to know what the vegetables contain so you can explain to the child. Much of that information is in Chapter 2. This vegetable gives you this vitamin and mineral. That vegetable gives you that one. Your body uses them all to create a healthy person.

Involving Children in Food Preparation

When you ask children to describe their earliest memories, they often talk happily about helping their grandmother make some kind of food. Many of the chefs in this book began cooking by their grandmother's or mother's side.

Preparing food together can be a great bonding experience between you and your child, and it also provides you with the opportunity to teach good nutrition. If your child helps you to prepare vegetables, he will want to try what he has prepared.

Have your child create his or her own nutrition plan for a day and discuss every part of it, pointing out what is carbohydrate, protein, fat, the balance among those foods, and how they affect his or her diabetes. Use the food guide pyramid or the child's nutrition plan as a guide for planning, showing the important role that vegetables play in the plan.

Never prepare one meal for your diabetic child and another for the rest of the family. Everyone can benefit from the better choices you make with your child's nutritious food. The child also realizes that eating isn't punishment for a person with diabetes because the whole family eats the same way.

Keeping Problem Foods Out of Sight and Good Foods in Easy View

If potato chips or creamy cookies sit on the kitchen counter, can you blame your child (or yourself) for grabbing a handful every time he or she goes by? Don't buy these foods in the first place. If you do, keep them out of sight. You know what happens when you walk up to a buffet table. You can more easily avoid what you don't see.

On the other hand, keep fruits and vegetables in plain sight. Have carrot sticks and celery sticks easily available. Keep some cooked broccoli and cauliflower in the refrigerator.

Again, your child follows your example. If you raid the freezer for ice cream, don't be surprised to see your child do the same thing. If you raid the refrigerator for broccoli or asparagus, that is what your child will do as well. The great benefit to you when you set an example for your child is the excellent nutrition that you get.

Growing a Garden

Even if all you have is a small box, you can show your child where vegetables come from, how they grow, when to pick them, and the fun of eating what you grow. Plus, foods that you grow and pick yourself, just at the peak of taste, are a totally different experience from what you get at the market. Only the farmers' market can come close. So if you can't possibly grow your own, take your child to a farmer's market. They are everywhere.

If you do have a little space, here are a few recommendations from an old farmer (me). Grow some bush beans from seeds for the beautiful flowers that precede the delicious and plentiful beans, and to demonstrate what can come from a tiny seed. They don't require staking up like pole beans. Grow some beets and carrots, also from seeds, to show that foods grow under the earth as well as above the earth, and they get pretty sweet at that. Grow some tomatoes and zucchini from plants to show how things can grow in abundance from only one or two plants that start very tiny.

Let your child do the picking. The thrill of picking your own food is not to be missed. If you can't pick in your own garden, pick where you can pay for the produce in another garden.

Finding Vegetable Recipes They Like

In the age of the Internet, the availability of great recipes is almost overwhelming. In this book you will find a tiny portion of what is out there. Brilliant chefs are working to produce recipes that make us salivate. Your children will love the results.

Appendix D has my recommendations for sources for great recipes, not just for people with diabetes, but for everyone. One of the central themes in all my books about diabetes is that people with diabetes can eat great food. They can eat just about anything as long as the portions are appropriate.

You don't have to go to vegetarian sources to find great vegetable recipes. Even restaurants that feature meat know how to cook vegetables. You'll be amazed at the creative ways that chefs prepare zucchini, carrots, squash, spinach, and so forth.

Try watching some of the cooking shows on TV as you exercise. Check the schedule and try to exercise when the vegetable cooking is being shown. The only problem is that you may want to stop exercising and start cooking. Resist until you have done your thirty minutes or more.

Stir Frying

One of the best ways to cook vegetables ending with a delicious dish without adding a lot of fat is to stir fry. You use very little oil and the vegetables come out hot and delicious. The natural tastes of the vegetables are sealed in. The

Chinese have been doing it this way for generations. Until they adopted our Western styles of cooking and eating, diabetes was not much of a problem among the Chinese.

Stir fry many different kinds of vegetables together to make a vegetable medley. Some may take a little longer or a little shorter to fry so put the ones together that take the same time. A meal made up just with stir-fried vegetables can be all your child needs to realize how delicious vegetables can be. You don't have to throw in any chicken or beef. That is an important message to send your child. A meal can be complete without animal protein. As I have tried to emphasize in this new edition, eating vegetarian is a very healthful way to go.

Using a Dip

Sometimes dipping the vegetables into a delicious dip that you prepare can make the vegetables even more delicious, desirable, and easy to eat. Here is a simple dill dip mix that your child will love:

- ✔ ½ cup dried dill weed
- ✔ ½ cup dried minced onion
- ✔ ½ cup dried parsley
- ✔ ½ cup Beau Monde seasoning

Combine the ingredients in a bowl and store in a tight container. Label it with instructions for use. When needed, combine 1 cup lowfat mayonnaise, 1 cup lowfat yogurt and 3 tablespoons of dill dip mix and blend well. Your child will love it with all vegetables.

Knowing the Right Sized Portion

A 2-year-old child requires a lot less than a 20-year old adult. The recommended serving size of vegetables for a toddler is a tablespoon per year of age. If you want to get your 2-year old to eat five of his servings of vegetables, all you have to do is get him to eat ten tablespoons during the course of the day. That's a lot easier than you thought. If your child wants more, don't stop him!

With so little that has to be eaten to reach the daily goal, it may be easier to stick to just one or two vegetables on any given day. Today is carrot and bean day while tomorrow is beet and zucchini day. Vegetables can be fun!

Giving Fruit Juice

You would never think of offering your child a cigarette, would you? Why would you ever offer your child a can of soda? Chapter 2 makes it pretty clear that there is little difference in the negative consequences of cigarettes or soda or fruit drink, for that matter. If you want to get some more fruit into your child and he won't eat enough solid fruit, give him juice. You can get juice from just about any fruit and many vegetables.

You can also make delicious fruit smoothies with lots of fruit, some juice, and a little yogurt. Kids love them!

Don't buy the canned variety, which always has too much salt in it for some dumb reason. Get a juicer and make your own. The wonderful possibilities of putting together all kinds of fruit flavors is easily available if you make your own. Connect the drinking of juice with some kind of celebration. In our house we have juice with breakfast every morning and clink our glasses together as we say, "To life!"

Part V
Appendixes

The 5th Wave   By Rich Tennant

"Sorry sir — we don't currently offer a 'Happy Hemoglobin Meal.'"

In this part . . .

The appendixes contain a lot of useful information, whether you're planning meals or curious about the restaurants and chefs that provided recipes for this book. Check out Appendix A to find out more about the restaurants that contributed many of the delicious recipes in this book. You find out about their particular style of cooking and the chefs who make this possible. Head to Appendix B for a glossary of key cooking terms, and use Appendix C to find guidelines for substituting other sweeteners for sugar, as well as cooking equivalents, such as how many tablespoons make up a cup. Appendix D offers other resources in books and on the Web for recipes and nutritional information for people with diabetes.

Appendix A

Restaurant Descriptions

• •

*A*fter you have had a chance to look over and try some of the wonderful dishes in this book, you'll never again think that people with diabetes can't enjoy terrific meals. The chefs who contributed these recipes are health- and nutrition-conscious, and you'll probably be able to find other choices on their menus that also fit your nutritional plan very well. However, note that we have tried to reduce kilocalories by reducing fat and sugar intake as much as possible — with the agreement of the chefs — as well as keeping salt intake on the low side.

The meal you receive in the restaurant may not be exactly what you find here, especially because chefs change often; also, chefs sometimes cook for 100 or more people, and their measurements may not be exact every time. Most food must be prepared rapidly in a restaurant and not the same way. You'll also receive a portion that is generally too large, so be prepared to take some home.

The restaurants that contributed recipes for this book are all fine restaurants that have been given the stamp of approval by various testing organizations. You will not be disappointed no matter what you eat in these establishments, but the kilocalories and the distribution of carbohydrates, protein, and fat may not fit your nutritional plan perfectly. You need to adjust other meals and snacks to get your overall nutrition plan to conform to the guidelines for a full day (see Chapter 2).

The difficulty of preparation for the recipes in this book varies greatly. For a few reasons, we include some recipes that are more labor-intensive and time-intensive than usual.

- ✔ First, many of you are excellent cooks and will try these recipes despite the difficulties because they're delicious and worth the time.

- ✔ Second, even if you choose not to try specific recipes, you'll find wonderful tips about foods and techniques to incorporate into whatever you cook.

- ✔ Third, you'll get an idea of what goes into the magical foods that these fine restaurants are turning out, and you can choose to order that dish if you go to that restaurant.

Whatever your pleasure, bon appétit!

Restaurant Descriptions

The following sections introduce the restaurants in this book and the recipes they contributed. Each establishment offers innovative cuisine and a quality dining atmosphere.

Barbetta

321 West 46th Street, New York, New York; 212-246-9171

Barbetta, the oldest restaurant in New York, still run by its founding family, recently celebrated its 100th birthday. In addition, it is the oldest Italian restaurant in New York and the oldest restaurant in New York's Theater District. It was started in 1906 by Sebastiano Maioglio, the father of the current owner, Laura Maioglio. Laura has transformed her restaurant into New York's first truly elegant Italian dining destination. Good nutrition is important to Laura Maioglio, and the following recipes from Barbetta confirm her focus on health:

✔ Fresh Mushroom Salad (Chapter 9)

✔ Risotta alle Erbe Made with Extra-Virgin Olive Oil (Chapter 10)

✔ Broiled Salmon with an Herb Sauce and Cucumbers (Chapter 12)

✔ Paillard of Chicken Breast with Fennel and Parmigiano (Chapter 13)

✔ Pears Baked in Red Wine alla Piemontese (Chapter 16)

Baricelli

2203 Cornell Road, Cleveland, Ohio; 216-791-6500

Baricelli, in the Baricelli Inn in Cleveland, has been a four-star restaurant almost since the Minnillo family welcomed their first dinner guests in 1985. Chef/owner Paul Minnillo is the third generation of a family of restaurateurs. His Italian and American food, featuring the freshest ingredients, has been pleasing gourmets for more than 20 years.

Baricelli provided the following delicious recipes:

✔ Haricot Vert (Chapter 11)

✔ Roast Free-Range Chicken Breast Stuffed with Porcini Mushrooms, Caramelized Leeks, and Pancetta (Chapter 13)

✔ Veal Tenderloin with Chanterelle Mushrooms in a Veal Muscat Reduction Sauce (Chapter 14)

Candle Café and Candle 79

Two locations: 1307 Third Avenue, New York, New York; 212-472-0970 and 154 E 79th Street, New York, New York; 212-537-7179

Candle Café serves local, organic, vegan food. It was started in 1984 by Bart Potenza who was joined in 1987 by Joy Pierson. Their food is dedicated to good health, using vegetables and fruits grown without pesticides and other chemicals. Their work together led to the *Candle Café Cookbook* in 2003.

They provided the following recipes:

- ✔ Live Cucumber and Avocado Soup (Chapter 8)
- ✔ Roasted Root Vegetables and Quinoa (Chapter 10)

Cetrella

845 Main Street, Half Moon Bay, California; 650-726-4090

Lewis Rossman, the executive chef at Cetrella, has rapidly turned this fine restaurant into a destination. The menu features elegantly rustic Northern Mediterranean cuisine inspired by the coastal villages of France, Italy, and Spain. Lewis emphasizes using the local produce, cheeses from nearby artisans, and seafood from the nearby Pacific Ocean. These are the recipes that Lewis Rossman has kindly provided for our readers:

- ✔ Vegetable Fritto Misto (Chapter 11)
- ✔ Pan-Roasted Salmon Fillet with Lemon-Dill Butter Sauce (Chapter 12)
- ✔ Rock Shrimp Ceviche (Chapter 12)

Clementine

126 Clement Street, San Francisco, California; 415-387-0408

Clementine features the delicious food of French chef and co-owner Didier Labbe. Chef Labbe has worked in some of the finest restaurants in the world including l'Arpege in Paris, one of a small number of three-star Michelin restaurants in that country. The restaurant features some of the classics of France, such as snails, along with delicious treatments of the fine fish, meat, and poultry locally available. You, of course, can't eat the snails, because they're swimming in butter, but you can try the following recipes. You won't be disappointed.

- Rhubarb Soup with Fresh Strawberries (Chapter 8)
- Roasted Lamb Sirloin with Herbes de Provence, Spinach, and Onion Ragout with Lamb Au Jus (Chapter 14)

DavidBurke and Donatella

133 East 61st Street, New York, New York; 212-813-2121

DavidBurke and Donatella features the cuisine of one of America's fastest rising young chefs, David Burke. He has received numerous other awards for his fine cuisine. David's training was at the Culinary Institute of America in Hyde Park, New York. Following that, he served in a number of great restaurants in the United States and went to France to fine-tune his skills. David's genius with fresh ingredients keeps his restaurant filled every night with VIPs and others. The restaurant provided the following recipe:

- Zucchini and Cucumber Linguine with Clams (Chapter 11)

Derek's Bistro

181 East Glenarm Avenue, Pasadena, California; 626-799-5252

Derek's is a casually elegant restaurant renowned for its superb California contemporary cuisine. It is a hidden gem located in a Pasadena mini-mall. The food is prepared in the tradition of classic French cooking. The executive chef, Juan Dominguez, utilizes the seasonal local produce along with fresh seafood, meats, game, and poultry. One highlight for the person with diabetes is that the desserts are offered in mini and regular sizes, so you can get a taste without wrecking your diet.

Derek's contributed the following recipes to this book:

- Watercress Salad (Chapter 9)
- Horseradish-Crusted Cod with Lentils (Chapter 12)
- Spiced Infusion with Tropical Fruits (Chapter 16)

Eccolo

1820 Fourth Street, Berkeley, California; 510-644-0444

Christopher Lee, an alumnus of the great Chez Panisse Restaurant, is following in the footsteps of his mentor, Alice Waters, with his Cal-Italian menu revolving around pristine local ingredients. The menu includes several seasonal fruit desserts that any person with diabetes would enjoy.

Here are the recipes contributed by Eccolo:

- ✔ Artichoke Frittata (Chapter 6)
- ✔ Pickled Vegetables (Chapter 11)
- ✔ Chicken Breasts with Lemon and Garlic (Chapter 13)

Hangawi

12 Park Avenue, New York, New York; 212-213-1001

Hangawi's owners, William and Terri Choi, started the restaurant 15 years ago because they believe vegetarianism is the healthiest diet. They translated many of their favorite Korean dishes for Western vegetarians. They use many ingredients that they bring back from Korea to produce food for which their restaurant has been voted the best vegetarian restaurant in New York. Hangawi provided:

- ✔ Organic Tofu and Shitake Mushrooms (Chapter 10)

Horizons

611 S 7th Street, Philadelphia, Pennsylvania; 215-293-6117

Horizons is the product of chef/owner Rich Landau and his wife and pastry chef Kate Jacoby. Together they have won numerous awards for their innovative vegetarian cooking including Restaurant of the Year and Top Ten Chefs. They have published a couple of best-selling cookbooks.

Horizons has provided:

- Mushroom Garlic Medley (Chapter 10)
- Mushrooms Stuffed with Fennel and Spinach (Chapter 10)
- Truffled Hummus (Chapter 7)

The Lark

6430 Farmington Road, West Bloomfield, Michigan; 248-661-4466

The Lark is a sophisticated European-style country inn located in the heart of West Bloomfield, Michigan. The award-winning cuisine is prepared with French cooking techniques. Chef Kyle Ketchum was trained at several fine restaurants after graduating from Le Cordon Bleu of Scottsdale, Arizona. He combines the finest local ingredients with his special skills to produce food that has consistently won awards, including *Bon Appétit* magazine's "One of America's 10 Best Special Occasion Restaurants" and *Condé Nast Traveler* magazine's "Best Restaurant in the United States."

Chef Kyle Ketchum from The Lark provided the following recipes:

- Watermelon Gazpacho (Chapter 8)
- Goat-Cheese-Stuffed Zucchini with Yellow Tomato Sauce (Chapter 11)
- Cantaloupe-Papaya Salad with Ginger Simple Syrup (Chapter 16)

Millennium

580 Geary Street, San Francisco, California; 415-345-3900

Millennium chef Eric Tucker and owner Ann Wheat have created a gourmet dining experience of vegetarian, healthy, and environmentally friendly foods. Many cultures are responsible for the delicious flavors and styles you will find there.

Millennium has provided:

- Baby Artichokes, Gigante Beans and Summer Vegetable Cartoccio with Cream Polenta (Chapter 10)
- Quinoa and Black Bean Salad over a Chilled Avocado Soup (Chapter 11)
- Vietnamese Style Stuffed Grape Leaves (Chapter 10)

Paley's Place

1204 NW 21st Avenue, Portland, Oregon; 503-243-2403

Vitaly Paley, chef of Paley's Place, was born near Kiev in the former Soviet Union. He studied at the French Culinary Institute in New York and fine-tuned his skills at fine restaurants in New York and France. Vitaly came to Portland and opened Paley's Place with his wife, Kimberly, in 1995.

The cuisine is French bistro fare. The ingredients are from the Pacific Northwest from local farmers and ranches. Vitaly uses them to produce classic food similar to the classic music he once performed. Paley's Place contributed the following recipes to this book:

- ✔ Truffle Vinaigrette (Chapter 9)
- ✔ Summer Tomato Salad (Chapter 9)
- ✔ B.B.Q. Cedar-Planked Salmon (Chapter 12)

Peristyle

1041 Dumaine Street, New Orleans, Louisiana; 504-593-0935

Peristyle in New Orleans has gone through a number of ownership changes in the last few years but has now settled in the very capable hands of chef/owner Tom Wolfe. He produces French-influenced cooking, to be expected since he grew up in New Orleans and most of his culinary experience is there, including at the famous Emeril's, where he worked for eight years.

Peristyle contributed these recipes to this book:

- ✔ Beer-Braised Pork and Crisp-Herb Cabbage with Apple-Tarragon Dipping Sauce (Chapter 14)
- ✔ Wolfe's BBQ Sauce (Chapter 15)

Poggio

777 Bridgeway, Sausalito, California; 415-332-7771

Poggio is the dream of famed restaurateur Larry Mindel, who has been creating great restaurants for 30 years. Past creations include Ciao and Prego in San Francisco; Guaymas in Tiburon, California; and MacArthur Park in San Francisco and Palo Alto. He also pioneered the concept of the Italian bakery and restaurant at Il Forniao. He has been recognized by the Italian government for his contribution to preserving the Italian heritage outside of Italy.

Larry is joined in the kitchen by chef and partner Chris Fernandez. At Poggio he uses the best of the local ingredients to make classic Italian food with care and respect.

Poggio provided these recipes for this book:

- ✔ Red-Wine-Braised Lentils (Chapter 10)
- ✔ Spit-Roasted Pork Loin with White Beans all' Uccelletto (Chapter 14)
- ✔ Spinach-Ricotta Gnocchi (Chapter 15)

Rathbun's

112 Krog Street, Suite R, Atlanta, Georgia; 404-524-8280

Rathbun's is the dream of executive chef Kevin Rathbun, who developed his great love for extraordinary food at a very young age. Kevin began in restaurants as an apprentice at age 14. Soon he was working for such famous chefs as Bradley Ogden and Emeril Lagasse at Commander's Palace in New Orleans. In 2004, Kevin opened Rathbun's, where he features a Modern American menu. Aware of the problems of obesity, Kevin offers small plates for those who limit their portions. Rathbun's contributed the following recipes for this book:

- ✔ Cauliflower-Parmesan Soup (Chapter 8)
- ✔ Zucchini and Parmigiano-Reggiano Salad (Chapter 11)
- ✔ Pan-Roasted Cod with Shrimp and Mirliton Squash (Chapter 12)
- ✔ Thai Rare Beef with Red Onion and Kaffir Lime (Chapter 14)
- ✔ Pan-Roasted Veal Chop with Corn and Gouda Ragout (Chapter 14)

Sublime

1431 N. Federal Highway, Ft. Lauderdale, Florida; 954-539-9000

Sublime is the vision of owner Nanci Alexander who wanted to show that plant-based food could be sublime. It has an award-winning menu featuring natural and organic foods and spirits from around the globe. The cuisine has received numerous awards.

Sublime has provided:

- ✔ Brown Rice Pudding (Chapter 18)
- ✔ Tuscan Quiche (Chapter 6)

Tanta Marie's Cooking School

271 Francisco Street, San Francisco, California; 415-788-6699

Tanta Marie's Cooking School was founded in 1979 by Mary Risley to provide all-day, year-round classes for people who want to cook well. She has been the recipient of "Cooking Teacher of the Year" and "Humanitarian of the Year." The school covers all cuisines. Their graduates serve as chefs, food writers, cooking teachers, pastry chefs, and caterers. Tante Maire's has provided a number of vegetarian recipes for this book, but you can learn whatever cuisine you are interested in at their school.

Tanta Marie's has provided:

- ✔ Asparagus Bread Pudding Layered with Fontina (Chapter 18)
- ✔ Asparagus Pizza with Fontina and Truffle Oil (Chapter 13)
- ✔ Breakfast Polenta with Apples, Walnuts, and Maple Syrup (Chapter 6)
- ✔ Cacit (Chapter 12)
- ✔ Fig, Mozzarella, and Mizuna Salad with Thai Basil (Chapter 7)
- ✔ Heirloom Tomato Soup with Fresh Basil (Chapter 8)
- ✔ Muesli (Chapter 6)
- ✔ Portobello Mushroom Sandwich (Chapter 12)
- ✔ Pumpkin Risotto (Chapter 11)
- ✔ Salad of Blood Oranges, Beets, and Avocado (Chapter 7)
- ✔ Summer Vegetable Stew with Egg (Chapter 8)
- ✔ Vegetable Frittata (Chapter 6)

Vegetate

1414 9th Street, NW, Washington, D.C.; 202-232-4585

Vegetate was voted Washington's best vegetarian restaurant in 2009. Owner Jennifer Redd believes in the best possible ingredients from local and regional farms. The menu changes regularly depending on what is currently in season. I visited there myself and can vouch for the delicious food.

Vegetate provided:

- ✔ Collard Greens (Chapter 7)
- ✔ Grilled Romaine Caesar (Chapter 7)
- ✔ Quinoa and Spiced Adzuki Beans (Chapter 11)

A City-by-City Restaurant Travel Guide

So that you can use this section as a kind of travel guide, we have listed the restaurants by cities, which are in alphabetical order.

Atlanta, Georgia

Rathbun's

Berkeley, California

Eccolo

Cleveland, Ohio

Baricelli Inn

Ft. Lauderdale, Florida

Sublime

Half Moon Bay, California

Cetrella

New Orleans, Louisiana

Peristyle

New York, New York

Barbetta

Candle Café and Candle 79

DavidBurke and Donatella

Hangawi

Pasadena, California

Derek's Bistro

Philadelphia, Pennsylvania

Horizons

Portland, Oregon

Paley's Place

San Francisco, California

Clementine

Millennium

Tante Marie's Cooking School

Sausalito, California

Poggio

Washington, D.C.

Vegetate

West Bloomfield, Michigan

The Lark

A Glossary of Key Cooking Terms

al dente: Cook to slightly underdone with a chewy texture, usually applied to pasta.

bake: Cook with hot, dry air.

barbecue: Cook on a grill, using charcoal or wood.

baste: Spoon melted butter, fat, or other liquid over food.

beat: Mix solid or liquid food thoroughly with a spoon, fork, whip, or electric beater.

bind: Add an ingredient to hold the other ingredients together.

blanch: Plunge food into boiling water until it has softened, to bring out the color and loosen the skin.

blend: Mix foods together less vigorously than beating, usually with a fork, spoon, or spatula.

boil: Heat liquid until it rolls and bubbles.

bone: Remove the bone from meat, fish, or poultry.

braise: Brown foods in fat and then cook slowly in a covered casserole dish.

bread: Coat with bread crumbs.

broil: Cook by exposing directly to high heat.

brown: Cook quickly so the outside of the food is brown and the juices are sealed in.

caramelize: Dissolve sugar and water slowly and then heat until the food turns brown.

ceviche: Placing raw seafood in an acid to "cook."

chop: Cut food into small to large pieces.

curdle: Cause separation by heating egg- or cream-based liquids too quickly.

deglaze: Pour liquid into a pan of meat — after roasting or sautéing and after removal of fat — to capture the cooking juices.

degrease: Remove fat from the surface of hot liquids.

devein: Remove the dark brownish-black vein that runs down the back of a shrimp.

dice: Cut into cubes the size of dice.

dilute: Make a liquid, such as a sauce, less strong by adding water.

drain: Remove liquid by dripping through a strainer.

drippings: The juice left after meat is removed from a pan.

dry steaming: Cooking foods such as vegetables in their own natural juices rather than adding additional moisture.

dust: Sprinkle lightly with sugar or flour.

emulsify: Bind hard-to-combine ingredients, such as water and oil.

fillet: Cut meat, chicken, or fish away from the bone.

fold: Mix together without breaking.

fry: Cook in hot fat over high heat until brown.

fumet: A heavily concentrated stock.

garnish: Decorate food.

grate: Shred food in a grater or food processor.

grease: Lightly cover a pan with fat to prevent food from sticking.

grill: Cook on a rack over hot coals or under a broiler.

hors d'oeuvres: Bite-sized foods served before dinner.

infusion: Extract flavor from a food into a hot liquid.

julienne: Cut vegetables and other foods into matchstick-sized strips.

knead: Work dough to make it smooth and elastic.

leaven: Cause to rise before and during baking.

marinate: Place in a seasoned liquid to tenderize.

meringue: Egg whites beaten with sugar and baked at 300 to 325 degrees Fahrenheit.

mince: Chop food very fine.

pan-roast: A two-step process that first sears and seals a thicker piece of meat or chicken in a pan on the stovetop and then finishes that piece in the oven, in the same pan you started with.

pan-broil: Cook on top of the stove over high heat, pouring off fat or liquid as it forms.

parboil: Partially cook food in boiling water.

pare: Remove skin from a fruit or vegetable.

phyllo: A tissue-thin layer of dough.

pickle: Preserve food by submerging in a salty brine.

pilaf: A rice dish seasoned with herbs and spices, combined with nuts, dried fruits, poultry, and vegetables.

pinch: The amount of food you can take between two fingers.

poach: Submerge food in a liquid that is barely boiling.

proof: Test yeast — to find out whether it's active — by mixing with warm water and sugar.

purée: Break food into small particles (examples are applesauce and mashed potatoes).

reduce: Boil down a liquid to concentrate the taste of its contents.

roast: Cook in dry heat.

sauté: Brown food in very hot fat.

sear: Subject foods such as meat to extremely high heat for a short period of time to seal in juices.

shred: Tear or cut into very small, thin pieces.

simmer: Cook over low heat, never boiling.

soufflé: A baked food made light by egg whites.

steam: Cook food over a small amount of boiling water.

stock: A liquid in which solid ingredients (like chicken meat and bones, vegetables, and spices) are cooked and then usually strained out.

steep: Place dry ingredients in hot liquid to flavor the liquid (tea is an example).

stew: Slowly cook meat and vegetables in liquid in a covered pan.

stir-fry: Quickly cook meat or vegetables in a wok with a little oil.

sweat: Cook over low heat in a small amount of fat (usually butter) to draw out juices to remove rawness and develop flavor.

toast: Brown by baking.

vinaigrette: A dressing of oil, vinegar, salt, pepper, and various herbs and spices.

whip: Beat rapidly to add air and lighten.

zest: The outermost colored peel of an orange or other citrus fruit.

Appendix C

Conversions of Weights, Measures, and Sugar Substitutes

· ·

Do you know how many tablespoons are in a cup? How many grams are in a pound? And how do you choose between all those sugar substitutes on the market? What if you need to convert an oven temperature from Celsius to Fahrenheit? This appendix offers some information to help you answer those questions.

Conversions

The following list provides some common measurement conversions.

1 teaspoon = ⅓ tablespoon

1 tablespoon = 3 teaspoons

2 tablespoons = ⅛ cup (1 ounce)

4 tablespoons = ¼ cup

5⅓ tablespoons = ⅓ cup

8 tablespoons = ½ cup

16 tablespoons = 1 cup

1 cup = ½ pint

2 cups = 1 pint

2 pints = 1 quart

4 quarts = 1 gallon

1 pound = 16 ounces

1 fluid ounce = 2 tablespoons

16 fluid ounces = 1 pint

Table C-1 explains how to convert specific measurements. For example, if you have 3 *ounces* of mushrooms, how many *grams* of mushrooms do you have? To find out, multiply 3 by 28.35 (you have 85.05 grams).

Table C-1	Conversion Methods	
To Convert	*Multiply*	*By*
Ounces to grams	Ounces	28.35
Grams to ounces (dry)	Grams	0.035
Ounces (liquid) to milliliters	Ounces	30.00
Cups to liters	Cups	0.24
Liters to U.S. quarts	Liters	0.95
U.S. quarts to liters	Quarts	1.057
Inches to centimeters	Inches	2.54
Centimeters to inches	Centimeters	0.39
Pounds to grams	Pounds	453.59

Table C-2 shows you the differences between Fahrenheit and Celsius temperatures.

Table C-2	Temperature (Degrees)
Fahrenheit	*Celsius*
32	0
212	100
250	120
275	140
300	150
325	160
350	180
375	190
400	200
425	220
450	230
475	240
500	260

Sugar Substitutes

The new approach to nutrition for people with diabetes doesn't emphasize the elimination of sugar from your diet entirely as long as you count the kilocalories that you consume. When a recipe calls for only a few teaspoons of sugar, you may want to use table sugar (also known as *sucrose*). When the recipe calls for ¼ cup of sugar or more, then substitution with a noncaloric sweetener of your choice will definitely save you kilocalories. There are also sweeteners besides glucose that do contain kilocalories but offer other advantages, such as not raising the blood glucose as fast. (We discuss your sweet options in more detail in Chapter 2.)

The following sweeteners contain kilocalories that are added into the total kilocalorie count. They're absorbed differently than glucose, so they affect the blood glucose differently.

- ✔ Fructose, found in fruits and berries
- ✔ Xylitol, found in strawberries and raspberries
- ✔ Sorbitol and mannitol, sugar alcohols occurring in plants

Non-nutritive or artificial sweeteners are often much sweeter than table sugar. Therefore, much less of this type of sweetener is required to accomplish the same level of sweetness as sugar. The current artificial sweeteners (from oldest to newest) include the following:

- ✔ Saccharin
- ✔ Aspartame
- ✔ Acesulfame-K
- ✔ Sucralose

If you plan to substitute another sweetener for sugar, check out Table C-3 to find the measurements needed to achieve equal sweetness.

Table C-3 Sweetener Equivalents

Sugar	*Fructose*	*Saccharin*	*Aspartame*	*Acesulfame-K*	*Sucralose*
2 teaspoons	⅔ teaspoon	⅕ teaspoon	1 packet	1 packet	1 packet
1 tablespoon	1 teaspoon	⅓ teaspoon	1½ packets	1¼ packets	1½ packets
¼ cup	4 teaspoons	3 packets	6 packets	3 packets	6 packets
⅓ cup	5⅓ teaspoons	4 packets	8 packets	4 packets	8 packets
½ cup	8 teaspoons	6 packets	12 packets	6 packets	12 packets
⅔ cup	3½ tablespoons	8 packets	16 packets	8 packets	16 packets
¾ cup	¼ cup	9 packets	18 packets	9 packets	18 packets
1 cup	⅓ cup	12 packets	24 packets	12 packets	24 packets

Appendix D

Other Recipe Sources for People with Diabetes

• •

So many cookbook recipes are available for people with diabetes that this book wouldn't have been written if it didn't offer a special feature, namely the recipes of some of the finest chefs in the United States. You can find a number of excellent books and even more recipes on Web sites. You can generally count on the recipes in books to contain the nutrients they list, but Web recipes may not be as reliable; you need to evaluate the site before accepting the recipes. You can trust the sites that we list here. You can find them by typing in the address or by going to Dr. Rubin's Web site at www. drrubin.com.

When you get to his Web site, click on the Related Web sites link, where you can find links to all the sites we mention here.

Cookbooks for People with Diabetes

No book like this one exists on cooking for people with diabetes. Those listed in this section offer recipes for home-grown meals, not the creative work of great chefs. However, plenty of useful information and tons of good recipes appear in the books we list here.

- ✔ American Diabetes Association and American Heart Association, *Diabetes & Heart Healthy Cookbook,* American Diabetes Association, 2004.

- ✔ American Diabetes Association and American Heart Association, *Diabetes and Heart Healthy Meals For Two,* American Diabetes Association, 2008.

- ✔ Bergenstal, Richard M., MD, *Betty Crocker's Diabetes Cookbook,* Wiley Publishing, Inc., 2003

✔ Cain, Anne, MS, MPH, RD, *All New Complete Step-by-Step Diabetic Cookbook,* Oxmoor House, 2006.

✔ Crocker, Betty, *Betty Crocker 30-Minute Meals For Diabetes*, Betty Crocker, 2008

✔ Editors of *Diabetic Gourmet Magazine, The Diabetic Gourmet Cookbook,* Wiley Publishing, Inc., 2004.

✔ Fisher, Helen V., *You Can Eat Well With Diabetes,* Running Press, 2004.

✔ Ginsberg, Art, *Mr. Food's Quick and Easy Diabetic Food Cooking,* American Diabetes Association, 2007.

✔ Good, Phyllis Pellman, *Fix-It and Enjoy-It Diabetic Cookbook,* American Diabetes Association, 2007.

✔ Grunes, Barbara, *Diabetes Snacks, Treats and Easy Eats for Kids,* Surrey Books, 2006

✔ Hall, Dawn, *Busy People's Diabetes Cookbook,* Rutledge Hill Press, 2005.

✔ Karpinske, Stephanie, RD, *Better Homes and Gardens Simple Everyday Diabetic Meals,* Mededith Books, 2004.

✔ Powers, Maggie, MS, RD, CDE, *American Dietetic Association Guide to Eating Right When You Have Diabetes,* Wiley Publishing, Inc., 2003.

Food and Recipe Web Sites for People with Diabetes

In this section, we list the best of the currently available Web sites. Things change so frequently on the Web that it's difficult to stay up-to-date. Look for newer listings on Dr. Rubin's Web site at www.drrubin.com.

✔ The nutrition section of the American Diabetes Association Web site begins at www.diabetes.org/nutrition-and-recipes/ nutrition/overview.jsp. Here you find discussions of nutrition as well as lots of recipes.

✔ The Web page Ask NOAH About Diabetes supplies links to many important articles about diabetic nutrition as well as diabetic recipes at www. noah-health.org/en/endocrine/diabetes/nutrion/index. html.

- Children with Diabetes includes a large amount of information on meal planning, sugar substitutes, and the food guide pyramid, as well as many recipes, at www.childrenwithdiabetes.com/d_08_000.htm.

- *Diabetic Gourmet Magazine* offers a valuable site at www.diabetic gourmet.com that contains information about diagnosis and treatment as well as numerous recipes that you can use.

- Diabetic-recipes.com has a huge collection of diabetic and heart-healthy recipes at www.diabetic-recipes.com.

- The Food and Drug Administration provides a lot of useful information on diabetes and food at www.fda.gov/diabetes.

- The Joslin Diabetes Center discusses many nutrition topics at its Web site, www.joslin.org/education/library.

- Three Fat Chicks on a Diet has complete calorie counts for most fast-food restaurants at www.3fatchicks.com/fast-food-nutrition.

- The Mayo Clinic has numerous delicious recipes for the person with diabetes at www.mayoclinic.com/health/diabetes-recipes/RE00091.

- The Vegetarian Resource Group maintains a large site at www.vrg.org/journal/vj2003issue2/vj2003issue2diabetes.htm that's filled with information for vegetarians who have developed diabetes.

Index

Business/Accounting & Bookkeeping

Bookkeeping For Dummies
978-0-7645-9848-7

eBay Business
All-in-One For Dummies,
2nd Edition
978-0-470-38536-4

Job Interviews
For Dummies,
3rd Edition
978-0-470-17748-8

Resumes For Dummies,
5th Edition
978-0-470-08037-5

Stock Investing
For Dummies,
3rd Edition
978-0-470-40114-9

Successful Time
Management
For Dummies
978-0-470-29034-7

Computer Hardware

BlackBerry For Dummies,
3rd Edition
978-0-470-45762-7

Computers For Seniors
For Dummies
978-0-470-24055-7

iPhone For Dummies,
2nd Edition
978-0-470-42342-4

Laptops For Dummies,
3rd Edition
978-0-470-27759-1

Macs For Dummies,
10th Edition
978-0-470-27817-8

Cooking & Entertaining

Cooking Basics
For Dummies,
3rd Edition
978-0-7645-7206-7

Wine For Dummies,
4th Edition
978-0-470-04579-4

Diet & Nutrition

Dieting For Dummies,
2nd Edition
978-0-7645-4149-0

Nutrition For Dummies,
4th Edition
978-0-471-79868-2

Weight Training
For Dummies,
3rd Edition
978-0-471-76845-6

Digital Photography

Digital Photography
For Dummies,
6th Edition
978-0-470-25074-7

Photoshop Elements 7
For Dummies
978-0-470-39700-8

Gardening

Gardening Basics
For Dummies
978-0-470-03749-2

Organic Gardening
For Dummies,
2nd Edition
978-0-470-43067-5

Green/Sustainable

Green Building
& Remodeling
For Dummies
978-0-470-17559-0

Green Cleaning
For Dummies
978-0-470-39106-8

Green IT For Dummies
978-0-470-38688-0

Health

Diabetes For Dummies,
3rd Edition
978-0-470-27086-8

Food Allergies
For Dummies
978-0-470-09584-3

Living Gluten-Free
For Dummies
978-0-471-77383-2

Hobbies/General

Chess For Dummies,
2nd Edition
978-0-7645-8404-6

Drawing For Dummies
978-0-7645-5476-6

Knitting For Dummies,
2nd Edition
978-0-470-28747-7

Organizing For Dummies
978-0-7645-5300-4

SuDoku For Dummies
978-0-470-01892-7

Home Improvement

Energy Efficient Homes
For Dummies
978-0-470-37602-7

Home Theater
For Dummies,
3rd Edition
978-0-470-41189-6

Living the Country Lifestyle
All-in-One For Dummies
978-0-470-43061-3

Solar Power Your Home
For Dummies
978-0-470-17569-9

Internet

Blogging For Dummies,
2nd Edition
978-0-470-23017-6

eBay For Dummies,
6th Edition
978-0-470-49741-8

Facebook For Dummies
978-0-470-26273-3

Google Blogger
For Dummies
978-0-470-40742-4

Web Marketing
For Dummies,
2nd Edition
978-0-470-37181-7

WordPress For Dummies,
2nd Edition
978-0-470-40296-2

Language & Foreign Language

French For Dummies
978-0-7645-5193-2

Italian Phrases
For Dummies
978-0-7645-7203-6

Spanish For Dummies
978-0-7645-5194-9

Spanish For Dummies,
Audio Set
978-0-470-09585-0

Macintosh

Mac OS X Snow Leopard
For Dummies
978-0-470-43543-4

Math & Science

Algebra I For Dummies
978-0-7645-5325-7

Biology For Dummies
978-0-7645-5326-4

Calculus For Dummies
978-0-7645-2498-1

Chemistry For Dummies
978-0-7645-5430-8

Microsoft Office

Excel 2007 For Dummies
978-0-470-03737-9

Office 2007 All-in-One
Desk Reference
For Dummies
978-0-471-78279-7

Music

Guitar For Dummies,
2nd Edition
978-0-7645-9904-0

iPod & iTunes
For Dummies,
6th Edition
978-0-470-39062-7

Piano Exercises
For Dummies
978-0-470-38765-8

Parenting & Education

Parenting For Dummies,
2nd Edition
978-0-7645-5418-6

Type 1 Diabetes
For Dummies
978-0-470-17811-9

Pets

Cats For Dummies,
2nd Edition
978-0-7645-5275-5

Dog Training For Dummies,
2nd Edition
978-0-7645-8418-3

Puppies For Dummies,
2nd Edition
978-0-470-03717-1

Religion & Inspiration

The Bible For Dummies
978-0-7645-5296-0

Catholicism For Dummies
978-0-7645-5391-2

Women in the Bible
For Dummies
978-0-7645-8475-6

Self-Help & Relationship

Anger Management
For Dummies
978-0-470-03715-7

Overcoming Anxiety
For Dummies
978-0-7645-5447-6

Sports

Baseball For Dummies,
3rd Edition
978-0-7645-7537-2

Basketball For Dummies,
2nd Edition
978-0-7645-5248-9

Golf For Dummies,
3rd Edition
978-0-471-76871-5

Web Development

Web Design All-in-One
For Dummies
978-0-470-41796-6

Windows Vista

Windows Vista
For Dummies
978-0-471-75421-3

Dummies products make life easier!

DVDs • Music • Games •
DIY • Consumer Electronics •
Software • Crafts • Hobbies •
Cookware • and more!

For more information, go to
Dummies.com® and search
the store by category.

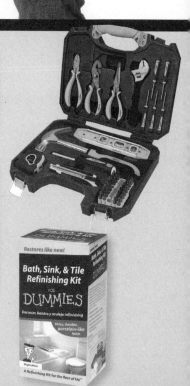

FOR
DUMMIES
Making everything easier!™